Also by Michael Holzman

Lukács's Road to God

Writing as Social Action (with Marilyn Cooper)

James Jesus Angleton: The C.I.A., and the Craft of
Counterintelligence

Pax 1934-1941 (novel)

Guy Burgess: Revolutionary in an Old School Tie

The Black Poverty Cycle and How to End It

Minority Students and Public Education:
A Resource Book (Two Volumes)

Donald and Melinda Maclean: Idealism and Espionage

The Chains of Black America

The Language of Anti-Communism

From Pius IX to Joseph McCarthy

Chelmsford Press   Briarcliff Manor, New York

Chelmsford Press
Briarcliff Manor, New York

ISBN-13:978-1546349976
ISBN-10:1546349979

For Jane

Acknowledgments

I would like to thank the participants in the Cold War Seminar at the Tamiment Library, New York University, especially Anthony Hiss, Michael Koncewicz, and Timothy Naftali. Shelley Glick of the Briarcliff Manor Public Library has been helpful beyond the call of duty. I would also like to thank Olivier Burtin, Randall Bytwerk, David Durant, Christopher Elias, Andrew Feffer, Richard Fliegel, Henry Hardy, Jeff Hulbert, Jane Rawlingson MacKillop, Kathryn McGarr, Evangeline Monroe, Gerald Monroe, Steven Rosswurm, Frances Stonor Saunders, Matthew Spender, and Clarence Taylor.

Errors are, of course, my own. I would be grateful to have them brought to my attention so that they might be corrected.

THE LANGUAGE OF ANTI-COMMUNISM

From Pius IX to Joseph McCarthy

Michael Holzman

Table of Contents

Introduction

But language does not simply write and think for me. It also increasingly dictates my feelings and governs my entire spiritual being the more unquestioningly and unconsciously I abandon myself to it . . . Words can be like tiny doses of arsenic: they are swallowed unnoticed, appear to have no effect, and then after a little time the toxic reaction sets in after all . . . Victor Klemperer[1]

Victor Klemperer was a Romance philologist, a practitioner of a scholarly discipline that seeks to understand literature, then society itself, through the study of a language's words and phrases. In the normal course of events he would have followed his teacher Karl Vossler and his contemporaries Erich Auerbach and Ernst Curtius in a lifelong study of Western culture through a close reading of its literature. But for a German son of a rabbi there was to be no normal course of events in the mid-twentieth century. Klemperer is now best known not for his studies of Montesquieu, but for his diaries, documenting life in Nazi Germany from the point of view of a secular Jewish intellectual married to a Christian woman and who therefore was—just—able to survive the Third Reich. Klemperer distilled the philological aspects of those diaries in *The Language of the Third Reich,* a study of the words and phrases used by the Nazi regime and their lingering effects on the mentality of the German people.

The present study applies this method to an examination of the language of Cold War Anti-Communism. The Communist Party of the United States was relatively insignificant politically, never enrolling more than a few tens of thousands members, viewed with characteristic contempt by its Soviet masters, at times a useful tool

---

[1] Klemperer, Victor. The Language of the Third Reich. Trans. Martin Brady. London: Bloomsbury, 2013, pp. 15-16.

for such as John L. Lewis and other union organizers, to be discarded when no longer useful, finally ostracized even among the revived Left of the 1960s. Anti-Communism, on the one hand, was a much more significant phenomenon, on the one hand part of the persistent American populist tradition, on the other an instrument ready for the use of corporations against unions, Republicans against the New Deal, segregationists against African Americans. The abusive language used both by Communists and Anti-Communists was similar, which is not surprising, as many of the more prominent Anti-Communists were themselves ex-Communists. As Robert Ivie summarized their language, "The nation's adversary is characterized as a mortal threat to freedom, a germ infecting the body politic, a plague upon the liberty of humankind, and a barbarian intent upon destroying civilization."[i] Although German has been to a great extent denazified (a term Klemperer hated), the language of Anti-Communism, even in the absence of Communism itself, is still present in American English, laying ready at hand to be put to new uses by politicians and others to proclaim the urgent need to sacrifice civil liberties in the cause of national security.

*　*　*

The struggle between two world-wide, ideologically-driven institutions, the Communist Party and the Roman Catholic Church, was a central factor in Cold War Anti-Communism. Although for a time it seemed unlikely, given the obvious answer to Stalin's question "How many divisions has the Pope?" in the end, the Church won. The first chapter of this book describes the language of that struggle, from its beginnings in early-nineteenth century Europe to its manifestations within mid-twentieth-century American political culture. The key term used by the Church in reference to Communism was "conspiracy." The second chapter concerns the American Legion, its connections with the Anti-Communist activities of the Church, on the one hand, and with government entities, such as the Federal Bureau of Investigation, on the other. The central terms for the American Legion were "Americanism" and its opposite: "Un-American." Next, the eponymous House Committee on Un-American Activities and the Senate Internal Security and Government Operations (McCarthy) committees are considered, along with other legislative units. These often deployed the Church's keyword, conspiracy, but with a legalistic interpretation, and also deployed a rich vocabulary of invective of their own.

The "liberal" establishment operated somewhat differently. In addition to some involvement with the Congressional committees, it produced an alternative ideology of Anti-Communism, the distorting effects of which in the universities and the schools and what passes for common knowledge, linger. The work of three once-famous exemplary figures are discussed from this point of view: the historian Arthur M. Schlesinger, Jr.; the theologian, Reinhold Niebuhr, and the professor of philosophy, Sidney Hook. Another aspect of this tendency, what Schlesinger called the Non-Communist Left, was internationalized by the Central Intelligence Agency by means of, among other activities, the London-based cultural and political magazine *Encounter,* with its pairing of American and British editors. *Encounter* rebroadcast, as it were, the American language of the Cold War from its London offices, from time to time adding its own terms and nuance, some of which was developed by the Information Research Department of the Foreign Office.

George Orwell famously wrote in his *Politics and the English Language:* "The English language . . . becomes ugly and inaccurate because our thoughts are foolish, but the slovenliness of our language makes it easier for us to have foolish thoughts.

The point is that the process is reversible. Modern English, especially written English, is full of bad habits which spread by imitation and which can be avoided if one is willing to take the necessary trouble. If one gets rid of these habits one can think more clearly, and to think clearly is a necessary first step toward political regeneration . . .

The Language of Anti-Communism is offered with that hope.

December 31, 2016

3

The Language of Anti-Communism

Notes

[i] Ivie, Robert L. "Cold War Motives and the Rhetorical Metaphor: A Framework of Criticism," in Medhurst, Martin J.; Ivie, Robert L.; Wander, Philip; Scott, Robert L. Cold War Rhetoric: Strategy, Metaphor, and Ideology. East Lansing: Michigan State University Press, 1997, p. 72.

The Language of Anti-Communism

The Catholic Church and Anti-Communism

In March, 1937, during the first year of the Spanish Civil War, Pope Pius XI issued two encyclicals. *Mit Brennender Sorge (With Burning Anxiety)*, which was addressed primarily to the hierarchy of the Church in Germany, was critical of the Nazi regime's campaign against the Church. It was a defensive document, intended to strengthen the morale of the German archbishops and bishops, in the first instance, and also that of the German Catholic community, in general. The other encyclical, *Divini Redemptoris*, had a wider, a worldwide range, and a different focus. It associated "Bolshevistic and atheistic Communism" with Satan. (Satan was not mentioned in relation to Nazism in *Mit Brennender Sorge*.) And while *Mit Brennender Sorge* dealt exclusively with current events, *Divini Redemptoris* traced the Church's opposition to Communism back to Pope Pius IX, who in 1846 had condemned "the unspeakable doctrine of Communism, as it is called," two years before the publication of *The Communist Manifesto*.

In his encyclical *Qui Pluribus* of November 9, 1846, Pius IX had called Communism "a doctrine most opposed to the very natural law. For if this doctrine were accepted, the complete destruction of everyone's laws, government, property, and even of human society itself would follow." *Qui Pluribus* linked government, property and the structure of society, associating the socio-economic status quo with natural law, that is, the word of God. And three years later, Pius IX again condemned "that infamous doctrine of so-called Communism." He wrote in the *Nostis Et Nobiscum* of December 8, 1849 that "the goal of this most iniquitous plot is to drive people to overthrow the entire order of human affairs and to draw them over to the wicked theories of this Socialism and Communism, by confusing them with perverted teachings . . . As regards this teaching and these theories, it is now generally known that the special goal of their proponents is to introduce to the people the pernicious fictions of Socialism and Communism by misapplying the terms "liberty" and "equality."

> The final goal shared by these teachings, whether of Communism or Socialism, even if approached differently, is to excite by continuous disturbances workers and others, especially those of the lower class, whom they have deceived by their lies and deluded by the promise of a happier condition. They are preparing them for plundering, stealing, and usurping first the Church's and then everyone's property. After this they will profane all law, human and divine, to destroy divine worship and to subvert the entire ordering of civil societies.

Among those perverted teachings, according to the Pope, was opposition to the Church's teaching that "the very nature of human society obligates its members to obey its lawfully established authority." The Pope's objection to Communism and Socialism, in these early condemnations, was not primarily religious, in the usual sense of the word. It was the threat that Communism and Socialism held for property rights and the existing class structure of civil society.

On December 8, 1864, in *Quanta Cura,* Pius IX wrote that enemies of the Church, "teaching and professing the most fatal error of 'Communism and Socialism,' they assert that 'domestic society or the family derives the whole principle of its existence from the civil law alone; and, consequently, that on civil law alone depend all rights of parents over their children, and especially that of providing for education'," as opposed to natural (Church) law and parochial schools. Pius IX, writing in the turbulent period of the mid-nineteenth-century revolutions, described Communism in the terms used for heretical sects (including, in places in these encyclicals, the Protestant churches among them). The Pope was particularly troubled by Communist theories about relations in the family and education, "the rights of parents over their children." The Church and hierarchical, authoritarian, state and society, the Pope taught, were mutually dependent. Communists (and Socialists), he wrote, subversively sought to convince the "lower" and working classes that they would be happier in a more equal society and that they should endeavor to bring this about. Notably, Communism was conceived of as "a plot" not only against the religious doctrines of the Church, but also against secular "laws, government, property." It is Communism's presumed essence, as it were, as a plot, a plot with this dual focus, that would be taken up by Anti-Communists in America ninety years later.

In 1878, Pius IX's successor, Pope Leo XIII, issued the encyclical, *Quod Apostolici Muneris,* "On Socialism," entirely devoted to "the deadly plague that is creeping into the very fibres of human society and leading it on to the verge of destruction"

> We speak of that sect [sic] of men who, under various and almost barbarous names, are called socialists, communists, or nihilists, and who, spread over all the world, and bound together by the closest ties in a wicked confederacy, no longer seek the shelter of secret meetings, but, openly and boldly marching forth in the light of day, strive to bring to a head what they have long been planning—the overthrow of all civil society whatsoever . . . the socialists would destroy the "right" of property, alleging it to be a human invention altogether opposed to the inborn equality of man, and, claiming a community of goods, argue that poverty should not be peaceably endured, and that the property and privileges of the rich may be rightly invaded, the Church, with much greater wisdom and good sense, recognizes the inequality among men, who are born with different powers of body and mind, inequality in actual possession, also, and holds that the right of property and of ownership, which springs from nature itself, must not be touched and stands inviolate.

While Pius IX had been writing in response to the revolutions of 1848, Leo XIII had before him the example of the annexation of Rome by the new Italian state and the example of the Paris Commune as well, with its much more sweeping critique of class and property. His reaction was to condemn democracy outright and to deem socialism a "plague."

Twelve years after *Quod Apostolici Muneris*, Pope Leo XIII was, if anything, more worried about Freemasonry than the Socialists, as in his view the government of the Italian state was pursuing an aggressively secular course under the influence of the Masons. The Pope promulgated the encyclical *Ab apostolici*, on October 15, 1890, condemning (not for the first time) Freemasons in Italy, whom he declares were "possessed by the spirit of Satan, whose instrument they are . . .." The Pope believed that the Masons controlled the Italian state and were determined to destroy the Catholic religion even there: "instead of the Catholic Faith, must now be substituted the most absolute freedom of examination, of criticism, of thought, and of conscience." But the Pope did not neglect to again warn against socialism as well:

> Moreover, one of the greatest and most formidable dangers of society at the present day, is the agitation of the Socialists, who threaten to uplift it from its foundations . . . So criminal is its nature, so great the power of its organization and the audacity of its designs, that there is need of uniting all conservative forces, if we are to arrest its progress and successfully to prevent its triumph. Of these forces the first, and above all the chief one, is that which can be supplied by religion and the Church: without this, the strictest laws, the severest tribunals, and even the force of arms, will prove useless or insufficient (*Ab apostolici*, 14).

These Popes associated the anti-Catholic activities of the Masons and Socialists with the Jews, and, sometimes, as we have seen, with Protestants as well, invoking Satan as a figure for these enemies of the Church and the established order.

Underlying and strengthening the rhetoric of these nineteenth-century encyclicals is something much older, the Ciceronian rhythms of the orator's denunciation of the conspiracy, the plot, of Catiline, which, according to Cicero, threatened to overturn the order of the Roman state and its gods. Cicero's example gave a classical resonance to the encyclicals' vocabulary of secret meetings, long laid plans, plots and conspirators, the appeals to nature and its laws, the differentiation of classes presented as natural, a virtuous condition, set against the worldwide iniquity of demands for economic and social equality. No doubt Pius IX and Leo XIII, Cardinal Spellman and the more learned among the Anti-Communist American priests were familiar with *In Catilinam I-IV*. It was not necessary for J. Edgar Hoover; Senators McCarthy, Eastland and McCarran; representatives Dies and Rankin, to have studied them. This much of the rhetoric of Anti-Communism came to them ready-packaged.

In January, 1930, seven years before *Divini Redemptoris*, in the midst of the economic paralysis and panic that followed the Stock Market Crash, a Canadian-born Roman Catholic priest, Father Charles E. Coughlin, serving a parish in the Detroit suburb of Royal Oak, "delivered a Sunday sermon, 'Christ or the Red Serpent,' recounting 'the news from Russia' that 'by government decree the mistletoe and holly of Christmas have been abolished.' He warned that the United States was being corrupted from within by the same 'purple poison of Bolshevism,' which was undermining, even destroying, family life . . .'"[ii] In March, Catholics were instructed by the Pope to pray on Sundays "for the reconversion of Russia, and until the 1960s such prayers would be the routine conclusion at every Catholic Mass."[iii]

Coughlin's radio programs reached all the major Midwestern and Eastern cities, giving him perhaps ten million listeners.[iv] The "radio priest's" broadcasts promulgated Anti-Communism and increasingly overt anti-Semitism, making nearly explicit the Vatican's more muted traditional, theologically-based, hostility to Jews by linking international finance capitalism to Communism, which must have been somewhat surprising for both. In any case, according to Richard Gid Powers, the historian of American right-wing Anti-Communism, by "January 1935 . . . Coughlin's organization was turning into one of the most dangerous anti-Semitic movements in American history."[v] Coughlin, working with other figures on the racist and anti-Semitic far right, such as Gerald L. K. Smith, went some way toward forming their own political party. Powers wrote that "Coughlin's rise was the almost predictable result of the Roman Catholic Church's willingness in the thirties to tolerate anyone—even Hitler—who could present himself as an effective fighter against communism . . .

The Pope's influential secretary of state, Eugenio Cardinal

Pacelli, believed that "Marxism was the greatest danger of all time to the Church" and that only authoritarian governments could hold out against revolution. As the Pope's ambassador to Germany in the twenties, Pacelli, who would become Pope Pius XII in 1939, had come to regard Germany as Christianity's bulwark against communism.[vi]

After Kristallnacht, November, 1938, Coughlin referred to Nazism as a "defense mechanism against Communism." He "then declared that the 'rising generation of Germans regard Communism as a product not of Russia, but of a group of Jews who dominated the destines of Russia.'"[vii] The following month Coughlin offered some advice to American Jews: "for his collective safety, the American Jew must repudiate the atheistic Jew. Communism must be stamped out, else an illogical world will build up a defense mechanism against it in these United States paralleling, if not surpassing, the same illogical defense mechanism which operates under Nazism."[viii] By early 1939 "the radio priest's weekly [publication] carried the front-page headline, 'Rome-Berlin Axis Is a Firm Rampart against Communist.' The article stated that 'it should never be forgotten that the Rome-Berlin axis . . . is serving Christendom in a peculiarly important manner.'"[ix] There are indications that Coughlin was receiving support from Nazi Germany in return for this work on its behalf, as well as reprinting material from Goebbels, in translation and unattributed.[x] This was one channel through which the vituperative Nazi language combining Anti-Communism with anti-Semitism entered American Anti-Communist discourse.

Coughlin eventually found himself in conflict both with President Roosevelt and with his own Church. The former took steps to remove him as a political threat, by, among other actions, effectively destroying his possible allies in the most important organizations publically exhibiting Nazi and Fascist sympathies. The Church asserted increasing control over Coughlin's broadcasts and publications. In early February 1940, the board of censors of Coughlin's immediate superior, Archbishop Mooney, "rejected [an] entire script on the basis of its anti-Semitic content. Coughlin had intended to broadcast these thoughts: 'We may say that very little of any consequence is taking place in Jewish life in this country without the participation, or even the initiative, of the Jewish communists.'"[xi] Finally, in May, 1942, the Church silenced Coughlin and ended his political career, leaving the its Anti-Communist work in the United States to more conventional clerics and its lay organizations.[xii]

The vocabularies of Anti-Communism and anti-Semitism merged in Coughlin's and other publications and broadcasts of the period. Labeling Communism as a poison, a plot, a plague chimed with similar labeling of Communists and Jews by Nazi propagandists, such as Robert Ley, who also happened to agree with Pope Leo XIII about the Masons: "In the modern era, the Jews have established major world organizations to conceal their criminal deeds, which are joined together under *Freemasonry*. World Freemasonry, which has gradually recruited many important Gentiles, is nothing other than a clever way of concealing Jewish crimes." Ley claimed that: "Judaism and Bolshevism were and are everywhere and at all times the same."[2] And most typically of Nazi propaganda, he figured Jews as non-human parasites bringing, or being, disease:

> Is it enough to destroy the louse, but leave the brood alive? Is it enough to free ourselves of the pest, yet deal with others who are still infested with the pest? *The brood that we leave alive is the Jewish world, the Jewish mentality, the Jewish spirit,* that still surrounds us, that follows us everywhere. And we still find infested neighbors in Europe, above all among our enemies, and in particular with Bolshevism.[xiii]

An essential point of Nazi propaganda was the identity of Jews and Communists and therefore the terms of opprobrium used against them were also identical. Although the emphasis in Nazi propaganda

---

[2] This equivalency had some resonance in American Anti-Communist circles: "in 1948, a letter circulated among members of the local chapter of the Confederate Daughters of America stating that 'nearly all the Communists in America are Jews, and . . . most of the funds and agitators used in stirring up your Southern Negroes are Jewish in origin." Dinnerstein, Leonard. Anti-Semitism in America. Oxford University Press: Oxford and New York, 1994, p. 188.

was on the Jews, with the Communists trailing on behind, other Anti-Communists deployed similar, if not identical, terms of disease and vermin about Communists, in some cases, as we will see, using them in an anti-Semitic fashion as well.

It is against this background that Pius XI's *Divini Redemptoris* had condemned the actions of Communists in Russia, Spain and Mexico against the Church and had gone further, claiming that "Communism . . . strips man of his liberty, robs human personality of all its dignity and removes all the moral restraints that check the eruptions of blind impulse . . . human personality . . . is a mere cog-wheel in the Communist system . . . The preachers of Communism are also proficient in exploiting racial antagonisms . . . [they] burrow into the universities . . . few are aware of the poison which increasingly pervades their minds and hearts . . ." These phrases, as well, became verbal tokens of American Anti-Communism, endlessly invoked and rearranged images of poisoning, burrowing, eruptions, cog-wheels, attacks on liberty, personality, dignity and moral restraints. While his predecessors had addressed their criticisms of Communism to the priesthood, requiring them to preach against it, Pope Pius XI went further, specifically charging the worldwide branches of the lay organizations of Catholic Action with responsibility for fighting Communism.

A supporter of Coughlin, Martin H. Carmody, the Supreme Knight of the Knights of Columbus, an American Catholic Action organization, had a role in organizing opposition to the revolutionary, anti-Catholic, government of Mexico. In 1938, the Knights of Columbus, answering the Pope's call, published a pamphlet on "The Peril of Communism" by George Hermann Derry, Director of its Department of Social Action. The pamphlet clearly stated that in its Anti-Communist efforts, "The Knights of Columbus . . . is following out the precepts of Pope Pius XI." After condemning Communism in the three countries, Russia, Spain and Mexico, that had most concerned the Pope and the Supreme Knight, Derry turned to North America. His estimate of Communist Party membership in the United States and Canada, 40,000 at that point in the late-1930s, left him with the problem of how to argue that this relatively small group could be an apocalyptic threat. Derry dealt with this with a move that would be taken up by other Anti-Communists, by describing the Communist Party in the United States and Canada as "an army of leaders," each an officer trained to mobilize hundreds of other people to their cause. (This was repeated by J. Edgar Hoover, twenty years later, when membership in the Communist Party had dwindled to 10,000, not all of whom were agents of the Federal Bureau of Investigation.[3])

On October 11, 1938, the House of Representatives Subcommittee of the Special Committee to Investigate Un-American Activities, usually called the Dies Committee, after its chairman, Representative Martin Dies of Texas, met in Detroit to investigate the sit-down strikes then occurring in the automobile industry. An investigator for the committee, Chester Howe, opened the session by stating that "We expect to show that the sit-down strikes originated here and were instigated by well-known Communist agitators." Paralleling Derry's "army of leaders" line of thought, Howe told the committee that "many reputable people attend meetings of affiliates of this party unknowingly because of a charitable or humanitarian instinct . . . the appeal of party leaders is subtle and usually hidden behind the name of an organization or a charitable cause."[xiv] Howe was followed by John D. McGillis, Secretary of the Detroit branch of the Knights of Columbus. McGillis stated that "the Knights of Columbus "became interested in this [Anti-Communist] work . . . primarily because of the activity of the Communist Party all over the world, and especially as it pertains to the Catholic Church . . . about two years" earlier. That is, responding to the directive of Pope Pius XI in *Divini Redemptoris* that Catholic action groups, like the Knights of Columbus, combat Communist and similar groups and governments, such as those of Mexico and the Spanish Republic, the

---

[3] CPUSA membership: January 1946: 52,500; 1947: 73,000; December 1949: 54,174; early 1953: 24,796; December 1955: 22,663; 3-6,000 in Summer 1958, cf. Mark R. Belknap. Cold War Political Justice: The Smith Act, the Communist Party, and American Civil Liberties. Westport, CT: Greenwood Press, 1977, pp. 190; 205.

American headquarters of the Knights of Columbus had begun an investigation of the efforts of the Communist Party of the United States to recruit Americans to fight on the side of the Republic in the Spanish Civil War.[xv] As International Brigade recruiters were especially active in Detroit, McGillis had been assigned that task.

The Vatican, then, supported Francisco Franco's Anti-Communist "crusade" in part by seeking to cut off the supply of American recruits to the International Brigade. It assigned this task to its American Catholic Action group, the Knights of Columbus, which developed "Americanism" experts, that is, Anti-Communist experts, who worked with American governmental entities— Congress, the Department of Justice and the F.B.I., state and local politicians—and non-governmental entities, such as the American Legion. They shared files, informers, other experts (especially ex-Communists), a worldview and a vocabulary.[4] In regard to informers, Whittaker Chambers, who must be accepted as an expert on these matters, stated that "To be an informer . . . Men shrink from that word and what it stands for as from something lurking and poisonous.

> Spy is a different breed of word . . . Spy as an epithet is a convention of morale; the enemy's spy is always monstrous; our spy is daring and brave. It must be so since all camps use spies and must while war lasts . . . The informer is different, particularly the ex-Communist informer. He risks little. He sits in security and uses his special knowledge to destroy others . . .[xvi]

Chairman Dies summed up McGillis's testimony in regard to the Catholic Church's Anti-Communism activities:

In addition to many other fundamental reasons why Catholics are so vigorously opposed to communism, is it not true that the

---

[4] In 1951 Senator McCarran stated that the Senate Internal Security Subcommittee "would rely heavily on the testimony of ex-Communists, who had 'no illusions about the Communist Party and its purposes, and have developed antibodies against further infection.'" Kutler, Stanley I. The American Inquisition: Justice and Injustice in the Cold War. New York: Hill and Wang, 1982, p. 199.

Catholic Church, which is world-wide, has seen the results of communism in other countries? . . . They know how, in Spain, little by little, there were inroads of communism. While they were ridiculed they finally, all of a sudden, found themselves under the control of the Communists. . . The same thing is true in Russia and in other countries . . . So, taking this experience and information from all over the world, they appreciate the grave danger, and they have been on the alert in their determination to expose it.[xvii]

The House Committee on Un-American Activities, and, more generally, the government of the United States, would continue to be suspicious of Americans who had either fought in Spain against the Roman Catholic Church-backed Falangists or those who had supported them. Indeed, U.S. Government agencies would sometimes take service in Spain on the side of the Republic, or support for those who had gone to Spain, as tantamount to membership in the Communist Party.

Coughlin, despite his some-time popularity, was a peripheral figure in the Church, his radio audience taken over by Monsignor Fulton J. Sheen's broadcasts, which also condemned those sympathetic with Communism or the Soviet Union or who supported Franco's Spain. Donald Crosby, S.J., observed that "As early as March 1946 [Bishop Fulton J. Sheen] warned of Communist subversion in America and condemned 'the fellow travelers in the United States and those whose hearts bleed for Red Fascism."[xviii] Another Catholic clergyman, Father John Cronin, was a more important figure connecting the Church and the American Anti-Communist activities of the mid-twentieth century. Cronin, a protégée of Archbishop Curley of Baltimore, was active among workers in that city during the 1930s, organizing against the local Communist-dominated unions. He was a master of behind-the-scenes maneuvers, both within the Church and nationally. Working through the National Catholic Welfare Conference and with such influential members of the hierarchy as Curley and Cushing of Boston,[xix] he obtained support for a large study of Communism in the United States, "The Problem of American Communism in 1945: Facts and

Recommendations," known as the Bishops' Report. His research on the report was supported, indeed, in large part performed by, the F.B.I., with which he had established connections at both the local Baltimore level and at the F.B.I.'s Washington, D.C. headquarters.[xx] Cronin also received information from J. B. Matthews, the professional Anti-Communist chief investigator for the House Committee on Un-American Activities and from the Chicago and New York City police departments' "Red Squads."[xxi] Cronin, through his work on the Bishop's Report and his later activities with the Social Action Department of the National Catholic Welfare Conference became a key liaison person for the Anti-Communist efforts of the Roman Catholic Church in the United States, the Federal Bureau of Investigation, the Congressional investigatory committees and their professional witnesses. According to Professor Steve Rosswurm, "Cronin played such an important role in the Anti-Communist movement that it is difficult to exaggerate its significance."[xxii]   If Coughlin had a successor as the leader of American Catholicism's Anti-Communist effort, Cronin would be a good candidate.

The Bishops' Report was the beginning, not the end, of Cronin's Anti-Communist activities. He helped establish the secular Anti-Communist periodicals *Plain Talk* and *Counterattack,* the bases for the blacklisting publication *Red Channels.* Although "In the concluding chapter of the [Bishops'] report . . . Cronin offered a judgment of the problem [that] . . . There was no chance that America would go Communist or even that the CPUSA would gain 'large numbers' who believed in Communism as a doctrine or accepted its discipline,"[xxiii] Cronin became increasingly radical, for example, working with the F.B.I. against J. Robert Oppenheimer, the director of the Manhattan Project, and Edward Condon, the distinguished physicist who directed the National Bureau of Standards.[5] "In 1941 [the F.B.I.] put [Oppenheimer] on its list of

---

[5] Another priest, Father Edward A. Conway, S.J., infiltrated and undermined the National Committee for Atomic Information and the Federation of Atomic Scientists as an F.B.I. informant from March 9, 1946.

potential subversives to be picked up for custodial detention . . .

In the November 1953 letter to J. Edgar Hoover that officially triggered Oppenheimer's fall, William L. Borden, the former executive director of the Joint Congressional Committee on Atomic Energy, claimed that "more probably than not," the physicist 'acted under a Soviet directive in influencing United States military, atomic energy, intelligence, and diplomatic policy . . . Borden also charged Oppenheimer with espionage . . . based on little besides the common assumption that "every American Communist is potentially an espionage agent of the Soviet Government."[xxiv]

Eventually, "Cronin's ideology led him to see Party members where there were only liberals and to conflate events that proved useful to the USSR with a conscious effort to aid it."[xxv]

If Cronin worked behind the scenes and, for the most part, within the Church (and the F.B.I.), the very public Francis Cardinal Spellman was treated by *The New York Times* as if he were an auxiliary mayor of the city, his travels documented day-by-day, his sermons summarized, his family's births, deaths and marriages noted.[xxvi]

But Spellman was not simply a prominent American. He was as well an important and powerful member of the world-wide hierarchy of the Roman Catholic Church. Spellman spent years in Rome, beginning in 1911 when he went there to study at the Pontifical North American College. He returned to Rome in 1925, where he became a Vatican official as Privy Chamberlain to the Pope and then secretary to Cardinal Lorenzo Lauri, not returning to the United States until his appointment as Auxiliary Bishop of Boston (with the title of Titular Bishop of Sila, in Algeria). In 1939 he was made Archbishop in New York City. When he was made a Cardinal in 1946 by his friend Pope Pius XII, it was as Cardinal-Priest of Santi Giovanni e Paolo in Rome. This was a conventional career path for an American member of the hierarchy, forging personal and official connections along the way at the Vatican, a career spent partly in the

---

He also worked against Oppenheimer. Russworm, Steve. *The F.B.I. and the Catholic Church, 1935-1962*, pp. 180ff; 186.

United States, partly in Rome.

The tight connections between the Roman Catholic Church and the Federal Bureau of Investigation can be illustrated by the fact that in late-1945 or early-1946 Spellman was made an F.B.I. "contact," a term of art for an informant, or, in another parlance, an agent, secretly providing information to the Bureau concerning the Catholic Church. The F.B.I. noted that "'This contact can be . . . of assistance in furnishing information concerning prominent Catholic priests and laymen'. . . . Foreign affairs was one of the areas in which Spellman provided help to the F.B.I.. Since he knew Latin American and South American prelates, the Bureau came to the cardinal on two occasions for help in gathering intelligence . . . ."[xxvii] As James Angleton said, "Once an agent, always an agent, for someone."

This career pattern has a perhaps ironic analogy with that typical of Communist figures, such as Earl Browder, the some-time leader of the Communist Party of the United States. Browder, like Spellman, was a frequent visitor to his world-wide organization's foreign headquarters, in his case that center was in Moscow, and with his partner, perhaps wife, Kitty Harris, spent time working for the Communist International in the Far East, before returning to high positions in New York. (Harris went on to a career in espionage, most notably as the liaison in London and Paris between the British diplomat Donald Maclean and the Soviet secret intelligence service.) Browder was the dominant CPUSA official until his expulsion from the Party in the mid-1940s. For both Browder and Spellman, the support of a foreign patron—Pacelli or Stalin—was vital to their careers in the United States, as vividly illustrated in the case of Browder when Stalin withdrew that support and Browder was forced into internal exile in Yonkers.

The Church did not lose its commitment to Falangist Spain with the end of the Spanish Civil War. Cardinal Spellman, for one, made known his support for Franco immediately after the end of World War II, when the Spanish government had not yet emerged from the opprobrium of its alignment, if not alliance, with Germany. However, ending the isolation of Spain was not solely a concern of the Catholic Church. There were those in the American military and business community, in the British and American secret intelligence services, and among conservative American and British politicians, who wished to bring Spain into the emerging Anti-Communist alliance. (Or to profit by trade with it, as with cotton broker and Undersecretary of State William Clayton.) More generally, on March 18, 1948, speaking at a meeting addressed by President Truman shortly after the latter had announced the Truman Doctrine, "Cardinal Spellman warned that the war did not end with V-J Day. He said that war was still threatening to overwhelm America, destroy her freedom and make her captive to atheistic communism. He charged that a *'conspiracy* of silence and appeasement' was enveloping those who feared communism but were afraid to speak out against it.

America is no safer from mastery by communism than was any European country. There we witnessed the killing and *enslavement* of whole peoples by communists, who, with the shedding of blood, became as if drunken with it . . . Fear must clutch your hearts as tightly as it grips my own, as we watch the towering glacier spread ceaselessly, mercilessly, across Europe and Asia, as powerful, aggressive, ruthless forces press to a finish the issues of *slavery* against democracy, *evil* against good, might against right, Stalinism against God . . . Soviet Russia *spews forth her Communist hordes* over the face of the earth, adding whole empires to her orbit of power . . . It is not alone in defense of my faith that I condemn *atheistic communism,* but as an American in defense of my country, for while communism is an enemy of Catholicism, it is also a challenge to all men who believe in God and in America" (Emphases added).[xxviii]

The Google Ngram Viewer,[6] is a useful tool for illustrating the frequency with which key words appear over time. It generates charts of the frequency with which words or phrases appear in published books in a variety of languages and a number of centuries. Specifying American (as opposed to, say, British) English and the period 1939 to 1960, the Ngram Viewer yields this graph for

---

[6] Google Books Ngram Viewer http://books.google.com/ngrams.

Cardinal Spellman's phrases "atheistic communism" and "Communist hordes":

The frequency of the appearance of "atheistic communism" parallels the progress of the Cold War, that of "Communist hordes" the tempo of the Korean War.

Cardinal Spellman added additional apocalyptic notes to those of the encyclicals of Popes Pius IX and XI and Leo XIII, warnings that would be heard again and again during the years of the Cold War. The war that had been against Germany and Japan and their allies continued, but the Soviet Union was now the enemy. Spellman called Communism a conspiracy and associated it with slavery, as against democracy, with murder, with (surely "oriental") hordes, and, finally, not to put too fine a point on it, with evil itself. On the other hand, he associates (somewhat blasphemously, one would think), belief in God with belief in America. At the end of April, 1948, in a speech to the American Legion, which had presented him with an "Americanism" award, Spellman urged his audience "to unite against men and women who abused their privileges as American citizens to impose on this country through 'intrigue and infamy the Communist pattern of serfdom, based on bloodshed, barbarism, suppression and slavery' . . . He emphasized each person's individual duty in stopping 'the lust-born hates of Communist bigotry and greed that are sweeping like scythes across our nation's face.'"[xxix] The Cardinal's ample use of alliteration at once strengthened and compromised his imagery.

Ann Durr pointed out that "The whole basis of the cold war was that communism meant dictatorship and capitalism meant democracy. [But h]ow could anyone say that capitalism was the best system in the world when the whole Southern part of the United States was segregated and Negros had no rights at all? It created a great dilemma for the United States."[xxx] Anti-Communists, like Spellman and especially politicians from the former Confederate states, dealt with this rhetorically by applying words like "serfdom," "slavery," and "bondage," words often heard in criticism of Jim Crow America, to Communism and the Soviet Union.

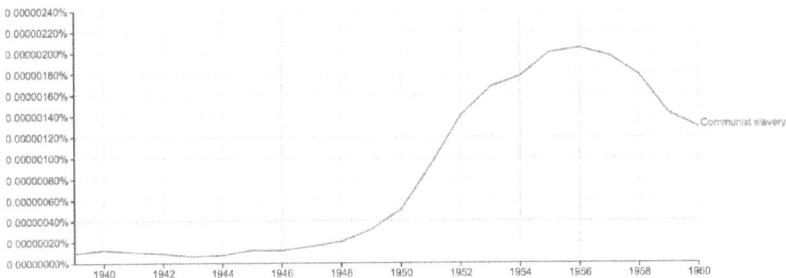

In order to clarify matters from the point of view of the Catholic Church, according to Msgr. Joseph F. Flannelly, administrator of Spellman's St. Patrick's Cathedral, "Americanism" is "'the preservation of God's order in government'. . . God's order 'is preserved by the Constitutional Government of the United States, which is based on belief in God as the omnipotent Ruler of the world and observance of His eternally just law.'"[xxxi] The authors of the Constitution put it differently, basing the document and the form of government it outlines on the will of the people, without any mention of God. Be that as it may, the officials of the Roman Catholic Church in America deployed a rhetoric of atheistic or godless Communism (or the godless Soviet Union, or godless Russia) on the one hand, and a tacitly Catholic, divinely-based government of the United States, on the other.

In February, 1949, "Cardinal Spellman . . . called . . . upon the American people to unite in prayer and protest to stop the

Communist penetration of our nation . . . the Cardinal declared the time had come when a strong and vigilant America should try to help save civilization from 'the world's most fiendish, ghoulish men of slaughter' . . . He declared that this country faced 'Communist conquest and annihilation'," a warning that he would repeat nearly word for word for the next decade.[xxxii] He specifically called for a purge of all Communists from the Government and other institutions.[xxxiii] ("Communist penetration," with its obvious sexual overtones, was a favorite term of Anti-Communist rhetoric, peaking in frequency in the early 1960s and then falling away.) The Knights of Columbus, the American Catholic Action group acting at the behest of the Pope, went further. In August, 1952, "Superior Judge John Swift of Boston, Supreme Knight of the Knights of Columbus, said . . . that the Communist party should be outlawed in the United States."[xxxiv] It was not clear whether Judge Swift was speaking as an official of the Commonwealth of Massachusetts or as an official of a lay organization of the Catholic Church. Perhaps one can make too much of the distinction between the various Anti-Communist entities. Their representatives themselves often elided the boundaries among them. For example, in May, 1953, when "Cardinal Spellman was honored . . . with a citation from the American Legion commending him for his leadership in fostering Americanism . . . [He] said that all Americans should recognize the threat of communism to this country and Christianity."[xxxv]

The mirror-imaging of the Communist International and the Catholic Church reached a *reductio ad absurdum* when the F.B.I. agent and journalist Jacob Spolansky wrote that the Communists International "is presently based on a fabulous estate just outside Bucharest, where 700 carefully selected party officials under the supervision of Jacques Duclos of France direct the Communist world-wide conspiracy,"[xxxvi] Spolansky figured Duclos as the Pope and a suburb of Bucharest as a kind of down-market Vatican, while Duclos was, in fact, just the acting Secretary General of the French Communist Party, in Paris, and the headquarters of the Communist International, under another name, remained as always, in Moscow.

In part, American Anti-Communism was a method for Irish

Catholic assimilation. The stereotypically Irish American Catholic Church became firmly identified with Anti-Communism in its most extreme forms.[7] "Americanism" experts and parades, with the Knights of Columbus well-represented among both, even Coughlin's anti-Semitism, served to transform a minority immigrant community, once barely differentiated from African-Americans in the prejudices of the Protestant ruling class, into the arbiter of patriotism. Cardinal Spellman, for example, explicitly associated himself with McCarthyism and its procedures: "No American uncontaminated [sic] by communism has lost his good name because of Congressional hearings on un-American activities. However, there are individuals who have seriously compromised themselves by a flat refusal to state whether they are now or have been Communists. It is impossible for me to understand why any American should refuse to declare himself free of Communist affiliation, unless he has something to hide."[xxxvii] When Senator McCarthy's power began to fade, Cardinal Spellman, as one of his main supporters, began to come in for criticism, even from within the Church. In April, 1954, Bernard J. Shell, senior Auxiliary Bishop of the Chicago Archdiocese, asked: "Are we any safer because the line between a liberal or a non-conformist, and a Communist or subversive is hopelessly blurred? I doubt it."[xxxviii] McCarthy's enemy, Senator Ralph Flanders of Vermont, criticized Cardinal Spellman directly: "Cardinal Spellman . . . shook hands with [Senator McCarthy] . . . Did this mean that the imprimatur of '*nihil obstat*' [nothing hinders] had been set by the church on these debonair campaigns to divide Americans from each other on religious lines?"[xxxix] There was this rather tin-eared response: "'Joe [Senator McCarthy] is a really sincere Catholic,' [Msgr. Edward R. Martin] declared. 'I personally know that over $5,000,000 has been pooled to kick Joe out of the Senate, and that's only a small portion of what is pouring into Washington. The reason is solely because of his Catholic ideals.'"[xl] Msgr. Martin, we might note, was the retired chief chaplain of the

---

[7] It was not for nothing that Cardinal Spellman's Cathedral in New York City was dedicated to St. Patrick, the Apostle to Ireland.

First Army and therefore may not have strongly differentiated between service to his Church and service to his country.

In Cardinal Spellman's speech to the American Legion on August 30, 1954, he ventured into foreign affairs, criticizing the idea of peaceful co-existence between the United States and the Soviet Union, asking, rhetorically: "How does one peacefully co-exist with men who mouth words of peace while waging treacherous war; men who wear the trappings of civilization while they indulge in the techniques of barbarism?"[xli] A week later, with no apparent irony, the "Cardinal called American Communists 'the host of traitorous men and women who, living beneath the protection of the American flag, enjoy the priceless privilege of being citizens of our Republic while their own allegiance is actually pledged to the emblem representing a theory of government opposed to everything for which Old Glory stands.'"[xlii] The Cardinal's "own allegiance" being pledged, presumably, in the first instance to the Keys of St. Peter and the Pope, representing a theory of government having little to do with the Will of the People, as enshrined in the Constitution of the United States. The Church, as Pope Leo XIII had put it, "with much greater wisdom and good sense, recognizes the inequality among men" as contrasted with Communism, "America's enemy, deadly, merciless, subjugating nations by infiltration and aggression, enslaving freedom-loving peoples by promises of plenty while murdering their bodies, their souls and their hopes."[xliii] Spellman again echoing the nineteenth-century encyclical's description of "The final goal shared by these teachings, whether of Communism or Socialism, even if approached differently, is to excite by continuous disturbances workers and others, especially those of the lower class, whom they have deceived by their lies and deluded by the promise of a happier condition."

The Protestant churches, at least in the north, sometimes attempted to keep their distance from the wilder shores of the Anti-Communist movement. "Dr. Reuben Nelson, general secretary of the American Baptist Convention, linked 'McCarthyism' with attempts to impose 'formulas of thinking' over religion and other aspects of life. He said he was 'deeply concerned' that Cardinal Spellman,

Roman Catholic Archbishop of New York, should 'advocate McCarthyism.'"[xliv] In addition to the statements by Dr. Nelson and Senator Flanders, the attitude of the Protestant establishment toward Anti-Communist Catholicism was indicated by David M. Potter's reaction to the young William F. Buckley's book, *God and Man at Yale*. Potter, then Yale's Coe Professor of American Studies, wrote that Buckley "wanted his college to do exactly the same thing which he wants his church to do—that it hand down to him a directive telling him what to believe. When [Yale professor] Mr. Gabriel gave him the facts and in effect asked him to stand on his own feet and use them for himself, he was disappointed, and he felt that if Mr. Gabriel did not try to control his thought, then Mr. Gabriel had no convictions."[xlv] People like Nelson, Flanders and Potter were only too aware of, and suspicious of, aspects of Catholicism such as the Jesuit fourth vow: "I further promise a special obedience to the Sovereign Pontiff in regard to the missions according to the same apostolic letters and Constitutions."[xlvi] They did not fear a new Gunpowder Plot, but until the election of John Kennedy, they were not shy in expressing their suspicions of the loyalty of Roman Catholic politicians.

Despite his Protestant background, J. Edgar Hoover was an admirer of the Roman Catholic Church's teachings and certain members of its hierarchy and favored the employment of Catholics as F.B.I. agents. In this way the F.B.I. and the American Catholic Church became mutually infiltrated. For many years the Church held retreats specifically for Catholic members of the Bureau. While the Bureau had its informants in the Church, such as Cardinal Spellman, the Church had in effect what the Communists called a "fraction" within the F.B.I. It was a very large fraction, perhaps a plurality. Edward Tamm, for a time number three in the Bureau, a devout member of the Church, worked closely with Father Cronin, on the one hand, and with the House Committee on Un-American Activities, on the other, transmitting the (anonymous) findings of the often illegal F.B.I. investigations of Communists and liberals to each.[xlvii] The Bureau and the Church shared a common vocabulary in respect to the perceived Communist danger. Steve Rosswurm in his book

The F.B.I. and the Catholic Church, 1935-1962, observed that "Images of surging water, or stagnant, contaminated water, or watery substances constantly endangered the boundaries of Hoover's real and metaphoric bodies.

In dozens of cases Hoover used the terms 'flood,' 'tide,' and 'wave' to refer to crime, juvenile delinquency, lawlessness, and Communism. 'Slime' and 'slimy' were employed for profits, politics, racketeering, subversion, corruption, and selfishness; 'cesspool,' 'morass,' and 'swamp' were used in the same contexts . . . Catholics just as frequently described danger as gushing water or as dank, contaminated fluid of some kind. 'Waves,' 'tidal waves,' and 'floods' referred equally to obscene literature, Communism, and the Protestant revolt. 'Swamp' described nineteenth-century society, while immorality was a 'cesspool.' Watching an indecent movie was to be immersed in 'slime' . . . The answer of Hoover and Catholics to all these watery dangers was to erect some sort of barrier. 'Bulwark' was an image in which Hoover found great comfort, for it signaled the solid, the impermeable, and the protective: in other words, the male . . . Catholics, too, used these metaphors of hardness, stability, and rigidity . . . Communism and crime were, among other things, a cancer, a malignancy, a disease, an epidemic, a growth, an illness, a malady, a pestilence, a plague, a sickness, a germ, a tumor, a contagion, and a virus.[xlviii]

The Roman Catholic Church and the Communist International shared a common multi-national, hierarchical structure, each with a European headquarters and primary loyalty to whomever ruled at their center. But while Browder had futilely declared that Communism was twentieth-century Americanism, "Most American Catholics had come to identify their religious values so completely with those of the American state that whatever they considered an attack on the latter was also an assault on the former."[xlix] For many Catholics, particularly for those employed by the Bureau, what was good for the Church they sincerely felt was good for the country. If organizations like the Knights of Columbus were analogous to such closely-held organs of the Communist Party as International Labor

Defense, so the F.B.I. in those years functioned for the Church something like the most thoroughly infiltrated unions, such as the United Electrical, Radio and Machine Workers and the International Longshore and Warehouse Union, did for the Party.

The Church was engaged in a worldwide struggle against Communism, a struggle which in the late 1940s and through the 1950s, it seemed in danger of losing. Poland, the great Catholic bastion in the East, had been over-run by the Red Army; France, the eldest daughter of the Church, and Italy, its very seat, seemed from one moment to the next likely to elect Communist governments. Hence the intensity of its support for Anti-Communism in the United States. The CPUSA was a small thing, but in the eyes of the Church it was simply a local manifestation of a worldwide enemy and therefore it had to be crushed. And it was.

Notes

ii Warren, Donald. Radio Priest: Charles Coughlin, The Father of Hate Radio. New York: The Free Press, 1996, p. 30.

iii Powers, Richard Gid. Not Without Honor: The History of American Anticommunism. New York: The Free Press, 1995, p. 110.

iv Powers, pp. 132-3.

v Powers, p. 135.

vi Powers, pp. 132-3.

vii Warren, p. 156.

viii Warren, p. 165.

ix Warren, p. 183.

x "[N]ew evidence strongly suggest that Coughlin did receive funding from Nazi sources . . . A portion of the Justice Department's internal case memorandum . . . was devoted to 'The Use of Nazi Propaganda in Social Justice': '. . . there is at least one occasion upon which Social Justice reprinted in almost identical form a speech delivered by Goebbels. The Social Justice article gave no credit to Goebbels and did not in any way indicated that it was a reprint of Goebbels' speech.'" Warren, p. 251

xi Warren, p. 222.

xii Warren, p. 269.

xiii Ley, Robert. Pesthauch der Welt (Dresden: Franz Müller Verlag, 1944) trans. Randall Bytwerk, used by permission.

xiv HUAC, Detroit, October 20, 1938, p. 1240. https://ia700409.us.archive.org/15/items/investigationofu193802unit/investigationofu193802unit.pdf

xv HUAC, Detroit, October 20, 1938, p. 1241-2. https://ia700409.us.archive.org/15/items/investigationofu193802unit/investigationofu193802unit.pdf

xvi Navasky, Victor S. Naming Names. New York: Hill and Wang, 2003 (Viking, 1991), p. xx.

xvii HUAC, Detroit, October 20, 1938, p. 1604. https://ia700409.us.archive.org/15/items/investigationofu193802unit/investigationofu193802unit.pdf

xviii "The Politics of Religion: American Catholics and the Anti-Communist Impulse," Crosby, Donald F., S.J. in Griffith, Robert and Athan Teoharis. The Specter: Original Essays on the Cold War and the Origins of McCarthyism. New York: New Viewpoints, 1974, p. 30.

xix Baltimore Archbishop Michael J. Curley's "Anti-Communism also matched Hoover's. The headlines of several newspaper articles reporting his speeches prior to Pearl Harbor illustrate this similarity: 'Awakening to the Foe—Communism,' 'Reds Blasted as U.S. Peril by Archbishop,' 'Communism Held Self-Condemning,' 'Archbishop Hits Pretense of the "reds,"' 'Communism, Birth Control Scored,' "Archbishop Hits Coddling of Reds,' 'Curely Flays Y.S. "Flop" to Stalin.' Support for the demagogic Father Charles Coughlin flourished in Baltimore . . ." Rosswurm, Steve. The F.B.I. and the Catholic Church, 1935-1962. Amherst and Boston: University of Massachusetts Press, 2010, pp. 57-8.

xx "By 1945 [Edward A.] Tamm had become very concerned about the Communist problem in the United States. Like Hoover and Tolson, he was well aware of the extent of Communist influence, especially in some CIO unions, as well as the operation of Soviet espionage rings. But he could do little about any of this because much of the Bureau's evidence of Communist activity had been obtained illegally. To get their message out, Tamm and his colleagues needed non-Bureau conduits. Along came Father John Cronin, S.S. . . . to whom the F.B.I. funneled hundreds of pages of information that later appeared in a report he wrote for the Catholic hierarchy." In May 1945 Cronin reported that "the top levels of [the F.B.I.] are doing my research for me . . .' Several weeks later the 'grapevine' had it that the F.B.I.'s research project for Cronin was 'tremendous': ninety-one typed pages of material had been gathered for just one section of one question." Rosswurm, pp. 5;160.

xxi Rosswurm, p. 154.

xxii Rosswurm, p. 133.

xxiii Rosswurm, p. 172.

xxiv Schrecker, Ellen. Many Are the Crimes: McCarthyism in America. Princeton University Press, 1998, p. 165.

xxv Rosswurm, p. 175.

xxvi The postwar "crisis over the Church in Eastern Europe saw New York's Francis Cardinal Spellman emerge as the American Catholic spokesman against Communist persecution, while Monsignor Fulton J. Sheen's nationally broadcast sermons warned Catholics against 'the fellow travelers in the United States and those whose hears bleed for Red fascism.'" Powers, p. 194.

xxvii Rosswurm, p. 91.

xxviii *The New York Times*, March 18, 1948, p. 30.

xxix *The New York Times*, April 29, 1948.

[xxx] Durr, Virginia Foster. Outside the Magic Circle. Ed. Hollinger F. Barnard. The Autobiography of Virginia Foster Durr. University of Alabama Press, 1985, p. 284.

[xxxi] *The New York Times*, July 5, 1948.

[xxxii] In re Cardinal Mindszenty, *The New York Times*, February 7, 1949.

[xxxiii] *The New York Times*, February 10, 1949.

[xxxiv] *The New York Times* August 18, 1952.

[xxxv] *The New York Times* May 10, 1953.

[xxxvi] Review of: *The Communist Trail in America* by Jacob Spolansky. *The New York Times,* April 15, 1951

[xxxvii] *The New York Times* October 25, 1953.

[xxxviii] *The New York Times*, April 10, 1954.

[xxxix] *The New York Times*, June 2, 1954.

[xl] *The New York Times*, November 8, 1954.

[xli] *The New York Times* August 31, 1954. Speech given 8/30/54

[xlii] *The New York Times*, September 7, 1954.

[xliii] *The New York Times*, December 4, 1954.

[xliv] *The New York Times* October 27, 1953.

[xlv] 11.10.54, Provost, Records of the Provost: Edgar S. Furniss, Group No. YRG 3-A, Series No. I, box No. 3, folder 29, American Studies 1946-51.

[xlvi] http://jesuitchurch.net/learn/the-society-of-jesus

[xlvii] Rosswurm, p. 106.

[xlviii] Rosswurm, p. 20.

[xlix] Rosswurm, p. 121.

The American Legion and Americanism

The American Catholic Action organization, the Knights of Columbus, and the Roman Catholic Church itself, as represented by such figures as Cardinal Spellman, were as strongly allied with the American Legion as with the F.B.I. The American Legion was founded at the end of the First World War as a veterans' organization by a group of wealthy and influential men concerned about the possibility of Communist-inspired activities by former soldiers.[1] These officers (they were all officers), at the founding dinner in Paris, February 16, 1919, included Theodore Roosevelt, Jr., a son of the former President, who took the lead in forming the American Legion, and, among others, William J. Donovan, a lawyer and future head of Office of Special Services (O.S.S.), the forerunner of the Central Intelligence Agency, the C.I.A. One of the founding documents of the American Legion made their concerns explicit: "For God and Country we associate ourselves together for the following purposes: To uphold and defend the Constitution; to maintain law and order; to foster and perpetuate a 100 Percent Americanism . . ."[li] Speakers at the organizational meetings in the United States referred to "Bolshevism . . . the germ of the world's greatest mental madness" and agreed on "the elimination of I.W.W.'s and Bolsheviki" from the American Legion.[lii] Accordingly, the representative of the Soldiers and Sailors Council of Seattle, where a general strike had taken place early in February, 1919, was shouted down and expelled from the meeting. "Americanism" was the touchstone sentiment during these first meetings of the American Legion. It was left undefined, simply equated, apparently, with patriotism. Communism, and the ideologies of similar political groups, were defined as diseases, mental illnesses.

During the late-1930s the American Legion repeatedly expressed an equivalency between Communism and Fascism, proclaiming in January, 1939, that "The Legion is no more and no less opposed to Communism than it is to Fascism and Nazism. As always it is for the historic democracy under which the nation has grown to greatness."[liii] In April, 1939, an editorial in *The American Legion Magazine* proclaimed that "The American . . . will battle to the last ditch against introduction here of either fascism or communism, which . . . are so far as the individual citizen is concerned as alike as peas in a pod."[liv] And toward the end of 1939 the "National Convention at Chicago reaffirmed the Legion's undying hostility to communism and asked Congress to outlaw the communist party . . ."[lv] The American Legion was somewhat early with this request. As can be seen on the following graph, calls to outlaw the Communist Party were relatively few during the Second World War, but then became increasingly frequent during the Cold War years, until it was actually done.

Toward the end of 1940, Attorney General Robert Jackson, following an initiative from the American Legion, created an "American Legion Contact Program." Under this heading, the F.B.I. recruited and supervised members of the American Legion who monitored "'groups or settlements of persons of foreign extraction or possible un-American sympathies.'

They were to identify "the leaders of these groups, the locations of their meeting places, the identities and scope of operation of their social clubs, societies, language schools, etc.; whether persons are sent into communities to spread propaganda do raise funds for various purposes, or for the purpose of agitating such foreign extraction groups." By the end of World War II, over forty thousand legionnaires had been recruited as F.B.I.

informers.[lvi]

The German invasion of the Soviet Union and the increasing involvement of the United States in the war necessitated a clarification of the American Legion's attitude. At the Legion's convention late in 1941, after voting to extend Lend Lease to the Soviet Union, "the delegates reaffirmed the Legion's traditional stand of opposition to communism, fascism, Nazism and all other totalitarian ideologies as repugnant to the principles of American democracy, and [again] demanded the outlawing of the communist party in the United States.

> Aid to Russia, it was explained in the plainest kind of language, must be accepted as one of the means to bring about the defeat and downfall of Hitler and the unholy Axis alliance. The action of the convention cannot, therefore, in any way be construed as an endorsement of any part of the communist philosophy or accord with Stalin, apostle of communism.[lvii]

Nonetheless, there was practically no American Legion Anti-Communist rhetoric during the war-time Grand Alliance years of 1942, 1943 and 1944. Then, as it became clear that Stalin intended to create a sphere of influence including those European territories occupied by the Red Army, the American Legion resumed its Anti-Communist efforts. The key for the Legion, as for the Church, was Poland. Journalist Hans von [H. V.] Kaltenborn wondered in *The American Legion Magazine* as early as August, 1945: "How shall we apportion blame for the failure of two years of persistent effort to solve the Polish problem . . . Why did we feel obliged to accept a Communist government for a Catholic country?"[lviii] Of course the question was easily answered: because it was occupied by the Red Army, but that did not keep Poland from becoming a primary focus of American Anti-Communism, heavily influenced as it was by the American branch of the Roman Catholic Church.

A year later, the National Commander of the American Legion restarted the organization's Anti-Communist efforts with a return to the pre-war equation of Communism, Nazism and Fascism: "There are those who say we have been invaded already by the agents of those forces which would destroy our form of government . . .

[T]here are titanic political struggles now being waged by those nations believing, as does ours, that a government guaranteeing individual liberties and tolerant of individual rights, is superior to an intolerant communistic nation. To those who believe in America, communism is just as repugnant as were the Nazism and fascism of Germany and Japan.[lix]

Fairly soon thereafter, Karl Baarslag, the American Legion's research director on subversion and un-American activities, editor of the *Firing Line* newsletter, and later a research director for Senator McCarthy, advised members of the American Legion on "How to Spot a Communist." Baarslag, referring to "the last strong, tell-tale odor of Communism" and the "Communist-infested United Electrical, Radio and Machine Workers union . . ." associated Communism and Communists with vermin.[lx] It was language reminiscent of that used in Nazi propaganda and used as well by Communists themselves, especially, but not exclusively, against others on the left.

Baarslag deployed similar language the following month in a description of "Slick Tricks of the Commies." "Communism attacks like a cancer . . . Communist-infested organizations." "A well-led Communist "Fraction" in action suggests a pack of snarling sheepdogs harrying, splitting, and driving where they will a great flock of thousands of milling, helpless bewildered sheep."[lxi] The use of the slang term "Commie" was a good indicator of the rise and decline of populist Anti-Communism during the height of the Cold War period. Note the very low frequency in American English of "commie" during the war years on the following Google Ngram graph.

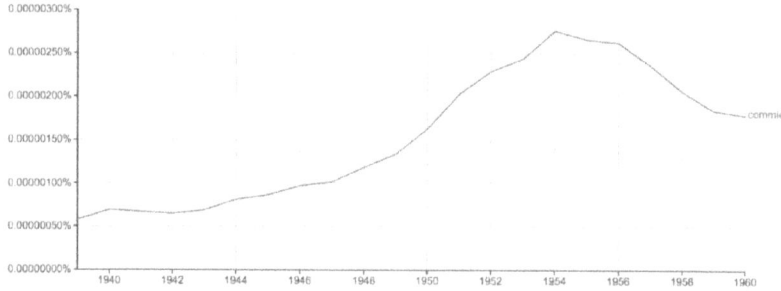

The use of the term "commie," rather than "Communist," had the satisfying effect of denigrating the group by a refusal to use its proper name, giving both Baarslag and his readers a feeling of superiority, just as, for example, Communists referred to members of the Fourth Communist International as "Trots." ("Reds" was less satisfactory for use by Anti-Communists, as the Communists themselves used that term and it had a certain residual positive valence from the wartime alliance with its celebrations of the victories of the Red Army.) Here we have again the Nazi Anti-Communist vocabulary of disease, especially cancer, and infestation. "Slick tricks" and "stooges" (also used by Baarslag) invite comparison with criminal swindlers, while the image of "snarling sheepdogs" and "bewildered sheep" refers to the "army of leaders" trope that would become increasingly frequent in Anti-Communist circles as actual Communist Party membership declined.

In the summer of 1947, then-National-Commander of the American Legion Paul H. Griffith, in an article entitled "Our Fight Against Communism," asserted that "This free republic is a capitalist state."[lxii] It was a phrase popular with members and staff of the House Committee on Un-American Activities, usually in the form of "our capitalist form of government." It was useful, as though American Communists were likely to assert their adherence to the Constitution, to democracy, they were unlikely to swear their allegiance to capitalism. In October, as the Hollywood purge got underway, Eric Johnston of the Association of Motion Picture Producers, informed member of the American Legion that, on the one hand, "American communists are treasonable and subversive. They are potential foreign agents," while on the other hand, "they are dupes and suckers for the fourteen men who sit in the Kremlin and pull the strings which make communists toe the party line everywhere."[lxiii] Treason, according to the Constitution and law, entails waging war against the United States or aiding a country with which the U.S. is at war. As the United States and the Soviet Union were never at war, American Communists, even if actual or potential foreign agents, were not treasonous and none were actually charged with treason. Subversion is another, and much contested, matter.

While the language of treason and subversion is intended to obscure the difference between these and place these charges on a high and serious plain, the vulgar jargon of "dupes and suckers," is intended to belittle Communist sympathizers and make them look foolish.

The summer before the 1948 election, in which the Communist Party very publicly supported Henry Wallace's Progressive Party, James F. O'Neil, that year's National Commander of the American Legion, using the disease metaphor, informed his members that Communists "are foreign agents in any country in which they are allowed to operate . . . Many newspapers and other publicity media have secret communists on their staffs who regularly slip in a neat hypodermic needle full of Moscow virus . . . Communist fifth columnists in this country are pure parasites."[lxiv]

In May, 1949, in the course of listing Communist writers and actors in a Hollywood film studio, Richard E. Combs used explicit vermin metaphors: "Just as vermin breed in filth and dark, so communism breeds behind closed doors . . . that studio at the time was heavily infested with communists . . ."[lxv] In the same issue of *The American Legion Magazine*, Irvin R. Snyder asked "Do you want the Communists in our midst to go unhampered in their spreading of their poisonous doctrines?"[lxvi] These phrases—parasites, virus, poison, vermin, filth—hung in the air from earlier in the decade, having been deployed continuously by the Nazis in reference, in the first instance, to Jews,[8] as well as to Communists. It may be

---

[8] For example: "Germany is urged to get rid of its 'Jewish vermin', in an

significant, in this regard, that the illustrations of the Anti-Communist articles in *The American Legion Magazine* almost always depicted Communist women as having dark hair, while the wives of the veterans were depicted as blonde.

George N. Craig, National Commander of the American Legion, used the vocabulary of vermin to refer to Communist members of labor unions, which, he wrote, were, "infested" with "red termites."[lxvii] Lawyers defending Communists he likened to criminals: they were "communist legal goons" or "commie stooges."[lxviii]

Benjamin Gitlow, a former Communist who had become an Anti-Communist, wrote a series of confessions and exposés in the 1940s (*I Confess: The Truth About American Communism,* 1940; *The Whole of Their Lives: Communism in America: A Personal History and Intimate Portrayal of Its Leaders,* 1948; *How to Think about Communism,* 1949). In June, 1949, he published a lengthy article in *The American Legion Magazine,* drawing on these. Its language, perhaps derived from that of intra-party struggles on the left, was vulgar and inflammatory, beginning with the title and subtitle of the article: "What Makes Them Commies? It's hard to figure out the crackpots and sharpies who make up the commie conspiracy."[lxix] Gitlow assured his readers that "Men, on party orders, abandon their families to live with communist amazons," and that in the Communist Party "we have the saboteur, the gangster, the sinister communist conspirator." The superior attractiveness of "amazons" to that of other women is not made clear. On a more serious level, Gitlow claimed that "The communist party of the United States is essentially a Soviet government party. Its leaders are Soviet agents," which was, in fact, true.

That autumn the Americanism section of the American Legion Convention "Denounced communism as an international conspiracy . . . requested sponsors to remove persons of communist sympathies from the radio and television programs."[lxx] An article by journalist

election article published in the "Hamburg Beobachter," Nazi organ, by Wilhelm Kube, leader of the Nazi fraction of the Prussian Diet." http://www.jta.org/1933/02/15/archive/nazi-leader-would-rid-germany-of-jewish-vermin

The Language of Anti-Communism

George Fielding Eliot, "How the States Are Dealing with Communism," reported on legislation in Maryland that containing "a definition of communism as not being a political movement but a world-wide conspiracy presenting

"a clear and present danger to the United States and to the State of Maryland," the act makes it a felony to advocate or conspire to bring about the overthrow of the national or state government by violence, or to "participate in the management or contribute to the support" of any subversive organization, or to remain a member of such organization "knowing it to be such."[lxxi]

Fielding went on to state that "People must be taught that they can't be communists and also be loyal American citizens."[lxxii]

The appearance of the term "international conspiracy," almost always referring to Communism, rose and fell in published American English with Anti-Communism itself:

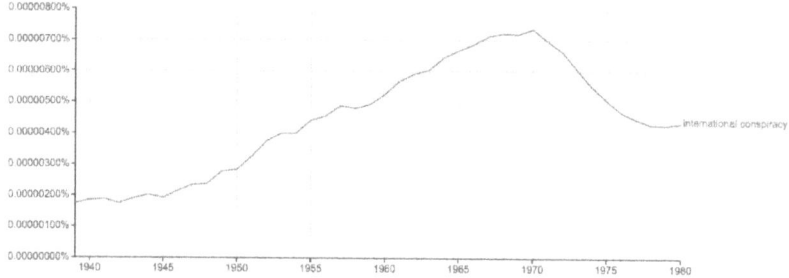

The adjective "international" appealed to the xenophobia of the populism of those years, when even employment by the United Nations was cause for suspicion.

At the end of 1949, Gitlow's fellow ex-Communist, J. B. Matthews, who became a familiar presence in the hearings of the House Committee on Un-American Activities and similar events, warned members of the American Legion that "The Commies Go After the Kids," deploying jargon similar to that used by Gitlow.[lxxiii] In the same issue of *The American Legion Magazine*, that year's National Commander of the organization compared Communists to insects: "Lashing out at the termites who are boring at our national life from within, Commander Craig pulled no punches. 'Our first job is to eliminate the enemy termites in our midst,' he asserted. 'There is no room in the United States today for both the American Legion and communism, and the Legion does not intend to move out.'"[lxxiv]

An article about Communist Party activist Steve Nelson, who was thought to have obtained information about the development of the atomic bomb, began: "The day the grim news broke that Soviet Russia has the atomic bomb, a stocky, dark-complexioned man with fanatical blue eyes, who calls himself an American citizen, smiled . . . The name of this dark-complexioned man is Steve Nelson."[lxxv] Nelson was born in Croatia. His parents were ethnic Hungarians. Although throughout this article he is referred to as "dark complexioned" photographs indicate that his skin color was typically European-American. Of course actual skin color was not what was meant when calling this organizer of "commie-fronts" dark complexioned.

Eugene Lyons, a former Communist sympathizer, if not a one-time member of the Communist Party, deployed an extensive Anti-Communist vocabulary including "Reds," "red conspirators," "Commies," "Pinks," "phony-liberal and self-styled progressive press," "crackpot Left," "stooges and sub-stooges," and "dupes ."[lxxvi] Although "Reds" is a term used by Communists themselves, "red conspirators" brings us back to the Papal, if not Ciceronian, denunciations. The remaining terms at once associate those who are not Anti-Communists with communism and denigrate them with modifiers implying a lack of sincerity or intelligence. In the vocabulary of Anti-Communism, liberals are most often "phony" or "so-called," or, as here, "self-styled." Lyons' use of "crackpot" to modify "Left," does not imply that there are people on the Left who are reasonable and sane, while some are not, but is meant to apply, perhaps, to the remaining adherents of the New Deal as a whole. As Richard Hofstadter observed, "What was involved, above all, was a set of political hostilities in which the New Deal was linked to the welfare state, the welfare state to socialism, and socialism to Communism. In this crusade Communism was not the target but the weapon."[lxxvii]

In another article Lyons assured his readers that a "true communist is, of course, simply a traitorous agent of the Soviet

Union, to be treated as such."[lxxviii] The key terms in this advice are "traitorous" and "agent." An agent is a spy, reporting, directly or indirectly, to a member of an intelligence service. A "traitorous agent" is, in this case, an American citizen working for an intelligence service with which the United States is at war. As the United States and the Soviet Union were not at war in 1950, Lyons' use of the term was figurative, but the suggestion to treat communists as if there were traitors at once strengthens the usage and makes it somewhat puzzling. How are figurative traitors to be treated?[lxxix] One answer was presented at that year's American Legion Convention, which "Urged that, for national security, all communists be placed in detention; all U.S. citizens who are communists be tried as traitors, and aliens treated as enemy spies."[lxxx]

Toward the end of 1950, another member of the team of ex-Communists, Louis Budenz, joined the American Legion's enterprise. He was presented as "the man who has probably done more than any other American to disrupt the plans of Stalin's spies and dupes plotting the overthrow of the United States from within,"[lxxxi] a person who had "renounced communism and returned to the Catholic faith" and was "well qualified as an expert on the communist conspiracy."[lxxxii] Budenz had been given an appointment at Catholic Fordham University in 1946 at the beginning of his career as an F.B.I. informant. Louis Frances "Budenz set the pattern for ex-communists. He recanted his previous political allegiances.

> To prove his sincerity—as it were therapeutic—he proffered names of others he knew or believed to be communists. In return the committee praised his conversion as well as his honesty in testifying, mutually satisfactory congratulations. Richard Rovere concluded that no one "has had any greater influence on the public view of the Communist problem than Louis F. Budenz." Joseph Alsop concurred: "Louis Budenz has played the decisive part in convincing numbers of our people that treachery teems in all departments of our national life." . . . To achieve the status of loyal citizen, Americans called before the committee had to engage in this kind of therapeutic rhetoric of confessing past sins and proving the therapy had worked by proffering names of others.[lxxxiii]

Communism, then, was a mental illness for which the appropriate therapy was informing, turning over the names of former associates for apprehension and punishment.

Budenz wrote in *The American Legion Magazine* in December, 1950, about "How the Reds invaded Radio: Seven years ago the head commies of the country got together to plot the best ways of penetrating the broadcasting industry. Here a leader of the conspiracy tells what happened."[lxxxiv] This was the first of a series of articles in the magazine describing Communist activities in various fields. In March, 1951, he described connections between the insurance organization, the International Workers Order, and the Communist Party: "I.W.O.-Red Bulwark: The inside story of an outfit that works hand in glove with the communist party and which now faces a crackdown that is long overdue."[lxxxv] By September he was negotiating with the C.I.A. to make his "services" available to General Eisenhower.[lxxxvi] In November, 1951, Budenz turned to Communist influence in colleges: "Do Colleges Have to Hire Red Professors? Uncover a red doing his stuff on a college faculty and a hue and cry is raised over 'academic freedom,' as though these people had a God-given right to infect our children with their made-in-Moscow virus."[lxxxvii] At this point Budenz routinely referred to communism as a "virus," equated "communists" and "pinkos" (the latter term usually referring to Socialists), and the "communist conspiracy." He claimed that it "is an incontestable fact that every communist educator or red sympathizer teaching in higher education is an active agent of the conspiracy, whose order he must obey. In his own field he is just as deadly as a Soviet agent." It is not clear whether Budenz meant literally that a professor sympathetic to Communism was a Soviet agent by virtue of that sympathy, which would imply a charge of espionage. The emphasis on "obedience" by a recent Catholic convert was a telling piece of mirror-imaging.

The journalist Irene Corbally Kuhn cautioned about "Some Book Stores [that] push red-slanted books because the owners or employees think that way. Other shops feature such books because left-wing reviewers have praised them." She noted that "the communist master plan that embraces every known means of influencing and dominating the human mind" was implemented by "homegrown left-wingers, bamboozled liberals or outright communists" owning or working in bookstores.[lxxxviii] It would be unusual for someone to call themselves a "left-winger." The rising frequency of the occurrence of the term in American English parallels the increasing activity of Anti-Communists like Kuhn.

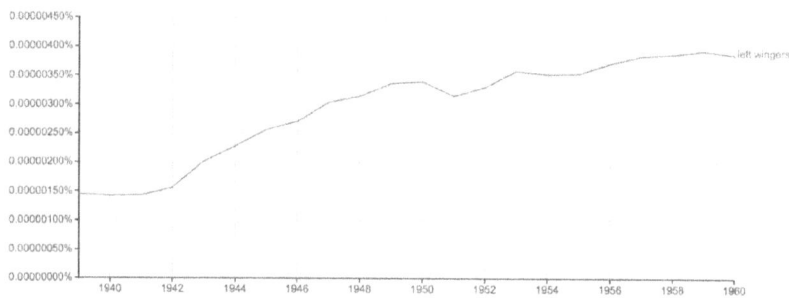

The Korean War heightened Anti-Communist emotions and fear. Erle Cocke, Jr., National Commander of the American Legion in 1951, asked: "Who is Letting our GIs Down?" and answered: "traitorous communists in our midst . . . Aiding these unspeakable traitors is a much larger group. Some of them are almost but not quite full-fledged communists; others are poor, deluded people who fancy themselves as intellectuals, liberals or what have you."[lxxxix] Apparently, not actual intellectuals or liberals, but people who mistakenly believe themselves to be such. No longer was it a matter of 40,000 or fewer members of the Communist Party, under Party discipline at that time. According to Cocke: "Today the United States has to cope with a Fifth Column of over 500,000 communists and fellow-travelers, working under the direct orders of Kremlin agents."[xc] (Again the assertion that sympathizers, "fellow-travelers," were necessarily obedient to Party orders.) The danger was world-wide. According to *The American Legion Magazine*, "The Nazis March Again: High-Pressured by the Soviet, Several of Hitler's Generals Have Formed An Army of 300,000 Men, Now Poised to Carry the Red Flag Across the Rhine."[xci] This was, of course, a fantasy. The generals in question were living in the West.

When that year's National Chaplain of the American Legion,

Rabbi David Lefkowitz, Jr., of Shreveport, Louisiana, spoke at the national convention he "told the delegates that communists posing as 'liberals' must be unmasked, but without smearing innocent persons or denying civil rights. 'The most futile way of combating reds would be to imitate them,' he said. 'Campaigns of character assassination, attempts at censorship, intimidation and suppression of opinion are police-state tactics, which create the very climate in which communism and fascism thrive.'"[xcii] In this atmosphere, his admonitions were disregarded. In an unusually direct attack on the New Deal, and former President Roosevelt himself, William LoVarre accused FDR of being pro-Communist. "On November 16th [1933] . . . while most good Americans slept, the President of the United States raised the 15-year quarantine against the disease of communism . . . [and] agreed to accept Stalin's ambassador."[xciii] The opposition LoVarre set up between "good Americans" on the one hand, and the late President of the United States, on the other, was clear enough.

Eugene Lyons and J. B. Matthews returned to their examination of Hollywood in the last quarter of 1951. Lyons, interestingly, attempted to incite class resentment, referring to "the red conspiracy" and "the pink past of a few actors, public officials, scientist and teachers . . . red mischief . . . an institution long infested by Kremlin termites . . . These *de luxe* proletarians and three-car peasants, paying the Union Square[9] racketeers for the fun of playing at cocktail communism."[xciv] J. B. Matthews asked: "Did the Movies Really Clean House? If you think that Hollywood's exposed reds were kicked out, this report on the present prosperity of many of them will probably surprise you." He went on to refer, as usual, to "the communist conspiracy" and the "seditious activities of the communist front organizations."[xcv]

The phrase "communist conspiracy" again appears in *The American Legion Magazine* in 1952 in articles on the Institute of Pacific Relations by ex-Communist Freda Utley; in an editorial, mentioning "the Kremlin's serfs in this country," and in an article by

---

[9] The New York City location of the headquarters of the Communist Party.

Irene Corbally Kuhn celebrating Alfred Kohlberg and the China Lobby.[xcvi] In October, Utley published an article criticizing anti-Nazi actions in Germany, referring to "the communist-Morgenthau line," the "communist conspiracy" and "the nazi-communist principle ."[xcvii] The name "Morgenthau" had associations that were no doubt not accidental in this context. Among other things, Henry Morgenthau, Jr., was at that point a recent past president of the United Jewish Appeal.

In the August, 1952, issue of *The American Legion Magazine*, William Fulton criticized the major philanthropic foundations for funding "outright communists, fellow travelers, socialists, do-gooders, one-worlders, wild-eyed Utopians, and well-meaning dupes . . . un-American and subversive activities. . . . Stalinites and their stooges . . . red-front organizations . . . Alger Hiss, the traitor . . . [and] a communist-infested outfit . . . the London School of Economics . . . [which] has been the principal culture medium for the breeding of communists, crypto-communists and socialists in England."[xcviii] E. Merrill Root, one of the founders of *The National Review*, in the course of warning against "left-wing super-salesmen operating under the slogan of 'academic freedom'" in colleges and universities who "exploit youth's desire to fight for the underdog and build a better world" asserted that "Communism . . . is the most reactionary conspiracy against man that the world has ever known" and that "[w]hatever the faults of slavery in the Old South, there was a human relationship, often a deep affection, and slaves were cherished as valuable property."[xcix] A description of people as "cherished property," cannot be left to stand, even in passing: "Cruelty was 'an innate, inextricable part of American Negro slavery, for [slaves] had to be maltreated, had to be made to suffer physical cruelty, had to be chained and lashed and beaten into producing for a profit. . . . Instead of a slave's value preventing cruelty, it was exactly because of that value, and that greater value he could produce—when forced—that cruelty existed.'"[c]

Vincent Hartnett, one of those who produced the blacklisting publication *Red Channels,* warned readers of *The American Legion Magazine* that "They've moved in on TV: Well aware of the tremendous power of television, the reds and pinks have not neglected this medium . . . A few communists or fronters may appear in the ordinary course of events on almost any network TV show." With typical vulgarity, Hartnett referred to a "communist biggie" and "Communist fellow travelers and stooges." He quoted "F.B.I. Director Hoover's further warning: 'What is important is the claim of the communists themselves that for every Party member there are 10 others ready, willing, and able to do the Party's work. Herein lies the greatest menace of communism. For these are the people who infiltrate and corrupt various spheres of American life." An editorial in the same, January, 1953, issue of the magazine referred to "communist hordes . . . [the] communist menace . . . communist police state mechanism . . . the communist or crypto-communist press "[ci]

The American Legion Magazine writer Felix Wittmer warned that "Many communities have been deluged with verbal torrents from lecturers with unsavory records. Who is responsible for procuring such people and for screening out speakers who favor traditional Americanism?" He referred to "communist and other left-wing stalwarts . . . communists and pinks . . . dissemination of the un-American and anti-American poison . . . communist contamination." Wittmer's linkage of Socialism with Communism was unusually strong.[10] "The equally great evil of socialism, which has wrecked England . . . The levelers, pinks, dupes, and crypto-communists . . . communist or socialist speakers."[cii] The following month Allen B. Willand, Director of the American Legion's National Americanism Commission, stated that "J. Edgar Hoover has estimated that 91.4 percent of the known militant communists in the United Stares are either aliens, married to aliens, or are illegally in the United States."[ciii] The remarkably precise percentage cited was apparently a rhetorical effort at validation of a reversion to the Palmer Raid rationales concerning bearded Eastern European Anarchists and Communists.

---

[10] The Kirkus review of Wittmer's book *The Yalta Betrayal* concludes: "The very purpose of this historical essay is destroyed by substitution of name-calling and abuse for an impersonal array of facts that might prove their own points."

The Language of Anti-Communism

Editorials in the May and June, 1953, issues of *The American Legion Magazine* referred to: "red traitors strategically placed in government, education, etc. . . . Kremlinites . . . the communist conspiracy . . . Communism or any other form of totalitarianism . . . communist, communist-front and other subversives . . . commies and commie-minded people" and claimed that "to support communism is to support treason ."[civ] "Commie-minded people" was an unusual formulation. In July, S. Andhil Fineberg noted that "The propaganda for the Rosenbergs is world-wide," A product, he found, of the "communist conspiracy . . . typical communist trickery . . . [by] communist schemers . . ."[cv] An August, 1953, editorial stated that: "teachers and professors . . . have shown their red, and yellow, colors by refusing to answer questions dealing with their communistic ties."[cvi] This association of those invoking the Fifth Amendment of the U.S. Constitution with Communism was a favorite tactic of Senators Joseph McCarthy and James Eastland.

J. Edgar Hoover reported to the American Legion in March, 1954, that "In January, 1947, there were approximately 74,000 members of the Communist Party in the United States . . . as of September 30, 1953, it numbered approximately 24,000."[cvii] These out of a population of more than 150 million. A letter to the editor in the same issue of *The American Legion Magazine* referred to "communists, fellow-travelers, eggheads and fuzzy-headed intellectuals who are knowingly and sometimes unknowingly attempting to undermine this great country of ours." "Fuzzy-headed intellectuals" may be a mistake for "fuzzy-minded." The anti-intellectual term "egghead" appears to have come into use in American English along with the period of Anti-Communist activity.

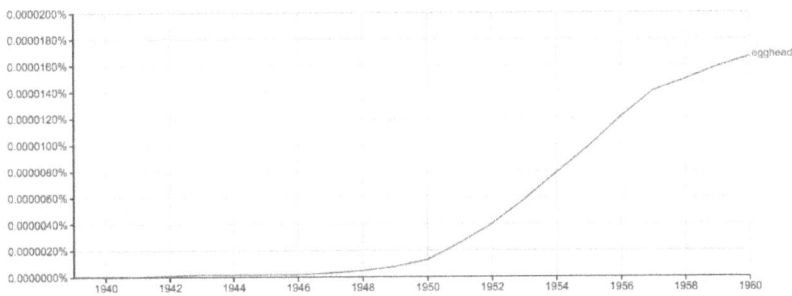

In May, Ralph De Toledano describing the American Civil Liberties Union, mentioned "the communist conspiracy," "communists and left-wingers, "communist perfidy and communist infiltration," "the communist menace," "communist shenanigans," "crypto-communists" and "disciplined communists."[cviii] In June a letter to the editor *The American Legion Magazine* continued to group "Communists and other liberals . . . that element . . ."[cix]

In the summer of 1954, as Senator McCarthy's troubles increased, following his attack on the U.S. Army, writers in *The American Legion Magazine* began to complain that *Anti-Communists* were being persecuted. Irene Corbally Kuhn wrote "Who are the Censors? If you want to learn about censorship, write a book that exposes communism," mentioning "the communist conspiracy," "anti-American pro-red books," "communists and their dupes."[cx] Robert Vernon Andelson claimed that in college, "You Conform . . . Or Else." He wrote that at the University of Chicago "left-wing professors operated as thought police, making a farce of academic freedom."[cxi] A letter to the editor of *The American Legion Magazine* in September referred to "so-called intellectuals . . . fuzzy-thinking eggheads"[cxii] and an editorial in the same issue referred to "Some of our most illustrious eggheads," warning that, in a remarkable grouping, "if you pal around[11] with crooks, thugs, gangsters, communists, second-story men, self-styled intellectuals, grave-robbers, professional liberals, pinks, punks or pickpockets people are

---

[11] "Palling around" was used in this way as late as the 2008 election by Sarah Palin in reference to President Obama's acquaintance William Ayers.

likely to think you're one of the boys."[cxiii] Along the same lines, in January, 1955, an editorial in *The American Legion Magazine* mentioned "leftie Louies" and stated, perhaps indicating at least one motive for this association between Communism and intellectuals, that "Every now and then Albert Einstein takes time off from his skull practice to take up some left-wing cause or other . . . the shaggy Herr Doktor . . . [is] troubled by all these investigations of scientists."[cxiv] Einstein, as nearly untouchable as Eleanor Roosevelt, frequently intervened in the investigations of scientists, whom he did what he could to protect, as he had in Germany a quarter of a century earlier.

After the fall of McCarthy and after the Supreme Court rulings setting aside most of the legal basis for the prosecution of Communists, the editorials in *The American Legion Magazine* became increasingly defensive and bitter. In the July, 1955, issue we find this: "Now that the communists and their ever-ready stooges have knocked off a few of our legally elected officials who were hurting them, they are giving more attention to those who have damaged them by daring to testify against the ringleaders of the red conspiracy."[cxv] And in December: The "claque of 360 clergymen, professors and other proletarians who signed a petition demanding that the Internal Security Act be declared unconstitutional . . . communist frauds and phonies . . . While these characters were whooping it up for the rosy red world of the commies . . . 'pseudoliberals' [quoting J. Edgar Hoover] . . . left-wingers and pro-communists . . . As their bedfellows these people have every communist and pro-communist in the country . . . . these reds and pinks"[cxvi] Even anti-racist statements were phrased in terms of Anti-Communism, as in an editorial in the February, 1956 issue of *The American Legion Magazine*: "The dangers of such attempts [by Gerald L. K. Smith and others] to divide the nation are in Cmdr Wagner's words that 'the communists will have won a major victory if the bloodstream of America is infected with the deadly poison of racial and religious bigotry and hatred.'"[cxvii]

An editorial in the May, 1956, issue of *The American Legion Magazine* referred to "this fight between godless communism and freedom" while one the following month warned "parents who don't want their children subjected to the possibility of red indoctrination" to avoid Sarah Lawrence, Harvard, M.I.T., Johns Hopkins, and the University of Chicago.[cxviii] An editorial in *The American Legion Magazine* issue of September, 1956, referred to the "Communist Conspirator," the "communist plot," the "communist conspiracy," and the "communist mess in the entertainment world."[cxix] And an editorial in December, 1956, asserted that "when a person allied himself with numerous communist fronts most sensible people recognized him as a traitor serving the Soviet conspiracy."[cxx] In April, 1957, an editorial quoted J. Edgar Hoover, who "declared that the weakest link in our security chain [sic] is the 'pseudo liberal.'"[cxxi] And in May, an editorial mentioned "left-wingers . . . familiar phonies . . . charlatans."[cxxii]

J. B. Matthews, explained in the October, 1957 issue of *The American Legion Magazine* "Why the communists and their accomplices are exulting over recent decisions of the Supreme Court." According to Matthews, "If the communist apparatus is not a conspiracy to commit an illegal act, it is nothing . . . At least 3,500 educators, in 639 institutions of higher learning, have public records of affiliation with communist organizations and enterprises . . . The Communist Party is not a political party in the American sense of the word . . . it is, on the contrary, an arm of the international communist conspiracy . . . Thousands of so-called intellectuals have been drawn into support of the communist-front apparatus."[cxxiii] An editorial in the same issue referred to "a highly pungent odor of communist propaganda."[cxxiv]

In the first half of 1958 the American Legion turned its attention to the scientists J. Robert Oppenheimer and Linus Pauling. According to an editorial in the March number of *The American Legion Magazine*: "Oppenheimer consorted with notorious communists for several years . . . Oppy [sic] knocked himself out to help develop an atomic bomb when the U.S.A. and the U.S.S.R. were co-belligerents, but after the war did everything possible to persuade this country to stop work on the H-bomb."[cxxv] And then in July: "One of the most ardent crusaders against our nuclear tests is Dr. Linus C. Pauling . . . The latest of his well-publicized squawks came in the form of a prediction that one of the by-products of nuclear fission, carbon 14, was going to send the entire human race to hell in a hand-basket, quick."[cxxvi] This was apparently something to be disregarded. *The Magazine* sarcastically noted that: "On August 4 the U.S. Court of Appeals in N.Y. threw out the conviction under the Smith Act of six Communist Party officials, on the grounds that their organized advocacy of the overthrow of the U.S. government had taught others only to 'believe' in overthrowing the U.S. and not to 'do' anything about it."[cxxvii]

The next article by Hoover in *The American Legion Magazine* was on Juvenile Crime, not Communism. After that, the emphasis of the magazine's Anti-Communist writers was virtually exclusively on foreign Communism, although in October, 1959, there was one last effort in the old style, by Eugene Lyons: "Why the Reds are Gaining in America. The Soviets' mammoth publicity campaign is making great gains for world communism." Lyons quoted HUAC claiming that the "'the communist apparatus in the United States is more treacherous and, in some respects, a greater menace than ever before' [quoting HUAC from 1955] and predicted that the Kremlin's claws will soon be deeper in the living flesh of America" even though "measured in numbers, the Communist Party is at its lowest ebb in nearly 40 years, with a membership under 10,000."[cxxviii] The U.S. population was then reaching 180 million. Counting, say, 90 million adults, Communists amounted to one-tenth of one percent of the total.

The American Legion had a variety of roles in the Anti-Communist effort. During World War II, 40,000 of its members were F.B.I. informers. No doubt many continued in that role afterwards. *The American Legion Magazine* and the Legion's conferences disseminated the Anti-Communist viewpoint among its millions of members and its officers served a validating function for others. Its Americanism officials were often called as expert witnesses during the congressional investigations, lending their authority to the views of legislators and informers. But that was not all there was to the Legion. The long columns of vitriolic Anti-Communist articles, editorials, and letters to the editor in the pages of *The American Legion Magazine* ran between advertisements for insurance; patent medicines; rifles and fishing tackle; business suits and girdles for men and illustrations of blonde women, presumably the wives of

Legionnaires, gazing into hand mirrors while clothed in demure negligees.

Notes

[l] "The [American] Legion was founded on May 5, 1919, by American officers in Paris who had watched thousands of French veterans carrying the red flag of revolution in that year's May Day parade . . . They feared bolshevism might infect demobilized American soldiers, and they had in mind as a model the German antiradical veteran's organization, the Freikorps, which had recently put down the Spartacist uprising in Berlin." Powers, Richard Gid. Not Without Honor: The History of American Anticommunism. New York: The Free Press, 1995, p. 28.

[li] Wheat, George Seay. The Story of the American Legion: The Birth of the Legion. New York and London: G. P. Putnam's Sons, 1919, p. 193.

[lii] Wheat, p. 89; p. 185.

[liii] "Editorial," *The American Legion Magazine*, January, 1939, p. 19.

[liv] "Editorial," *The American Legion Magazine*, August, 1939, p. 25.

[lv] Editorial, *The American Legion Magazine*, November, 1939, p. 23.

[lvi] Theoharis, Athan. The F.B.I. & American Democracy: A Brief Critical History. Lawrence, Kansas: The University Press of Kansas, 2004, p.33.

[lvii] "United in the Will To Win," by Boyd B. Stutler, *American Legion Magazine*, November, 1941, p. 15

[lviii] "What About Poland? H. V. Kaltenborn, *The American Legion Magazine*, August, 1945, p. 50.

[lix] "To Secure the Blessings of Liberty," by John Stelle, National Commander, *American Legion Magazine*, September, 1946, p. 28

[lx] How to Spot a Communist." *American Legion Magazine*, January, 1947, pp. 9ff.

[lxi] *American Legion Magazine*, February, 1947, p. 19ff.

[lxii] *American Legion Magazine*, July, 1947, p. 28ff.

[lxiii] *American Legion Magazine*, October, 1947, p. 68.

[lxiv] *The American Legion Magazine*, August, 1948, pp. 16ff.

[lxv] *American Legion Magazine*, May, 1949, p. 14; 42.

[lxvi] *American Legion Magazine*, May, 1949, p. 31

[lxvii] *American Legion Magazine*, April, 1950.

[lxviii] *American Legion Magazine*, July, 1950, p. 14ff.

[lxix] *American Legion Magazine*, June, 1949, pp.11ff.

[lxx] *American Legion Magazine*, October, 1949, p. 41.

[lxxi] *American Legion Magazine*, October, 1949, p. 47.

[lxxii] George Fielding Eliot, "How the States Are Dealing with Communism," *American Legion Magazine*, October, 1949, p. 49.

[lxxiii] *American Legion Magazine*, December 1949, pp. 14 ff.

lxxiv *American Legion Magazine*, December, 1949, p. 36.

lxxv Donald Robinson, "Steve Nelson: Unwelcome Guest," *American Legion Magazine*, February, 1950, P. 20 ff.

lxxvi "Who's Hysterical?: From The Howls Of The Reds, Echoed And Amplified By The Pinks, You'd Think Outraged Americans Were Stringing Commies Up On Every Pole, But No One Really Bothers Them." *American Legion Magazine*, March, 1950, p. 20ff

lxxvii Hofstadter, Richard. Anti-Intellectualism in American Life. New York: Vintage Books, 1963, p. 41.

lxxviii "What the Russian 'A' Bomb Means to You," *American Legion Magazine*, February, 1950, p. 55.

lxxix Later in the year Lyons' vocabulary descended to a yet lower register in an article entitled "The Men the Commies Hate Most: The House Committee on Un-American Activities has always been Number One on the commie hate parade. This article tells why it rates red venom and our gratitude." Lyons refers to those who "With inexcusable stupidity, most of them were blithely unaware that they were stooging for communists and fellow-travelers . . . [reaching the] lower depths of communist skullduggery" *The American Legion Magazine*, October, 1950, pp 15ff.

lxxx *The American Legion Magazine*, November, 1950, P. 41

lxxxi *The American Legion Magazine*, November, 1950, pp. 18ff.

lxxxii *The American Legion Magazine*, November, 1950.

lxxxiii Hinds, Lynn Boyd; Windt, Theodore Otto, Jr., The Cold War as Rhetoric: The Beginnings, 1945-1950. New York: Praeger, 1991, pp. 114-5.

lxxxiv *The American Legion Magazine*, December, 1950, p. 14ff.

lxxxv *The American Legion Magazine*, March, 1951, p. 14ff.

lxxxvi C.I.A., Director's Log, 22 September 1951. Freedom of Information Act Electronic Reading Room, /specialCollection/DCI/Smith FOIA/1951-July to September/1951-09-01.pdf

lxxxvii *The American Legion Magazine*, November, 1951, pp. 11ff

lxxxviii *The American Legion Magazine*, January, 1951, pp. 19ff

lxxxix *The American Legion Magazine*, May, 1951, p. 29ff

xc *The American Legion Magazine*, February 1951, p. 40.

xci *The American Legion Magazine*, April, 1951, p. 58.

xcii *American Legion Magazine*, May, 1951, P. 34.

xciii *The American Legion Magazine*, August, 1951, p. 53.

xciv *The American Legion Magazine*, September, 1951, p. 11ff.

xcv *The American Legion Magazine*, December, 1951, pp. 13ff.

xcvi *The American Legion Magazine*, March, 1952, pp. 16ff.; *The American*

Legion Magazine, May, 1952, p. 7; *The American Legion Magazine*, July, 1952, p. 14 ff.

xcvii *The American Legion Magazine*, October, 1953, pp. 15ff.

xcviii *The American Legion Magazine*, August, 1952, p. 22ff.

xcix *The American Legion Magazine*, December, 1952, p. 18ff.

c Murrell, Gary. "The Most Dangerous Communist in the United States": A Biography of Herbert Aptheker. Amherst, MA: University of Massachusetts Press, 2015, p. 49, cf. American Negro Slave Revolts.

ci *The American Legion Magazine*, January, 1953.

cii *The American Legion Magazine*, February, 1953, pp. 18ff.

ciii *The American Legion Magazine*, March, 1953, pp. 33ff.

civ *The American Legion Magazine*, May, 1953, June, 1953, p. 6; p. 29.

cv *The American Legion Magazine*, July, 1953, p. 43; p. 46; p. 48. Dr. Fineberg was president of the Association of Jewish Community Relations Workers and director of community service of the American Jewish Committee. He advocated the death penalty for the Rosenbergs, as their activities encouraged anti-Semitism.

cvi *The American Legion Magazine*, August, 1953, p. 6.

cvii *The American Legion Magazine*, March, 1954, pp. 14ff.

cviii *The American Legion Magazine*, May, 1954, pp. 20ff.

cix *The American Legion Magazine*, June, 1954, p. 5.

cx *The American Legion Magazine*, July, 1954, pp. 14ff.

cxi *The American Legion Magazine*, August, 1954, pp. 24ff

cxii *The American Legion Magazine*, September, 1954, p. 4.

cxiii *The American Legion Magazine*, September, 1954, p. 7.

cxiv *The American Legion Magazine*, January, 1955.

cxv *The American Legion Magazine*, July, 1955, pp. 6ff.

cxvi *The American Legion Magazine*, December, 1955, pp. 6ff.

cxvii *The American Legion Magazine*, February, 1956, p. 32.

cxviii *The American Legion Magazine*, May, 1956, p. 17ff.; *The American Legion Magazine*, June, 1956, p. 6.

cxix *The American Legion Magazine*, September, 1956, p. 7. More criticism of the Fund for the Republic, report on Black Listing.

cxx *The American Legion Magazine*, December, 1956, pp. 6ff.

cxxi *The American Legion Magazine*, April, 1957.

cxxii *The American Legion Magazine*, May, 1957, pp. 6 ff.

cxxiii *The American Legion Magazine*, October, 1957, pp. 14ff.

cxxiv *The American Legion Magazine*, October, 1957, pp. 6ff.

cxxv *The American Legion Magazine*, March, 1958, p. 7.

cxxvi *The American Legion Magazine*, July, 1958, p. 7.
cxxvii *The American Legion Magazine*, September, 1958, p. 35.
cxxviii *The American Legion Magazine*, October, 1959, pp. 18ff.

Government Committees

The popular memory of the Anti-Communist activities of the mid-twentieth century focuses on the questioning of suspected Communists by Congressional committees: "Are you now or have you ever been?" There were 111 of those investigations between 1945 and 1955, rising in a crescendo, in step with the declining membership of the Communist Party of the United States, from four investigations during the 79th Congress (1945-47) to 51 during the 83rd Congress (1953-55).[cxxix] Although the most famous investigations were those of Senator McCarthy's Senate Permanent Subcommittee on Investigations, those of the Senate Judiciary Committee and its Internal Security Subcommittee, both led by Senator James Eastland, and those of the House Committee on Un-American Activities, were more numerous. In addition to these investigations by committees of the Congress of the United States, there were many more by committees of the various state legislatures and local authorities, such as school boards. All of these were supported, usually *sub rosa,* by the Federal Bureau of Investigation, and more publicly, by the American Legion, the Knights of Columbus and a network of professional individual investigators, witnesses and publicists. The key terms in these investigations included "conspiracy," that ancient term of opprobrium for suspect organizations, and "Un-American."

"Un-American" was first used in an 1846 translation (by William W. Turner) of Friedrich von Raumer's *Die Vereinigten Staaten von Nordamerika,* published in New York as *America and the American People.* Raumer, who was an admirer of the United States and particularly of its public libraries, used the term to object to the anti-immigration movement of the period (directed against Irish Catholics). "When even in the dangerous times of the French revolution, the Alien Law was rejected as imprudent, unjust, and un-

American, how can it now be sought, in quieter times and on weaker grounds, not merely to revive it, but to render it more severe?"[cxxx] The term was rarely used in American English thereafter until 1880, after which its use became increasingly frequent, reaching a peak in 1921 at the time of the Palmer Raid arrests of radicals and immigrants (as "un-American," lower case), then becoming less frequently used until the late-1930s, when it was revived, chiefly in reference to Nazi propaganda, surpassing the 1921 peak in the late-1930s, and reaching a level nearly twice that in 1950, by that time in reference to Communism, as shown on the following Ngram chart.

"Un-American" was used to designate a remarkable range of activities and organizations in the period of the First World War and the early 1920s. It was often used about Socialism and Socialist organizations, labor unions and other working class and ethnic organizations. It was more generally applied to mandates, regulations, and requirements of any kind, whether by government or corporations, including compulsory school attendance laws.[cxxxi] It was used in reference to the Anti-Saloon League and to President Wilson. At the same time it retained its nineteenth-century application to manifestations of ethnic prejudice.[cxxxii] Un-American was perhaps most frequently applied to labor union activities, but also to Wall Street and to the professional training of athletes: "It is un-American because it is aristocratic." It was applied in a rather literal way to people not of American birth (as well as, ironically enough, to American Indians) and, again, to manifestations of ethnic prejudice. The term in this last sense was frequently used by Jewish organizations. Alfred E. Smith, Governor of New York, used it of the Ku Klux Klan. By 1935 it was said that "The word 'un-American' is so broad that it covers almost any advanced social, political or economic reform,"[cxxxiii] but it continued to have the opposite application, for example being used by the United Mine Workers in regard to the practices in the bituminous coal industry and by the New York State Federation of Labor to William Randolph Hearst. President Roosevelt, in 1938, referred to "selfish and un-American employers, and other mongers of fear."

The *locus classicus* of the term in the middle years of the twentieth century is the House of Representatives Special Committee to Investigate Un-American Activities (usually abbreviated as HUAC). The committee was established on March 20th, 1934, as the "Special Committee on Un-American Activities Authorized to Investigate Nazi Propaganda and Certain Other Propaganda Activities," out of concern that foreign, primarily German, propaganda might subvert the U.S. Constitution.[cxxxiv] Although from its beginning it also investigated organizations favorable to "Russian Communism," the committee at first focused on the organization and activities of the right-wing *Friends of New Germany* and the indigenous *Silver Shirts of America.* However, after Congressman McCormick of Massachusetts was replaced as chairman by Congressman Dies of Texas, the committee concentrated on people and organizations on the left. Thus, although the committee held hearings on the German-American Bund on August 12, 1938, it immediately turned its attention to Communism the following day. John P. Frey, the President of the Metals Trades Department of the American Federation of Labor (AFL), a friendly witness, informed the committee that the rival Committee for Industrial Organization (CIO)'s membership was "a carrier for the virus of communism."[cxxxv] "Fortunately," Frey testified, "I am convinced that communism [sic] cannot live in the United States if it is exposed to the light of day. Sunlight kills the virus, kills the germ."[cxxxvi] At another point in his testimony Frey changed his metaphor from virus to mental illness: "That is one trouble with the Communists; they have become mentally diseased."[cxxxvii]

It is interesting to compare

The Language of Anti-Communism

British and American usage of the phrase the "virus of Communism." In British publications usage of the phrase peaked in the years 1946-47:

This may have had something to do with the Attlee Government's internal conflicts between those in favor of and those opposed to participation of Communists in the Labour Party. In American publications, on the other hand, the frequency with which the phrase was used followed the trajectory of the Cold War, peaking in 1952-53:

Walter S. Steele, Chairman of the American Coalition Committee on National Security (which included the Veterans of Foreign Wars and the Daughters of the American Revolution), evoked "conspiracies" of Communists, who, like termites, "bore from within"[cxxxviii] and referred to the Communist Party as a "Trojan Horse."[cxxxix] As we will see, Steele was an early adapter of the term "conspiracy" in American English as applied to the Communist Party.

Here again, the frequency with which the term was used followed the fortunes of Anti-Communism itself:

Steele was also critical of others on the left, particularly contemptuous of the American Civil Liberties Union and "so-called" liberals. The "Trojan Horse" metaphor was comparatively unusual in the jargon of Anti-Communism. "So-called" usually was an attempt to delegitimize its object; for example, "so-called liberals," were not actually liberals in any positive sense. "So-called," was virtually a hallmark of Anti-Communist rhetoric, and not only in the United States. The German equivalent of so-called, *sogenannt,* peaked in frequency during the Second World War:

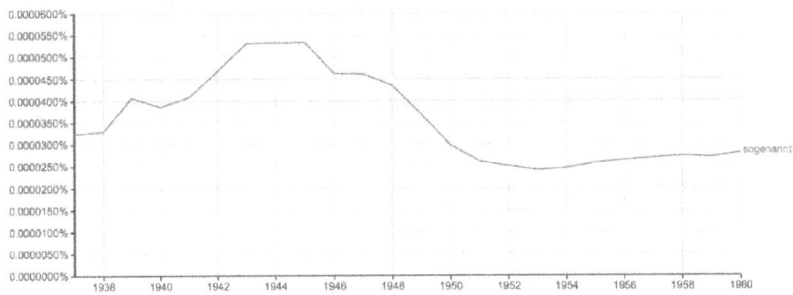

It was used by Joseph Goebbels, for example, in his weekly newspaper, *Das Reich,* on July 19, 1942, headlining an article on "The So-Called Russian Soul."[cxl]

The House Committee on Un-American Activities' hearing on

August 19, 1938, was devoted to the Federal Theater Project in New York City, part of a national program established in 1935 providing work for actors, directors, writers and others involved with the theater who were unemployed because of the Depression. The star witness was Hazel Huffman, a clerical employee of the Project, who used the disease metaphor for Communism: "To prove that communism exists and dominates the Federal Theater Project, it might be well to tell when it started and how it obtained its foothold. To correct a disease we must first know what is causing it." [12][cxli] With her, as with Steele, committee members asked for the names of Communists: "Give us some more names . . . name some names."[cxlii] HUAC was particularly sensitive to communism, actual or fictitious, in the African-American community. While questioning an actress called Sallie Saunders, who testified that she had been upset when asked by "a Negro" for a date, Congressman Dies, the Chairman, stated that "Communists are working among the Negroes in certain sections of the country, and . . . their appeal is racial equality."[cxliii] Chairman Dies did not believe that racial equality was a good thing.[13] When the Committee returned to the Federal Writer's Project during its hearings in September and October, 1938, Edwin P. Banta, a librarian with the project and a former member of the Communist Party, provided a list of names of Communists in the Federal Writer's Project and informed the Committee that the writer "Richard Wright was "a colored Communist," but that Ralph Ellison was "O.K.'d by the Communist Party, but not a member."[cxliv] (On July 13, 1949, Alvin Stokes, a HUAC investigator of "Negro" organizations, testified that there were then 1,400 Negro Communist Party members.[cxlv])

---

[12] Goebbels liked to refer to Communism as "this world disease." See, for example, his speech "Communism with the Mask Off" of 13 September 1935.

[13] "'Of course,' the chairman of a [Post Office] departmental loyalty panel admitted, 'the fact that a person believes in racial equality doesn't *prove* that he's a Communist, but it certainly makes you look twice, doesn't it? You can't get away from the fact that racial equality is part of the Communist line.'" Schrecker, Ellen. Many Are the Crimes: McCarthyism in America. Princeton University Press, 1998, p. 282.

The August, 1938, hearing was notable for an early appearance by Dr. Joseph Brown (usually J. B.) Matthews, identified at this point as a writer for the Federal Theater Project. Matthews, a journalist and graduate of Union Theological Seminary (where he may have encountered fellow Socialist Party activist Reinhold Niebuhr) had been a member of what seems to have been all possible Communist Party front organizations. He was to be one of the star expert witnesses of the HUAC, McCarthy, and other hearings until 1953.[14] On this occasion, he defined "fellow-traveler" for the Committee as "one who sympathizes very closely with the party's aims, but who generally, for strategic reasons, does not hold a party card."[cxlvi] This was a slightly unusual use of the term "fellow-traveler," adopted from Communist usage, which more often was applied to those with left-liberal, but non-Communist, opinions and activities. In any case, in 1938 the term was just beginning to come into common use in American English. It, too, would peak with Cold War Anti-Communism in the early 1950s.

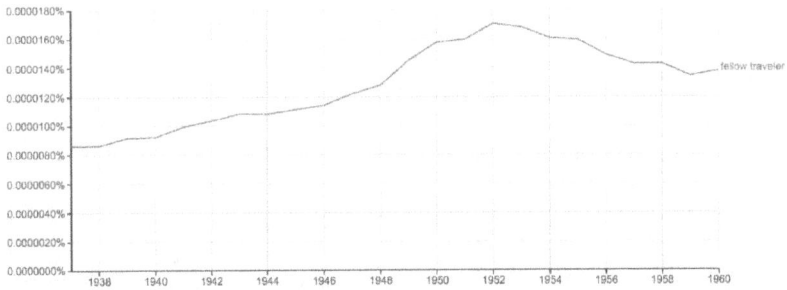

Matthews deployed a rich vocabulary of derogatory terms, referring to the "usual left-wingers," "innocent dupes," "Communists and their sympathizers," "pink intellectuals," "dupes, stooges, and decoys," and, in the Münzenbergian phrase for front organizations, "innocents' club[s]."[cxlvii] His influence may have played a part in the absorption of Communist invective into the lexicon of Anti-

---

[14] As we have seen, he was also a contributor of Anti-Communist articles to *The American Legion Magazine.*

Communism.

The House Committee on Un-American Activities held hearings in Detroit in mid-October, 1938, when they were told by Chester Howe, one of their investigators, that the union organization efforts in that city were "communistically inspired" and spreading "un-Americanism."[cxlviii] John D. McGillis, of the Knights of Columbus, who, as we have seen elsewhere, testified in regard to recruiting for the Spanish Republic in the Detroit area, gave the opinion that Communists were "a band of racketeers making suckers out of the people of the city of Detroit."[cxlix] A former F.B.I. agent, Jacob Spolansky, working as a detective for Wayne County, in which Detroit is located, referred to the "Communist [sic] Farmer-Labor Party" and stated that the Communist Party in Detroit "advocates the use of force and violence as a method of over-throwing our form of government, as well as any other organized form of government."[cl] Mr. Spolansky seems to have been uncertain about the distinction between Communism and Anarchism, as well as that between the progressive Farmer-Labor and Communist parties. Walter S. Reynolds, a representative of the American Legion, stated that the "Friends of Spanish Democracy," which recruited volunteers to fight in Spain, "has been guilty not only of subversiveness, but of actual treason against the United States." In his testimony Reynolds frequently used the phrase "so-called" to refer to intellectuals, left-wing organizations and even the Ford hunger strike. A fellow member of the Americanization Committee of the American Legion in Detroit, Clyde Morrow, referred to "so-called fellow travelers" and in typical locutions stated that he wished to "bring out a little incident there" and "We have something here which is quite interesting." [cli] Labeling statements and events as "interesting" during Anti-Communist investigations carried a subversive connotation. "Little" in this context quite often meant "significant."

Morrow spoke of an "infestation" of Communism, which had contaminated Detroit with "the Communist doctrine of non-discrimination between the white and black races," maintaining "Camp Liberty, [a] Communist camp of racial equality and free love."[clii] The association of racial equality with sexual relations between members of "the white and black races" has been carefully nourished by racists throughout American history. The objection has almost always been that of sexual relations between Black men and White women, without regard to the situation during the centuries of slavery, when sexual relations between White men and Black women were, aside from the usual motivations on the part of the men, an economic matter, an investment, as it were. Murrow, like his colleague Reynolds, found the inter-racial gatherings of Communists "interesting," believing that "one of the prime requisites of communism [is] racial intermixture." [cliii] We have then the theorem: racial equality equals sexual relations between Black men and White women, which in turn equals Communism. The use of the rather awkward phrase "racial intermixture," that is, sexual relations between African-Americans and European-Americans, was most frequent during the Cold War period, coinciding with the Civil Rights legal activity in the *Brown v. Board of Education* period, as can be seen from this Ngram chart:

If the Communist Party had intended to take power in the United States, 1938 would have been the year to do it. The United Auto Workers was strong and radical in Detroit; the docks on the West Coast were controlled by the longshoremen's union with Communist leadership; public transportation in New York City was controlled by another union with Communist leadership and the miners were led by anti-Communist, but radical, John L. Lewis. However, no such effort was made and the moment passed.

In hearings beginning on May 18, 1939, the committee investigated various right-wing and fascist organizations, taking testimony from some of their leaders including George E. Deatherage of the Knights of the White Camellia, who spoke about "Jewish Communism" and "communist Jews,"[cliv] and Major General George Van Horn Moseley, who spoke of "the disease of communism in America," and how "organized Jewry controlling this country."[clv] In August, 1939, there was testimony from Fritz Kuhn, the leader of the German-American Bund and William Dudley Palley, the leader, among other things, of the Silver Legion. President Roosevelt was preparing for war with Nazi Germany, Fascist Italy and Japan and had no patience for these men. Kuhn was imprisoned for tax evasion at the end of the year; Palley was imprisoned for treason.

Between 1940 and 1942 the Joint Legislative Committee on the [New York] State Educational System, with a subcommittee usually called the "Coudert committee," investigated political subversion in the public schools and municipal colleges of New York City. More than five hundred witnesses were interrogated in the Coudert committee hearings and an additional seven hundred were interviewed by committee staff. Andrew Feffer estimates that in this process perhaps eighty faculty members and staff, mainly at City and Brooklyn colleges, lost their jobs and over 600 names of teachers in the schools and colleges were placed on a list of suspected communists, sympathizers and others, which was subsequently made available to other investigators.[clvi] As with other Anti-Communist investigations, the Coudert committee's efforts resulted in the destruction of unions believed to be controlled by or infiltrated by Communists, in this case, the American Federation of Teachers's Local 5 (public school teachers) and AFT Local 537, representing college faculty and staff in New York City. David Caute calculated that 321 school teachers and 58 college teachers lost their jobs "as a result of the political purges of the 1950s."[clvii] In *Reds at the Blackboard: Communism, Civil Rights, and the New York City Teachers Union,* Clarence Taylor observes that "One of the crucial issues in the campaign against the T[eachers] U[nion] was anti-Semitism.

The suspension of the eight teachers in May 1950 unleashed several anti-Semitic verbal attacks, sometimes equating Jews with Communism. According to TU officials and some of their supporters, these opponents targeted the union because of their hatred of Jews. But the TU did not only blame those who used racist attacks. They contended that the board used a double standard, attempting to fire Jewish teachers while ignoring the antics of anti-Semitic and racist teachers. Although there is no evidence that board [of Education] members were motivated by anti-Semitism, some of those involved in the campaign did target union members because they were Jewish. In fact, some opponents [of the union] took part in a letter-writing campaign that attacked the teachers because they were Jews.[clviii]

Whether the investigations of New York educators were motivated by Anti-Communism, opposition to unions or anti-Semitism, or some combination of these, the effect was to destroy the unions and drive the Communist Party underground.

HUAC was relatively quiet during World War II, except for such routine matters as financial investigations and investigations of the desert internship camps for Japanese and Japanese-Americans. However, as soon as the war ended, the Republic party and its candidates declared that "the insidious poison of communism has been injected into the blood and sinew of the Democratic Party . . . [by] agents of Moscow who deny God and seek to destroy the American system of government."[clix] In 1946 "House Republican leader Joseph W. Martin declared: 'The people will vote tomorrow between chaos, confusion, bankruptcy, state socialism or communism, and the preservation of our American life.'"[clx] In his campaign for the Senate from Pennsylvania in 1946, Republican Edward Martin said that "A victory for the Democratic Party would be a victory for the [CIO]PAC. A victory for the PAC would be a victory for Communism."[clxi] He grouped together "parlor pinks, so-called intellectuals, fellow travelers and radicals."[clxii] The Anti-Communist alliance between the Catholic Church, the corporations, and the Republican Party was particularly strong and long-lasting in Pennsylvania.

HUAC resumed its investigation of the Communist Party of the United States of America after the war. On September 26, 1945, Jacob Stachel, a member of the editorial staff of the Communist Party newspaper, *The Daily Worker,* was asked if he could "name a country that has a better system than we have," defined as one "that has got as high a standard of living."[clxiii] A month later, on October 17, it was the turn of William Foster, the Party's National Chairman. Congressman Rankin, again implicitly defining the governmental system of the United States in economic terms, asked: "Your Communist Party today is dedicated to the overthrow of what it calls the 'capitalist system' isn't it?"[clxiv] The Committee's counsel, Ernie Adamson, in reply to Foster's protests that he was being injured by the hearings, asked Foster to tell "us how [the hearing] is hurting you?" Foster replied: "I will tell you how it is hurting me and how it is hurting the workers of this country.

> This system of red baiting that this committee is organizing and is the chief spearhead for that in the United States, is one of the greatest social menaces in our country. It serves to cultivate precisely those ideas of anti-Semitism and Fascism, anti-Negroism, the very ideas the Hitler came to power on, by inculcating them in the minds of the people.[clxv]

In November, 1946, the Committee heard frequent Anti-Communist witness Louis Budenz, who told the members of the committee that there was "conspiracy to establish Soviet dictatorship throughout the world," the Communist Party is "a quisling organization," and that there was a "Communist conspiracy'" managed by the "conspiratorial apparatus of the party."[clxvi] ("Quisling," a World War II term for traitor, was to rapidly drop out of use after the late-1940s.) Committee member J. Parnell Thomas asked Budenz to confirm that "every Communist in this country is a Russian fifth columnist," which he obligingly did.[clxvii] This assurance was repeated by committee member Rankin, who then deployed the metaphor of Communists as insects: "There are too many Reds and fellow travelers that have crept into the Department of Justice, and we are going to need to clean house and fumigate."[clxviii] In 1946, also, the Attorney General said: "There are today many Communists in America . . . They are everywhere—in factories, offices, butcher shops, on street corners, in private businesses—and each carries with him the germs of death for society."[clxix]

In February, and then again in July, of 1947, the committee held hearings "regarding Communism in Labor Unions in the United States." The committee was told by various witnesses from Milwaukee that there were "Communist influences" in the "Communist-dominated" unions, which, somewhat redundantly, were said to use "Communist tactics." Congressman Rankin saw a "National pattern or program" of strikes "to undermine and destroy this Government." Addressing a witness from the United Electrical, Radio and Machine Workers of America, CIO, Bridgeport, Connecticut, local, then-Congressman Richard M. Nixon, asked: "do you mean that an attempt . . . was made in your union by the Communist bloc to divert union funds to Communist-front organizations?" Nixon referred later to members of the Communist Party as "Commies."[clxx]

In a hearings on March 24, 1947, on H. R. 1884 and H. R. 2122, "which seek to curb or outlaw the Communist Party of the United States," Congressman Rankin referred to "a death grapple between oriental communism and western civilization" and to "the dangerous and pernicious organization in America known as the Anti-Defamation League."[clxxi] The congressman's use of the term "oriental" was not intended simply as a geographic identifier, but to signify an alien and mysterious (probably Jewish) force, while the Anti-Defamation League had as its specific mission precisely that of countering the influence of anti-Semites like Rankin, which is perhaps why, for him, it was dangerous and pernicious. A witness at this hearing, James Green, then-Chairman of the Americanism Commission of the American Legion, used the term "Red Fascist."[clxxii] "Red Fascism," rarely used in British English, was increasingly deployed as a term of opprobrium in American English as the wartime Grand Alliance frayed in 1944, then declining in frequency as the term "fascism" itself lost its currency, reviving somewhat at the height of the Cold War, then falling out of use again.

71

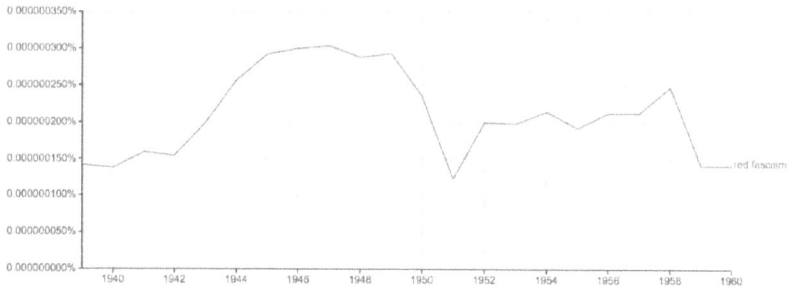

On the 26th of March, Dr. Emerson P. Schmidt, Secretary, Committee on Socialism and Communism, Chamber of Commerce of the United States, deploying a set of metaphors with sexual overtones, stated that the Communist Party had engaged in "secret penetration into areas where it is not recognized" [sic] and that "Communists have penetrated certain parts of the labor movement." He, too, referred to "Red-fascism" as well as to "left-wing and pink circles."[clxxiii] Jack B. Tenney, California State Senator, chairman, State Committee Investigating Un-American Activities (usually referred to as "the Tenney Committee"), stated his beliefs about the Communist Party, piling on an entire thesaurus of terms for Communists, in the style of Queen Victoria's rhetorical decrescendos: "if anything should happen internationally . . . you will have the greatest fifth column, the greatest group of traitors, assassins, terrorists . . . conspirators, saboteurs, and agents of a foreign government the world has ever seen."[clxxiv] (Tenney also exhibited this vocabulary in the title of his publication *Red Fascism: Boring from Within By the Subversive Forces of Communism.*) Testifying on March 27, Louis E. Starr, Commander in Chief, Veterans of Foreign Wars of The United States, saw "a growing menace" from "Communist Party members and their spineless, brainless stooges and fellow travelers."[clxxv] It is interesting that "zombies," usually depicted as brainless, but infrequently as fellow travelers, increasingly appeared in American English during this period:

72

Ambassador William C. Bullitt testified on March 24, 1947. He, too, stated that "communism is Red fascism."[clxxvi] He went on to observe with Tenney that "the Communist Party of the United States [is] composed, in the first place, of potential traitors," then, going one better, "I should consider it a conspiracy to commit murder on a mass scale."[clxxvii] Further, "The Soviet Government . . . stands for . . . slavery" and "there are more than 10,000,000 human slaves today in those forced labor camps working under the NKVD in the Soviet Union at this time[15] . . . It is worse than at the worst moment of Negro slavery. There were never so many slaves as there are today in the Soviet Union actually working in slavery."[clxxviii] This statement brought in Representative Rankin of Alabama, who had an interest in slavery: "In other words, the masses are the slaves of the state or the commissars."[clxxix] The frequency with which the phrase "forced labor camps" was used in American English was much higher during the Anti-Communist period than it had been during World War II, when it would have applied to Nazi Germany as well as to the Soviet Union:

---

[15] A few years later this number was claimed to have doubled. See below.

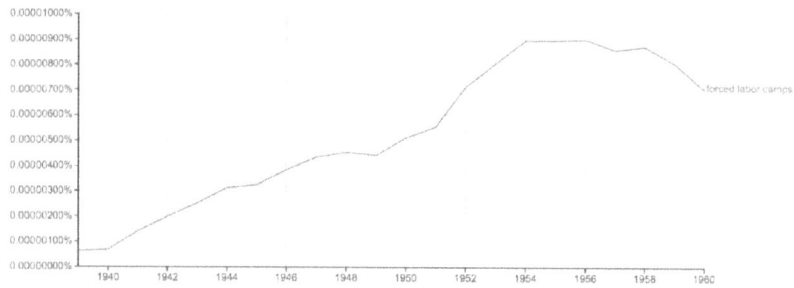

After this Rankin returned to one of his usual themes: "The information we have is that 75 percent of the members of the Communist Party in this country are Jews . . . If you will talk to these high-class American Jews, you find just what I am telling you," that Jewish Communists are inciting Southern Negroes to revolt. Rankin then asked: "Zionists . . . Isn't that a Communist front?'" On July 21, in regard to another organization, he was more certain, claiming flat out that the NAACP "is a Communist front organization,"[16] while referring later in the hearing to "New Dealers, Communists, pro-Communists, and 'One Worlders.'"[clxxx] As Sartre observed: "The Jew only serves [the anti-Semite] as a pretext; elsewhere his counterpart will make use of the Negro or the man of yellow skin."[clxxxi] The conspiracy, then, according to Rankin, and, perhaps, Bullitt, was one of Communists and their front organizations, Jews and their front organizations (some of which were the same), and "Negroes" and *their* fronts, all waiting for the opportunity to rise up as a Fifth Column facilitating an invasion by the Red Army.

J. Edgar Hoover, testifying on March 26th, had a less apocalyptic view, merely bringing out the disease metaphor while informing the committee that "Communism . . . is . . . an evil and malignant way of life. It reveals a condition akin to disease that spreads like an

---

[16] On September 2, 1947, the Committee issued a report on the "Civil Rights Congress as a Communist Front Organization." It asserted that "Having adopted a line of militant skullduggery against the United States with the close of World War II, the Communist Party has set up the Civil Rights Congress for the purpose of protecting those of its members who run afoul of the law" (p. 1).

epidemic and like an epidemic a quarantine is necessary to keep it from infecting the Nation."[clxxxii] He did not at this time specify the nature of the quarantine, although he would later advocate detention camps for the thousands of Americans on his list of those to be arrested in time of a national emergency. A report issued as early as the last day of 1948 noted that at HUAC's offices "files are maintained on the activities of some 3,040 persons. Five cabinets are devoted to information concerning these individuals, many of whom are top leaders in subversive groups or prominent fellow travelers of the Communist Party."[clxxxiii] The committee referred to the Communist Party as "this sinister, conspiratorial apparatus."[clxxxiv]

HUAC, famously, held "Hearings Regarding the Communist Infiltration of the Motion Picture Industry" in October, 1947.[clxxxv] Studio executive Jack L. Warner, also deploying the Anti-Communist jargon of disease and insect infestation, informed the committee that "Our American way of life is under attack from without and from within our national borders" and that "a pest-removal fund" was needed to deal with "ideological termites" and "subversive germs [that] breed in dark corners."[clxxxvi] Congressman Nixon, using a by now familiar verbal strategy of denigration, referred to "so-called freedom of expression."[clxxxvii] Adolph Menjou, a motion-picture actor, utilized Congressman Rankin's xenophobic vocabulary, mentioning "an oriental tyranny, a Kremlin-dominated conspiracy."[clxxxviii] References to "the Kremlin," as a syndoche for the Soviet Union were, as we will see in a later chapter, encouraged by those in the British and American governments in charge of Anti-Communist propaganda. In American English, its usage tracks the activities of HUAC and similar efforts.

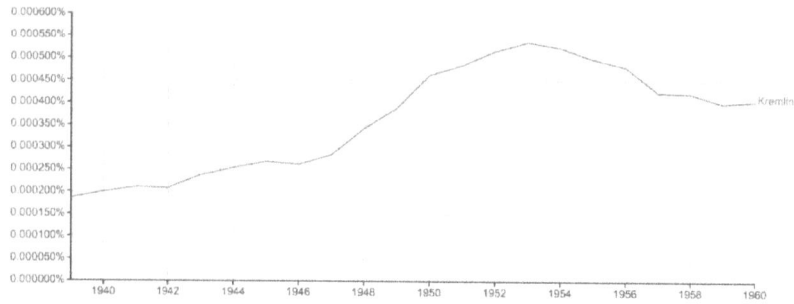

Victor Navasky tells us that "Walter Goodman gives a fair summary of the Rankin-HUAC heritage . . .

> 'The source of Rankin's animus against Hollywood—and he made no particular effort to conceal it—was the large number of Jews eminent in the film industry. "I have no quarrel with any man about his religion," he explained after a Committee investigator was reported to have warned some liberal Jews [in 1945] to "watch their steps" lest the fate of Germany's Jews overtake them. "Any man who believes in the fundamental principles of Christianity and lives up to them, whether he is Catholic or Protestant, certainly deserves the respect and confidence of mankind."' In Rankin's mind, to call a Jew a Communist was a tautology.[clxxxix]

Rankin was not alone in this: "Arnold Forster, general counsel of ADL (the Anti-Defamation League), recalls. 'There was an evident quotient of anti-Semitism in the McCarthy wave of hysteria. Jews in that period were automatically suspect. Our evaluation of the general mood was that the people felt if you scratch a Jew, you can find a Communist.'"[cxc]

During the House Committee on Un-American Activities hearings in Hollywood, Ruppert Hughes, a motion-picture writer, went so far as to claim that "any Communist is an enemy spy or agent."[cxci] James K. McGuinness, a MGM executive, agreed with Ambassador Bullitt, that "we have in our midst an active fifth column, a group of Quislings who intend to destroy our form of government in the service of a foreign ideology."[cxcii] Walter E. Disney (identified in the hearing transcript as a motion-picture cartoon producer), who was enraged by union activity in his studio, spoke of "Commie front thugs."[cxciii] A series of "hostile" witnesses—people who did not agree with the stance of the committee—refused to testify or were cut off. They were cited for contempt and under the marquee of the Hollywood Ten, many more than ten were jailed. The legal nuance with this was that, on the advice of Communist lawyers, they had relied on the free speech guarantees of the First Amendment for protection. Later witnesses knew better, and "took the Fifth," which states in part: "No person . . . shall be compelled in any criminal case to be a witness against himself . . ." The wording is of interest, as it does not include the words "incrimination" or "truthfully," as was often asserted by, for example, Senator McCarthy.

On May 10, 1948, HUAC issued a "Report on the Communist Party of the United States as an Advocate of Overthrow of Government by Force and Violence."[cxciv] The frequency of the appearance of the phrase "force and violence" in American English was on the rise in 1948, moving toward a peak with HUAC's own influence in the mid-1950s.

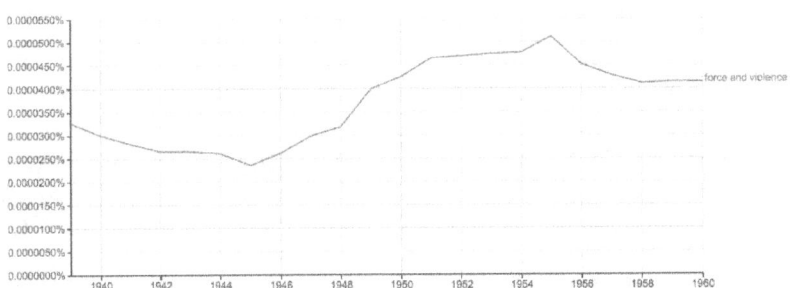

The committee's report found that "Communism . . . is a powerful force for evil," not, for example, a political party, and that "duplicity is innate in the Communist movement." [cxcv]

Elizabeth Bentley, a former Communist courier who named many names for many governmental and non-governmental investigators and committees, testified to HUAC on July 31, 1948. Congressman Rankin was an active interlocutor during her testimony, asserting that "It is about time that they . . . helped to clean this proposition up and drive these rats from the Federal, State, and the municipal pay rolls . . . weed out those enemies within our gates . . . who are plotting constantly for the overthrow of this Government."[cxcvi] "Rats" was a usual term of opprobrium for Communists, outside of labor circles where it had a wider application, "weeds," less common than, say, "termites." Russian Communism, Rankin said on this occasion, "is nothing but a system of abject slavery, dominated by a racial minority [that is, Jews] that has seized control."[cxcvii] And then, referring to civil rights, he deplored "all this communistic bunk."[cxcviii] In early August there was testimony from Whittaker Chambers, another former Communist, who said that "In [Alger Hiss's] walk there is a slight mince" and that Hiss's son "was a slightly effeminate child," thus adding insinuations of homosexuality to his accusations of Communism in regard to Hiss.[cxcix] (The child, however, was not accused of Communism.) On August 24th, Louis Budenz named several people as members of the Communist Party, including Alger Hiss, an accusation that Nixon reinforced, referring to "several mentions of Mr. Hiss as being under Communist discipline."[cc] Nixon's pursuit of Hiss was facilitated by the Congressman's connection with Father Cronin, and through him, with the F.B.I. According to Athan Theoharis, "Working indirectly through the Catholic priest John Cronin, F.B.I. officials provided Nixon with 'the results of the Bureau's investigation into Hiss.'

> Whenever the "F.B.I. turned up" such information, Cronin telephoned Nixon's private line—something he did "frequently between August and December 1948"—to supply "the F.B.I tidbits."[cci]

The 1948 Republican Party platform pledged "a vigorous enforcement of existing laws against Communists and enactment of such new legislation as may be necessary to expose the treasonable activities of Communists and defeat their objective of establishing here a godless dictatorship controlled from abroad. (On the other hand, the platform also called for anti-lynching legislation, an end to segregation in the armed forces, the abolition of the poll tax, "a revision of the procedure for the election of the President and Vice President which will more exactly reflect the popular vote" and a constitutional amendment providing equal rights for women.)

The phrase "Communist discipline," much used in the Congressional hearings, was infrequent in American English until the hey-day of those hearings.

HUAC held hearings "regarding Communist Infiltration of Radiation Laboratory and Atomic Bomb Project at the University of California, Berkeley, California," on April 22, 26, May 25, June 10 and 14, 1949.[ccii] One of the witnesses, David J. Bohm, then an assistant professor of physics at Princeton University, "took the Fifth." Bohm, who was to become one of the most important theorists of quantum mechanics, was hounded out of the country. He was to spend much of his career in exile first in Brazil, then in Britain, as a result of Anti-Communist persecution. Frank Oppenheimer, another physicist and the brother of J. Robert Oppenheimer, also took the Fifth during some of his testimony. Unable subsequently to pursue his profession, he became first a rancher, then well-known for his development of the Exploratorium science museum. Kenneth May, then an associate professor of mathematics at Carleton College, did not cooperate with the committee's efforts to connect J. Robert Oppenheimer with Soviet espionage. He, too, went into exile. The May Prize in the History of Mathematics is named for him. HUAC, and Senator McCarthy, were particularly suspicious of scientists, perhaps because of the Rosenberg espionage group, perhaps because of Albert Einstein's highly publicized opposition to Anti-Communist investigations, perhaps simply from the tradition of anti-intellectualism in American life.[17] The Congressional and local hearings and the loyalty oath controversy at the University of California were greatly damaging to scientific research at that university (which for many years after this had difficulty recruiting scientists) and more generally throughout the American scientific community.[cciii]

As HUAC was investigating physicists and mathematicians at Berkeley, an investigation that included agents climbing trees so as to peer into second floor windows and to claim that Steve Nelson, a Communist with a grade four education, had been handed "the secret formula" of the atomic bomb on a scrap of paper, a subcommittee of the Senate Committee on the Judiciary was holding hearings on "Bills to Protect the United States Against Certain Un-American and Subversive Activities." Senator Pat McCarran of Nevada chaired the Judiciary Committee while Senator James Eastland of Mississippi chaired the subcommittee.[cciv] The bill that became the McCarran Act was a compromise version of a draft by Senator Karl Mundt and Richard Nixon. The core of the law declared that "It shall be unlawful for any person knowingly to combine, conspire, or agree with any other person to perform any act which would substantially facilitate or aid in the establishment within the United States of a totalitarian dictatorship, the direction and control of which is to be vested in, or exercised by or under the domination or control of, any foreign government, foreign organization, or foreign individual."[ccv] The compromise had added to the draconian Republican drafts a provision by the liberal Democratic senator Hubert Humphrey and other members of the Americans for Democratic Action providing for the incarceration without trial of citizens at the initiative of the Attorney General.

---

[17] "In indoctrinating the masses of the people with Communist ideology and the pro-Soviet interpretation of current events, the Communist Party . . . uses not only Party members, but also fellow-travelers and members of Communist adjuncts and periphery organizations . . . Our so-called 'intellectual' classes—members of the arts, the sciences and the professions—have furnished the Communist Party USA with the greatest number in these classifications." American Business Consultants, Inc. Red Channels. New York: Counterattack, 1950, p. 2.

The "Necessity for the Legislation" section of the "Subversive Activities Control Act, 1949" contains the following language: "There exists a world Communist movement which . . . is a world-wide revolutionary political movement whose purpose it is . . . to establish a Communist totalitarian dictatorship in all the countries of the world . . .

> The establishment of a totalitarian dictatorship in any country results in the ruthless suppression of all opposition to the party in power, the complete subordination of the rights of individuals to the state . . . the maintenance of control over the people through fear, terrorism, and brutality . . . [ccvi]

The frequency of the term "totalitarian dictatorship" in British English, which chiefly applied it to Fascist governments, steadily declined from a peak in the early years of World War II, while that in American English peaked in 1953 with the Anti-Communist hearings.

Senator Mundt said in regard to his bill that "We can define communist accurately by saying it is an international conspiracy."[ccvii] He further defined "fellow travelers" as "communists in disguise."[ccviii] As "fellow travelers" were usually understood to be sympathizers with this or that objective of the Communist Party, but not members of the Party *per se,* the McCarran Act could be said to outlaw "communism" as being by definition a conspiracy, rather than, say, the ideology of a political party, and with it brought into criminal jeopardy many who thought of themselves simply as liberals. Senator Eastland,[18] heir to a vast plantation in the Mississippi Delta and with a family history including the lynching of the plantation's share croppers, indicated his suspicions of the administration of his fellow Democrat, President Truman, with a question to Senator Mundt: "Do you not believe there is in the city of Washington somebody high in this Government with great power that [sic] is aligned with the Communist movement who places these people in

---

[18] During a Judiciary hearing on subversion, Senator Eastland said: "I say that I am a racist. Say that I am an extreme racist, which I am." Committee on the Judiciary, United States Senate, 80th Congress, Hearings on H. R. 5852, May 28, 1948, p. 271.

strategic positions in the Government?" To which the Republican Senator Mundt replied "I think there is no question about that."[ccix] The powerful official "aligned with the Communist movement," is not named. Perhaps it was meant as Secretary of State Acheson. Perhaps it was thought better to leave the question hanging.

The May, 18, 1949, session of the subcommittee saw the participation of some of the leading members of the Anti-Communist network, including James F. Green, the National Americanism Chairman of the American Legion, who spoke of "the Communist conspiracy" and asserted that "The selling of Communism is the criminal salesmanship of confidence men and crooks."[ccx] Senator Olin Johnston of South Carolina referred to Communists as "traitors who know no allegiance except to the bloodthirsty Russian dictatorship."[ccxi] On the other hand, former New Deal official Clifford Durr, at that time the president of the National Lawyers Guild, testified that "these bills . . . will go far toward destroying the very foundations of our democratic system."[ccxii] At the hearings on May 19 and 20, 1949, Thomas Harris, Assistant General Counsel, Congress of Industrial Organizations and Arnold Johnson, Legislative Director of the Communist Party, spoke against the Mundt bill, as did Joseph Rainey, retired president of the Philadelphia branch of the NAACP. The conclusion of Rainey's speech expressed ideas seldom heard in these hearings: "I am hoping that there will be no passage of the Mundt-Nixon or a Mundt-Ferguson bill; so that there shall be no forestalling of the fight against Jim Crowism;

> so that there shall be no curtailment where the repealing of the Taft-Hartley Act is concerned; so that there will be no stopping of the building of low-cost homes for people to live in; so that there will be no stopping of the FEPC law; that there will be an advance among the national health lines in this country of ours; that we shall be able to fight to defeat the North Atlantic Pact, and that, above all things, neither the militarists nor the Wall Street trusts will be able to dictate to the millions of people who live in America as to what their future may be, but that the great masses of people in America themselves shall dictate the policies of how this country shall be

run; and, finally, I feel certain that these millions of people who should dictate the policies of the United States will dictate that there must be peace here in the United States, and there must be peace in the world. [ccxiii]

On the other hand, Donald R. Richberg, an attorney whose career slid precipitously from left to right across the political spectrum, reached for the disease metaphor, informing the subcommittee that it is "necessary and proper to identify and isolate Communists as moral lepers. They are no more entitled to secret their disease and to associate freely with healthy persons than are persons afflicted with infectious and loathsome physical diseases . . ."[ccxiv]

The 1952 Republican Party platform, like that four years earlier, proposed an equal rights amendment, the elimination of the lynching and the poll tax and desegregation in the District of Columbia. Otherwise, it was much different in tone and content. "We assert that during the last twenty years, leaders of the Government of the United States under successive Democrat Administrations, and especially under this present Administration, have failed to perform these several basic duties; but, on the contrary, that they have evaded them, flouted them, and by a long succession of vicious acts, so undermined the foundations of our Republic as to threaten its existence." The platform included an entire section on "Communism": "By the Administration's appeasement of Communism at home and abroad it has permitted Communists and their fellow travelers to serve in many key agencies and to infiltrate our American life.

When such infiltrations became notorious through the revelations of Republicans in Congress, the Executive Department stubbornly refused to deal with it openly and vigorously. It raised the false cry of "red herring" and took other measures to block and discredit investigations. It denied files and information to Congress. It set up boards of its own to keep information secret and to deal lightly with security risks and persons of doubtful loyalty. It only undertook prosecution of the most notorious Communists after public opinion forced action . . . We have always recognized Communism to be a world conspiracy against freedom and religion. We never compromised with Communism and we have fought to expose it and to eliminate it in government and American life.[ccxv]

It was against this background of mainstream Republican Party Anti-Communist militancy that HUAC's Anti-Communist activities were eclipsed in the early 1950s by those of the junior senator from Wisconsin, Joseph McCarthy, who in 1953 became chairman of the Permanent Subcommittee on Investigations of the Committee on Government Operations of the United States Senate. McCarthy, with the subcommittee counsel, Roy Cohn, selected various aspects of the federal government for investigation, sometimes for waste, sometimes for incompetence, sometimes for sabotage and occasionally for espionage. Senator McCarthy began with the State Department, which he had criticized in his initial national appearance on February 9, 1950, in Wheeling, West Virginia, continuing with the Department's International Information Program and its Voice of America broadcasting unit, through to the Army's research facility at Fort Monmouth, New Jersey, and then to the Army itself, with occasional brief forays elsewhere, including an abortive campaign against the Central Intelligence Agency.[ccxvi] The touchstones for the investigations were Communist influence in government departments and, especially in regard to the State Department, homosexuality.

The issue of homosexuality was framed in a circular manner. Homosexuals were deemed to be security risks as it was claimed that they were vulnerable to blackmail, because, if it became known that they were homosexuals, they would be designated as security risks and forced out of government service. Much of the emphasis on homosexuality by McCarthy and other Anti-Communists was consistent with the populist resentment of northeastern elites, the traditional old American ruling class, a resentment which McCarthy shared and exploited. The manners, and mannerisms, of men (always men) like Dean Acheson, President Truman's Secretary of State, and Alger Hiss (and his child), were assimilated to images of homosexuals.[19] "McCarthy . . . vowed that nothing would deter him

---

[19] "Joe McCarthy led the charge with his diatribes against the 'Communists

84

from exposing the 'egg-sucking phony liberals' and the 'Communists and queers' who inhabited the State Department."[ccxvii]

Senator McCarthy, in a departure from his usual formal vocabulary during the hearings themselves, often referred to homosexuals as "perverts."

The CHAIRMAN [Senator McCarthy]. We will not make the names of any of the perverts public . . . but I would like to have that name. I may say, one of the reasons for it is that one of the men from the American Legion Americanism Committee[20] . . . indicated that apparently a sizable number of the perverts who had lost their jobs in the State Department had shown up in Paris in jobs that paid better, with living conditions better than they are here. So, at some time, it will be necessary for us to get the names of all the four hundred-some homosexuals who were removed from the State Department and find out if they are in other government positions where they may be giving this government a bad name and bad security risks abroad.[ccxviii]

Senator McCarthy also sometimes referred to homosexuals as "homos." "Let me ask you this: Let us take 'A,' who is proven to your satisfaction to be a homosexual, either by way of conviction or something, and 'B,' who is a suspect. You allow both of them to resign . . . what appears in 'A's' file to show he was a homo?" [ccxix] During a brutal executive session interrogation of an accounting expert, Eric Kohler, who testified that he was, as it were, a non-practicing homosexual, Senator McCarthy asked if Paul Hoffman, industrialist and former director of the Economic Co-operation Administration, for whom Kohler had worked, knew "of this affliction of your?"[ccxx] as if homosexuality was a disease, rather than, say, a "moral failing," as often then defined. Kohler said he did not. (Kohler, who was self-abasing and cooperative in the hearing, was not forced to testify in public.)

Senator McCarthy's Sub-committee on Investigations devoted

---

and queers' in the State Department and his macho disdain for its leader, 'the Red Dean [Acheson] of Fashion.'" Schrecker, Ellen. Many Are the Crimes: McCarthyism in America. Princeton University Press, 1998, p. 148.
[20] Karl Baarslag, head of the Americanism Committee.

considerable attention to the State Department's International Information Program—which was responsible for what the British would call a "white propaganda" Cold War effort. (Information, as opposed to "black propaganda": disinformation.) According to Charles Arnot, Director of the International Press Service, International Information Administration, it had four major program objectives:

> One is to develop resistance to Soviet tyranny and imperialism and to deter the Soviets from further acts which destroy peace and freedom. Secondly, to stimulate on the widest possible popular basis support for the building of great strength in the free world, as the sole guarantee of the preservation of freedom and peace. Thirdly, to spread confidence in the U.S. as a strong and enlightened power with which other free nations will freely cooperate in their own interest. And fourthly, to strengthen the unity of the nations of the free world.[ccxxi]

As this Ngram chart shows, the phrase "free world" in American English was a Cold War term, barely used before the 1950 elections, peaking during the McCarthy period and then dropping off. It had returned to its pre-war low rate of frequency by 1995.

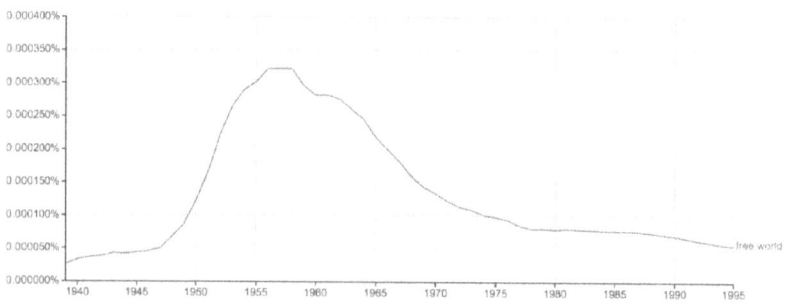

The phrase was apparently deployed as a deliberate counter to the Soviet use of "peace" in their propaganda efforts. The "free world," in this usage, did not designate a collection of democracies, but, rather, those nations and empires (such as those of Britain, France, Spain and Belgium) aligned with, often in military alliances with, the United States.

Communism was not mentioned in the Cold War objectives of the International Information Program. Instead, the issues were presented in terms of the Great Game, as it were, the contest between "Soviet tyranny and imperialism" and "the unity of the nations of the free world," terms congruent with those used in Britain, circa 1900, to describe the contest between Tsarist tyranny and imperialism and the civilizing mission of the British Empire: plus ça change, plus c'est la même chose.[21] On the other hand, the Senators on the subcommittee strongly suggested to Arnot that he use the term "International Communism" or some such variant rather than "Soviet tyranny." Arnot agreed, of course.

Sub-committee counsel Roy Cohn asked Mary van Kleeck, a prominent social reformer who had been involved with Henry Wallace's 1948 presidential campaign, if she was "a believer in our form of government today?" She responded: "Emphatically." Cohn was not satisfied: "My question was: You are a believer in the capitalist form of government?" van Kleeck replied: "Is the United States essentially and forever capitalist? It has changed its form of organization through the years. I am a believer in political democracy, which is the essence of the United States of America."[ccxxii] There was a sense in which Cohn was right. In the early Cold War period it would not have been too far afield to speak of the capitalist form of government of the United States, the higher reaches of the government being occupied by businessmen, like Studebaker's Hoffman at the Marshall Plan, William Clayton, a cotton trader, as Undersecretary of State for Economic Affairs and Charles Wilson of General Motors at Defense. Decisions such as that to recognize Franco's Spain were driven, at least in part, by their business interests as well, perhaps, some sympathy for the Spanish "form of government" of the day. The phrase, "capitalist form of government," unknown in British English, was used in American

---

[21] It is useful for the interpretation of this statement of objectives to compare it to that of the 2016 Bureau of International Information Programs iteration: "The Bureau of International Information Programs (IIP) supports people-to-people conversations with foreign publics on U.S. policy priorities."[21]

English through the McCarthy period, then died out with the Cold War.

McCarthy investigated employees of the International Information Program's broadcast service, the Voice of America, for Communist sympathies. Defending the use of Communist materials, against the implication that they should not be read by Voice of America employees, one official testified that "We read it because we wanted to get the Commie line."[ccxxiii] Another said, while declining to identify people thought to be Communists, "If I mention their names, it is perhaps accusing them of something that I have no right, since I can't say that they are Communists. [But t]here is that smell."[ccxxiv] When asked by Senator Symington whether a youth program broadcast to South America was "a good way to spend the taxpayers' money," a Voice of America official responded: "Senator, if by putting that show on you show the Russians, the Commies, up as evil, and if it means that it has to be done in a syrupy, corny way, and you win friends for the United States, the answer is 'yes,' Senator."[ccxxv] Just as one official testified that he could tell Communists by their "smell," and another equated Russians with "Commies," a State Department official, Edward W. Barrett, referred to "these Communist gangsters."[ccxxvi]

McCarthy held executive (closed) hearings on "File Destruction in the Department of State" beginning in late January, 1953. Senator McCarthy's theory was that the personnel files of the Department had been altered, possibly by John Stewart Service, to conceal Communist sympathies of State Department officers. Service was one of the primary targets of the group claiming that the Department's "China Hands" had "lost China" to the Communists. This inconclusive set of hearings was followed by one into the location of radio transmission towers for the Voice of America and more general questions about personnel and policies of the Voice of America. McCarthy repeatedly asked witnesses "who got that job for you" and the equivalent, implying that a Communist cabal had placed its sympathizers in government employment. Raymond Gram Swing, a political commentator and advisor to the Voice of America, was faced with the question: "How come your brother-in-law is a Commie?"[ccxxvii] David Cushman

Coyle, an employee of the State Department's Public Affairs section (who was fired), said under questioning: "I know my sister pretty well. She is no Commie." ccxxviii Troup Mathews, assistant chief, French Unit, Voice of America, was asked by Senator Jackson "Have you ever been an advocate of Marxism?"ccxxix Mathews denied having advocated Marxism.

A few months later Senator McCarthy and sub-committee counsel Cohn addressed witnesses on April 28 and July 1, 1953 on some matters of intellectual history. Senator McCarthy said to Theodore Kaghan, Deputy Director of Public Affairs for the United States: "You seem to distinguish between the Marxian concept of history and the Communist line. I do not quite follow your distinction."ccxxx Counsel Cohn, did seem to understand the nuances at hand, asking Edwin Burgum, a professor of English at New York University, whether "Would you agree that you have praise for Hegelian and Marxist dialectics and condemnation for everything else along those lines?"ccxxxi Burgum agreed. His fervently Anti-Communist colleague at NYU, Sidney Hook, consistently called himself a Marxist, perhaps somewhat decontaminating the term, at least for Cohn, if not for Senator Jackson. In March, while interrogating the poet Langston Hughes, Cohn gave his "own definition of a Communist as one who is a believer in communism, a believer in the Soviet form of government" and not necessarily a member of the Communist Party.ccxxxii Cohn asked one witness: "Have you ever been a Communist? I am not referring to party membership."ccxxxiii For Cohn, Communism was a matter of belief, not necessarily an activity.

In response to statements in Parliament by Clement Attlee and Prime Minister Winston Churchill advocating a summit conference to find a way to end the Korean War, Senator McCarthy in May, 1953, referred to Attlee as "Comrade Attlee" and

> accused him of having joined Dean Acheson . . . in past compromises "with treason" . . . Mr. McCarthy likewise accused former President Harry S. Truman of a "treasonable" act in his order, at the outbreak of the Korean war, that put the United States Seventh Fleet in the Strait of Formosa . . . to neutralize the Chinese National [sic] island.ccxxxiv

On the one hand, it was a common Labour Party practice to refer to members as "comrade," while, on the other, it is quite possible that Senator McCarthy did not know that and was simply tarring Attlee as a Communist, as he seemed to be accusing the former Prime Minister of the United Kingdom of treason to the government of the United States and former President Truman of treason to the Chinese Nationalist government. A few months later an Anti-Communist witness, Florence Fowler Lyons, referred to Ellen Wilkinson, a Labour Party member of Parliament, as "a notorious Socialist of England," which was undoubtedly true, as she had been a member of Attlee's cabinet and the Labour Party was often referred to at that time by its members as the Socialist Party, but without the implication intended by Lyons. [ccxxxv]

Richard Hofstadter observed that "The right–wing crusade of the 1950's was full of heated rhetoric about 'Harvard professors, twisted-thinking intellectuals . . . in the State Department;

> [T]hose who are "burdened with Phi Beta Kappa keys and academic honors" but not "equally loaded with honesty and common sense"; "the American respectables, the socially pedigreed, the culturally acceptable, the certified gentlemen and scholars of the day, dripping with college degrees . . . the 'best people' who were for Alger Hiss"; "the pompous diplomat in striped pants with phony British accents"; those who try to fight Communism "with kid gloves in perfumed drawing rooms"; Easterners who "insult the people of the great Midwest and West, the *heart* of America"; those who can "trace their ancestry back to the eighteenth century—or even further" but whose loyalty is still not above suspicion; those who understand "the Groton vocabulary of the Hiss-Acheson group."[ccxxxvi]

During the interrogation of Helen B. Lewis, a teacher married to the classics professor Naphtali Lewis, in connection with the State Department's Teacher-Student Exchange Program, Lewis challenged Senator McCarthy's habitual summary of the Fifth Amendment:

> The CHAIRMAN. "You decline to answer on the ground that if you give a truthful answer, the answer might tend to incriminate you?"
> Mrs. LEWIS. "No, sir. As I

90

understand it no such inference can be drawn . . . I am declining under the protection of the Fifth Amendment which says that I may not be a witness against myself."[ccxxxvii]

The following month, Senator McCarthy said: "If you ask a man whether he's a Communist, he's under oath, if his answer were to be 'no'—a truthful answer—that would not incriminate him. The only way he could be incriminated is if he were a Communist. So, when a man comes before our committee and says 'I won't answer because if I told the truth I might go to jail,' it means, of course, that he obviously is a Communist."[ccxxxviii] In spite of Senator McCarthy's interpretation, with its implication that any recourse to the Fifth Amendment was prima facie proof of guilt, Mrs. Lewis was correct, the Fifth Amendment does not include the words "truthful" or "incriminate." It simply states that a person cannot be forced to testify against themselves. The force of the prohibition is on the side of the accusers, in this case, the Senate Sub-Committee, which would be constitutionally barred from asking any witnesses to testify against themselves. They nonetheless habitually did so.

A few weeks later Senator McCarthy's interpretation of the Fifth Amendment was again challenged, on this occasion by Clarence Hiskey, a chemist, who was accused of espionage, repeatedly investigated, possibly guilty, but never charged:

The CHAIRMAN. "That is about as definite proof as we can get here that you were an espionage agent, because if you were not, you would simply say no. That would not incriminate you. The only time it would incriminate you would be if you were an espionage agent. So when you refuse to answer on the ground it would incriminate you, that is telling us you were an agent."

Mr. HISKEY. "I don't think you understand the whole purpose of the Fifth Amendment, Senator. That amendment was put into the Constitution to protect the innocent man from just this kind of star chamber proceeding you are carrying on."

The CHAIRMAN. "You object to being asked these questions?"

Mr. HISKEY. "Yes, I do."

The CHAIRMAN. "For your information, the provision of the Fifth Amendment came down from the old English law. The purpose of that is to avoid making a man convict himself of a crime, the theory being that no man should convict himself. That is the purpose of the provision of the Fifth Amendment."

Mr. HISKEY. "Yes."[ccxxxix]

Apparently, at least on this occasion, Senator McCarthy conceded the point, whether or not he was aware of it. Later in that hearing, he reverted to his usual interpretation: "The Chairman. 'You understand, of course, that when you refuse to state whether or not Doris Walters was a Communist on the ground a truthful answer might tend to incriminate you, you are in effect, so far as the committee is concerned, saying she is a Communist.'"[ccxl] Leonard E. Mins, a technical writer at the Fort Monmouth Laboratory, took the Fifth, quoting the relevant phrases verbatim "I cite the text of the Fifth Amendment, that no person shall be compelled to be a witness against himself"[ccxli] as opposed to McCarthy's usual construction "a truthful answer would tend to incriminate you."

References to the Fifth Amendment in American English steadily increased in frequency throughout the period of Anti-Communist legislative investigations.

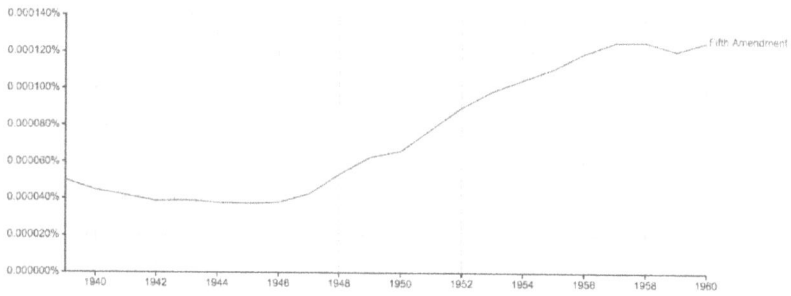

The Anti-Communist investigators and their allies coined the term "Fifth Amendment Communist" as an attempt to invalidate the use of the Fifth Amendment.

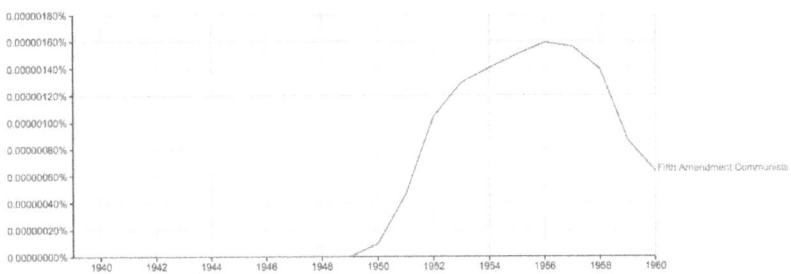

Perennial Anti-Communist witness J. B. Matthews committed professional suicide in July, 1953, by publishing an article in *The American Mercury* magazine entitled "Reds and Our Churches." The article began—and it is likely that few read further—"The largest single group supporting the Communist apparatus in the United States today is composed of Protestant clergymen." He claimed that there were "at least seven thousand Protestant clergymen in the . . . categories—party members, fellow-travelers, espionage agents, party-line adherents, and unwitting dupes," listing dozens of those he thought guilty of such sins by name and affiliation. Matthews had previously put the number of college professors in these categories at just 3,500. The criticism of the Protestant clergy was too much for the three Democratic members of the Senate Permanent Subcommittee on Investigations, who demanded, and finally got, Matthew's removal as the Subcommittee's Executive Director.

Senator McCarthy always denied accusations of anti-Semitism. His assistant, Roy Cohn, offered cover in this, which became the subject of a colorful exchange with a witness, who began by stating:

"My name is William Marx Mandel, and to save you the trouble of bringing out any possible pseudonym, as you did in the matter of Mr. Auerbach, I would like to make clear that I am a Jew."

Cohn: "That you are what?"

Mandel: "That I am a Jew."

Cohn: "So am I, and I don't see that that is an issue here."

Mandel: "A Jew who works for McCarthy is thought of very ill by most of the Jewish people in his country."

Some Anti-Communists, such as John Rankin, were quite frank about their anti-Semitism and their assumption that Judaism and Communism were intertwined. McCarthy was not one of those. And yet his investigations showed a consistent shading of that kind. Aviva Weingarten found that during McCarthy's investigation of U.S. citizens on the staff of the United Nations in early 1953, "of the 124 people questioned, seventy-nine appear to have been Jews, thirty-two were non-Jews and the ethnic origins of the remaining thirteen is uncertain."[ccxlii]

The extensive investigations of the Fort Monmouth, New Jersey, U. S. Army Signal Corps complex of laboratories, both by the Army and by McCarthy's committee, also seemingly focusing on those members of the staff identifiable as Jewish. Many of the Fort Monmouth engineers had attended City College at the time that Julius Rosenberg had studied there. During McCarthy's investigation of the Fort Monmouth laboratory, "Of the forty-two [Fort Monmouth] laboratory staff suspected of communist activity, thirty-nine were Jewish; one of them, who was not Jewish, was married to a Jewish woman."[ccxliii] Roy Cohn suggested sarcastically to one of the witnesses, Jacob Kaplan, "Maybe they are suspending everybody with the name of Kaplan," who replied "That is what it seems like to me."[ccxliv] There actually were, or had been, spies at Fort Monmouth. Joel Barr and Alfred Sarant, Communists who later defected to the Soviet Union, had worked there, but their activities were not discovered until after they reached Moscow.

Senator McCarthy's practice during these hearings was to assert suspicions as facts:

"The Chairman [McCarthy]. 'Did you know Alger Hiss?'"

"I must invoke the Fifth, sir." . . .

"The Chairman. 'You understand, of course, that means to us you know Alger Hiss.'"[ccxlv]

McCarthy asked William Ludwig Ullman, a former Treasury Department official, "Did you know that [the late Assistant Treasury Secretary Harry Dexter White] was an espionage agent at that time?"[ccxlvi] Roy Cohn asked an electronic engineer, Benjamin Zuckerman, "Who would you say was in that clique with you and Sobell?" Zuckerman replied: "I wasn't in a clique with Sobell. I discussed technical subjects with him."[ccxlvii] A meeting with someone became "a connection," with that person; seeing someone twice, over a year, became "a continuing association." Taking papers home to work on became theft of government property.

> "The Chairman. 'Did you live with [Coleman] when the apartment was raided by army security?'"
>
> "Senator, the apartment was not raided. He had been called and asked whether he would let them search the apartment."[ccxlviii]

In October, 1953, Senator McCarthy attacked John J. McCloy, former United States High Commissioner in Germany, Chairman of the Board of the Chase National Bank, President of the Ford Foundation, sometimes called "the Chairman of the U.S. Establishment," as a "bleeding heart" for opposing McCarthy's methods. "Mr. McCarthy said he did not 'give a tinker's dam what the bleeding hearts say' about his methods. 'We can't treat these people with a lace handkerchief,' he said. 'You can't go on a skunk hunting expedition with a top hat and silk handkerchief."[ccxlix] McCarthy often referred to his childhood chore of removing skunks from under the family chicken coop, contrasting his class origins with the "top hat and silk (or lace) handkerchief" which symbolized those of McCloy, Acheson and their colleagues. Similarly, in November, 1953, he referred to "the smelly mess" at Harvard arising from the refusal of President Pusey to fire faculty members McCarthy accused of being Communists.[ccl] Richard Hofstadter thought that "The real function of the Great Inquisition of the 1950's was not anything so simply rational as to turn up spies or prevent espionage . . . or even to expose actual Communists, but to discharge resentments and frustrations, to punish, to satisfy enmities whose roots lay elsewhere than in the Communism issue itself . . .

> The McCarthyite fellow travelers who announced that they approved of the senator's goals even though they disapproved of his methods missed the point: to McCarthy's true believers what was really appealing about him were his methods, since his goals were always utterly nebulous. To them, his proliferating multiple accusations were a positive good, because they widened the net of suspicion and enable it to

catch many victims who were no longer, or had never been, Communists; his bullying was welcomed because it satisfied a craving for revenge and a desire to discredit the type of leadership the New Deal had made prominent.[ccli]

This is something once more all too familiar at the time of this writing.

On November 24, 1953, Senator McCarthy gave, what was, in effect, a Republican campaign speech containing many of his best-known phrases:

- "[A] foreign policy so carefully shaped by the Alger Hisses, Harry Dexter Whites, the Owen Lattimores, the Dean Achesons, the John Carter Vincents"
- "Communists and traitors"
- "Communist slavery"
- "The Stygian blackness of Communist infiltration"
- "Phony, deluded, fuzzy-minded liberals"
- "The Black Death of Communism"
- "The Truman democrat [sic] administration was crawling with Communists"
- "Communists and fellow-travelers sold out"
- "Perfumed notes following the fashion of the Acheson regime"
- "[The] free half of the world and the Communist slave half"
- "[The] filthy Communist dungeons" in China
- Truman's "choir of deceit"[cclii]

In November and December of 1953 McCarthy threatened, first, philanthropic foundations and then colleges and universities by claiming to be preparing a bill that would deny tax deductions to donors to those institutions that employed "Fifth Amendment Communists." With the new year he turned on the Democratic Party, charging that "'the Democratic Administration over the past twenty years has deliberately and knowingly allowed Communists to take any position in Government they desire' . . . He said the record showed there was an 'unbelievable, inconceivable, unexplainable record of the deliberate, secret betrayal of a nation to its moral [sic] enemy, the Communist conspiracy.'"[ccliii] He was then joined in this description of the Communist Party as a "conspiracy" by the

American Civil Liberties Union. *The New York Times* reported on March 18, 1954, that "A strongly worded Policy statement denouncing the American Communist movement as 'an international conspiracy to seize power' was issued yesterday by the board of directors of the Civil Liberties Union. At the same time, the organization reaffirmed its traditional policy of defending anyone whose civil liberties were violated, regardless of his political or other affiliations."[ccliv] There seemed to have been a contradiction in the ACLU's policy. Highlighting those contradictions, *The New York Times* published a letter the same day by a New York City resident, Lorraine Hill, on the "Use of Emotional Phrases." She wrote: "The people who defend the tactics and attitude of Senator Joseph McCarthy have, it seems, a vocabulary as limited and ill-defined as the Communists . . .

> those who unthinkingly follow McCarthy . . . have a vocabulary which leaps spontaneously into their minds, suspending reason and eliminating the need for individual thought. All who oppose McCarthy for any reason are "soft-brained pseudo-intellectuals," "left-wingers," "pinkos" or "fellow-travelers." These are closely associated with "internationalists" and "subversives" of all kinds . . . These words have becomes so generalized that they no longer have any meaning other than a "bad word." People who defend McCarthy use these words lavishly, because they conjure awesome images and save time and thought. The words themselves answer all arguments and stop all reasonable approaches. The words are emotional ones, convenient because they cause reason to fly and emotion to conquer. It is impossible to discuss the moral issues of McCarthyism if one is automatically labeled a "soft-brained, pseudo-intellectual internationalist who follows the Commie line."

Mary McAuliffe concluded that "instead of helping to block and stop McCarthyism, the [American Civil Liberties] Union faltered in its defense of civil liberties and contributed, in part, to the national hysteria over Communism."[cclv]

On March 9, 1954, Edward R. Murrow, the most famous broadcast journalist in the United States, aired a "Report on Senator Joseph McCarthy" on his "See

It Now" television program. That program, McCarthy's response and Murrow's rejoinder, were devastating for the reputation of the Senator. By this time, not only the distinguished newscaster, Murrow, and the ordinary citizen, Lorraine Hill, but increasing numbers of individuals and institutional establishment groups were losing their fear of him. Finally, he was condemned by the Senate as a consequence of his attacks on the Army, and soon sank into obscurity and alcoholic dissolution.

Senator McCarthy had used little of the vitriolic jargon of Anti-Communism in the hearings themselves (although he was less restrained when discussing homosexuality). He rarely referred to "Commies,"[22] rarely used the metaphors of disease and vermin. Outside the hearing rooms he was less restrained. During his televised rebuttal to Edward R. Murrow's "See It Now" attack, McCarthy repeatedly stated that the members of the Soviet and Chinese governments were "slave-masters," who held "800 million people in Communist chains." But it was not Communists, but reporters, whom he called members of a "jackal pack" opposing Anti-Communists like McCarthy himself.[cclvi]

Meanwhile, the House Committee on Un-American Activities had begun its hearings on "Communist Methods of Infiltration (Education) in late-February, 1953. The hearings focused on colleges and universities, with particular attention to Harvard. Robert Gorham Davis, of Smith College, an ex-Communist and charter member of Sidney Hook's (and the CIA's) American Committee for Cultural Freedom, was one of the first witnesses. Committee chairman Harold Velde of Illinois told him that "The committee was greatly concerned with the evidence developed in the Hollywood hearings with respect to the type of 'thought control' practiced by the Communist Party upon its members. Screen writers were told how and what they should write."[cclvii] The phrase "thought control" was little used in American English before the period of Anti-Communist

---

[22] In contrast, "Commie" was in common usage in official State Department communications, especially, but by no means exclusively, in regard to the Chinese Communist Party and the People's Republic of China. See: Foreign Relations of the United States, passim.

hearings, but then rose to a peak during the HUAC hearings on education.

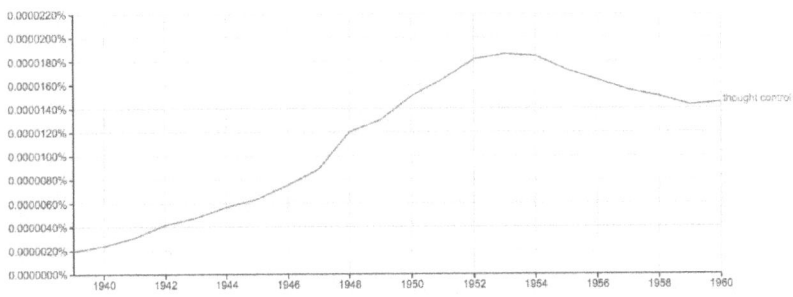

Davis told the committee, as would many others, that contrary to its assumption, members of the Communist Party did not try to influence their students in favor of the Party or its positions: "So far as my own experience goes, there was not direct attempt to influence teaching. There was never in the unit to which I belonged any discussion of what we did in class." For example, on February 26, Daniel J. Boorstin, then of the University of Chicago, also an ex-Communist, was asked to "'state . . . what, if any, influence this group of Communist Party members [at Harvard] exerted over the students who were members of the classes of various professors, if you know?' Mr. Boorstin. 'As a matter of fact, it was a curious sort of thing . . . that there was, as best as I can recall, never an effort made to affect what one said in the classroom, or to the student.'"[cclviii] On the other hand, Boorstin said that "no one should be employed to teach in a university who was not free intellectually; and in my opinion membership in the Communist Party would be virtually conclusive evidence that a person was not intellectually free.'" [cclix]

The interrogation of Wendell Hinkle Furry, an associate professor of physics at Harvard, was especially sharp. Representative Clardy, of Michigan, who was in the habit of addressing uncooperative witnesses as "Witness," or "Mr. Witness," without name or title, said to Professor Furry, when the latter invoked his rights under the Fifth Amendment: "Witness, do you conceive a straightforward answer that you are not a member of the Communist

Party could in any way incriminate you?"[cclx] Clardy, like McCarthy and Eastland, was attempting to delegitimize the use of the Fifth Amendment. His colleague, Congressman Donald L. Jackson, asked Furry "Do you make a distinction in your mind as between one who seeks the overthrow of the Government of the United States by force and violence in this country, and one in the lines of North Korea who seeks the overthrow of the United States of America by force and violence in Korea?"[cclxi] There had not been any testimony that members of the North Korean infantry thought they were attempting to overthrow the government of the United States.

On March 17, 1953, Hulda Rees Flynn, when asked by Congressman Kearney, "Do you believe this committee is interfering with your so-called [sic] academic freedom when they ask you concerning your membership in the Communist Party?" Mrs. Flynn replied: "I certainly do."[cclxii] A member of the committee later asserted that a member of the Communist Party "can't teach freely because his own thinking is under the domination and control of the Communist theories, procedures, and the subversive Communist conspiracy that is abroad in the world."[cclxiii] When asked if she knew that "the American Communist Party is part of a world conspiracy to overthrow the American constitutional form of government by force and violence," Flynn consulted with her attorney and then replied that she had "no considered opinion on that."[cclxiv] "World conspiracy" was a variant on the usual "conspiracy" *per se,* in American English.

On March 18, 1953, a quite uncooperative witness, Abraham Glasser, observed that "it is evident to me that in this hearing I am on trial, and not only I [sic], but the entire administration of the National Government which was in office during the late thirties, middle forties, and it is just what we thought would happen. This is an attack on the New Deal."[cclxv] Virginia Durr later observed in her memoir that "The opponents of the New Deal and of labor's efforts fought the labor unions on the Communist charge, they fought the New Deal on the Communist charge, they fought Mrs. Roosevelt on the Communist charge. They used it against everything."[cclxvi] Theodore S. Polumbaum, a writer and photographer, was asked: "Do you believe that the Communist Party of the

United States is a subversive organization . . . designed to overthrow our form of government?" ^{cclxvii} Congressman Clyde Doyle told Polumbaum that his was a "frank question, as an American man to an American man."cclxviii These phrases were, perhaps, to distinguish the Anti-Communist members of HUAC, frank American men, from the presumably less frank, less manly, possibly un-American, witnesses.

On April 22, 1953, Dr. William T. Martin, a professor and chair of the Mathematics department at M.I.T., who was an ex-communist, named those who had been with him in the Communist Party. Representative Clyde Doyle of California asked: "How long did it take you to discover that the Marxist literature and theory, philosophically, was only totalitarian Soviet communism's scheme to rule the world, and that it should rule the world?"cclxix This was a question that seemed intended to delegitimize, in this case, "Marxist literature and theory" as objects of scholarly interest. The committee chairman, Representative Harold Velde of Illinois, elaborated on this during the testimony of another scientist, physicist Paul R. Zilsel of the University of Connecticut: "Well, now, there is abundant evidence before this committee and other administrative agencies of Government and other investigating committees that the Soviet Government is now a totalitarian form of government and in some ways similar to Nazism . . . the Soviet system and American Communist party is a part of the dictatorial, totalitarian system." cclxx

Kit Clardy, the aggressive congressman from Michigan, interrogating M.I.T. chemistry professor Isadore Amdur, an ex-Communist, first asked: "You fell for the line then, to use the vernacular?" then asserted: "you fell for this phony line . . ." and "I presume you have read Das Kapital so that you know the economic theories or nonsense that Karl Marx advanced?"cclxxi Interestingly, Clardy had made himself well-versed in Marxist and Communist theory (or nonsense). During his questioning of a later witness, Clardy asked: "Do you not recognize the fact that today any active member of the Communist Party does not have freedom of thought? . . . [must] slavishly follow the Communist Party line?"cclxxii The phrase "slavishly follow," in American English, was more frequently used during the peak years of Anti-   Communism than earlier or later.

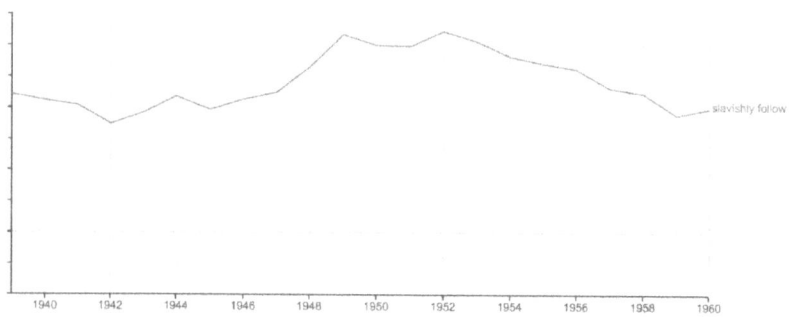

slavishly follow

The ex-Communist M.I.T. professor of Mathematics, Norman Levinson, a cooperative witness, said "I think that most people recognize that the leaders of the Soviet Union are essentially a bunch of gangsters . . ." And departing somewhat from his specialty, "I think in this country [the Communist Party] consists of a group of largely maladjusted crackpots, and I think perhaps a psychiatric examination would reveal . . . a man with serious—with serious personal deficiencies somewhere." [cclxxiii] These statements were part of the effort to change the definition of Communism from a political movement, that is, an activity in the public realm, to a legal and psychological matter, by placing it under the rubric of the criminal law and psychiatric causation. If the Communist leaders were "gangsters," then the Communist Party was by definition a criminal conspiracy, not a political party, and if its ordinary members were "maladjusted crackpots," their activities could be defined as arising from their personal problems and not from societal issues.

At these hearings in 1953 the committee was investigating Communist influence at Harvard in the late 1930s and early 1940s, not any that might have existed at the time of the hearings. HUAC also looked into the history of Communist activities at the University of Michigan. Representative Clardy, during the testimony of a friendly, ex-Communist, witness, Francis X. T. Crowley, commented about a Marxist study group meeting that "They identified it more or less as a meeting of liberals and progressives and all the other words the Communists ordinarily use . . . Trying to suck in as many as they could discover as to who would be vulnerable to further Communist Party indoctrination."[cclxxiv] The presumably Communist attorney Robert H. Silk was asked "Why don't you get out of that outfit? Why don't you clean house and get out of any association that makes you feel it is right to come in before a congressional committee and refuse to help your Congress clean up on these subversives?"[cclxxv] Representative Clardy, as if he had read Hofstadter as well as Marx, while questioning anthropologist Jack Lucas, asserted that "it is the so-called intellectuals, the people who have had the advantage of college and university educations that furnish the sparkplugs for this conspiracy."[cclxxvi]

In March, 1953, William Jansen, Superintendent of Schools of New York City, testified before the Senate Internal Security Committee. Jansen had decided that the school district would not employ Communist teachers. He told the committee that New York City would have four standards for teachers: Loyalty to Country; Scholarship; Love of Children and Respect for all Individuals, and High Ethical Standards (perhaps referring to homosexuality). Jenner said that Communists could not meet these standards because they had given their allegiance to "an international conspiracy that had the destruction of American democracy as its aim"; because their "mental processes were circumscribed by [the] party line and [that they were] under strict discipline"; because individuals do not count in a Communist state, and because Communists "definitely advocate lying when it is deemed to achieve their objectives." Further, refusal to answer questions about communism (that is, invoking Constitutional protections under the Fifth Amendment) "was taken as an act of insubordination and a ground for dismissal by the Board of Education."[cclxxvii] This was the rationale for a second purge of radical teachers from the New York City schools.

The House Committee on Un-American Activities held hearings on "Communist Political Subversion" during the Second Session of the Eighty-Fourth Congress, November and December, 1956.[cclxxviii] A friendly witness, Archibald B. Roosevelt, of Cold Spring Harbor, NY, an investment banker, involved with The Alliance, the American Coalition of Patriotic Societies, Sons of the American Revolution, testified about "the Communist Conspiracy" and stated that "the Kremlin has already invaded America . . . These Red forces are a political army which is civilian in appearance and walk the streets of America indistinguishable from the rest of the population." He also referred to "Red tyranny," "alien Reds," "the bleeding hearts of the 'liberals'," and "Red hordes."[cclxxix] "Red hordes, in American English, were associated with the Korean War. "Red tyranny" had a less definite association, and therefore its frequency was not as sharply defined by the fighting in Korea.

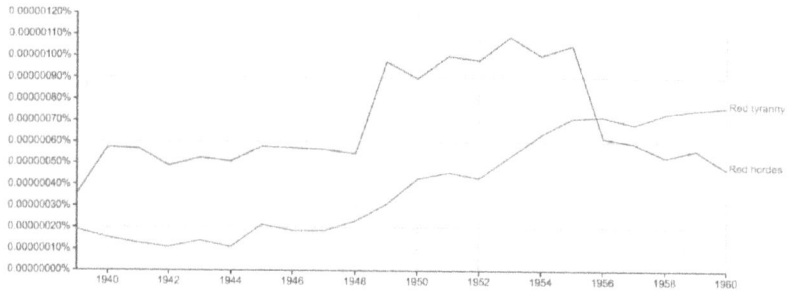

The then-Director of the committee, Richard Arens[23], was particularly persistent in asking witnesses if they were members of "the Communist conspiracy," as if it were simply a synonym for the Communist Party.[cclxxx]   On November 14, 1956, Arens asked a witness who had just invoked the Fifth Amendment against self-incrimination: "Why don't you stand up like a red-blooded American and deny you have ever been a member of the Communist conspiracy?"[cclxxxi] He used these phrases—"why don't you stand up" and "red-blooded American"—repeatedly during this and other investigations. On November 28, 1956, Arens threatened a New York City social worker, Evelyn Abelson, with the loss of her job and laughed about having stolen her mail. She did, in fact, lose her job. Arens said to Bessie Steinberg, of Pittsburgh, "Now, why don't you serve your Government by telling your Government what knowledge, if any, you have of the participation of the Communist conspiracy in undertaking to procure the enactment of these

---

[23] Sometimes spelled "Ahrens."

resolutions?' having to do with the McCarran-Walter Act. [cclxxxii] "Help your government" was a phrase often used sarcastically by Arens. On December 3, 1956, he said to Reverend Charles Hill, of the (Black) Hartford Avenue Baptist Church in Detroit, "Then stand up and tell this committee whether or not you were chairman of the Communist-controlled peace crusade" [cclxxxiii] On December 4th, in Chicago, he asked Ernest DeMaio, district president, United Electrical, Radio & Machine Workers of America, who had taken the Fifth: "Are you this moment a member of the Communist conspiratorial apparatus?"[cclxxxiv]

There was an unexpected, dramatic, moment in the hearing on December 6, 1956 in Los Angeles. Frank J. Whitley, a Black real estate broker, refused to answer questions, invoking his rights under the Fifth Amendment.[cclxxxv] When asked to explain himself, he began by stating that "Both of my parents were slaves here in America, and I have been persecuted ever since the day of my birth. And this committee or no other committee has taken up my cause. Congressman Clyde Doyle responded with: "You are directed to answer."

Mr. Whitley. On the basis of the first and fifth amendments of the United States Constitution, I refuse to answer.

Mr. Doyle. This is right. So the United States Government is protecting you and your constitutional rights.

Mr. Whitley. They are killing me and my people all over this country, and you know it. And you know it.

Mr. Scherer [Congressman Gordon H. Scherer]. What? They are killing you and all your people?

Mr. Whitley. What about Emmett Till? What about Mr. Moore in Florida a few years ago? And I don't have to go that far. I can start right in Los Angeles. The same thing is happening.

Mr. Doyle. You don't charge the United States Government with killing?

Mr. Whitley. For doing nothing about it. That is why I charge them.

Mr. Doyle. But I deny your statement, sir. The United States Government has done everything it could in the Till case to discover—it   ascertained there was no transporting across State lines.

Mr. Whitley. Yes. It's been 90 years since Abraham Lincoln signed the Emancipation Proclamation. They are begging to go to school in Texas even, right here by us. What are you doing? You are searching for some subversion you talk about.

Whitley, who was self-employed, does not seem to have suffered from his encounter with the committee.

On December 7, 1956, Arens asked Jerome Land, who was in the automobile business in Los Angeles, "Are you a member of a conspiracy that is based on deceit and lies, perversion of the truth?"[cclxxxvi] This question seems to have had only one implied answer, although as a matter of fact the response was not an answer, but the invocation of the Fifth Amendment. And Arens asked the Reverend Stephen H. Fritchman "are you now, or have you ever been, a member of a godless conspiracy controlled by a foreign power?"[cclxxxvii]   The term "godless conspiracy" was peculiar to the Cold War period in American English during the years in which God was enlisted by the Eisenhower Administration in its conflict with the Soviet Union.

In contrast, according to Google's Ngram system, it was unknown in British publications of the period.

Arens gave a full account of his understanding of his mission during the House Committee on Un-American Activities hearings on "Communist infiltration and Activities in the South." On July 31, 1958, he said that "A Communist is a person who is part and parcel of the Communist Party, either aboveground or belowground in the United States, the Communist operation.

About 100 years ago there

was a German scholar, Karl Marx. He evolved a philosophy of world revolution, an atheistic, communistic program. That was given a catalytic response by Nicolai Lenin, 50 years ago, at which time he and a band of revolutionaries seized control of the government. That movement has spread over the world. It has 33,000,000 agents over the world, in a death grip with all the God-fearing people, all that God-fearing people believe in. In the United States, 25 or 30 years ago that movement got a start. It is a movement than now has enmeshed in its grip 900 million people. It is the movement that proceeds by violence and deceit and subversion to corrupt and destroy. It is the movement within Soviet Russia itself which has, in its ascendancy, destroyed over 10 million human souls. It has at least 20 million in slave labor camps. It is a movement in Red China, according to the best advices, that has destroyed approximately 40 million souls. It is a movement that is heading toward a total war against the United States of America. It is a movement that has enlisted within the United States a fifth column, dedicated to destroy this Government, which is the last bastion of freedom of any potency to resist this movement in the world.[cclxxxviii]

This was two years after Khrushchev's "secret speech," four years after the death of Stalin, six years before the passage of the Voting Rights Act.

Anti-Communism and Segregation
The language of Anti-Communism—the "free world" as against "Communist tyranny" and the like—was compromised for its American sponsors, as was Anti-Communism itself, by the condition of the descendants of enslaved Africans in the United States, particularly in the South. The efforts of officers in the U.S. Army to impose segregation in Britain and France during the Second World War and the publicity given to the prevalence of segregation, "Jim Crow," by the Communists from the 1920s were continually at hand as, and used as, accusations of American hypocrisy.[24] This mattered

---

[24] The efforts to maintain segregation of the U.S. military in Britain did not go well. "When, for example, white Americans remonstrated with a

little in the South. After the end of the Second World War "white supremacists regarded all agitation against segregation as Communist-inspired and used this notion to gain acceptance for their positions . . ."[cclxxxix]

> Because the CPUSA had advocated civil rights for black southerners at least since it led the fight for the Scottsboro defendants in the early 1930s, and since many Communists had supported Henry Wallace's refusal to speak before segregated southern audiences in 1948, identification of integrationists with the Communist Party made sense to many southerners.[ccxc]

It did not make sense only to southerners. Albert Canwell, the chairman of a Washington State legislative committee, had "announced: 'If someone insists there is discrimination against Negroes in this country . . . there is every reason to believe that person is a Communist.'"[ccxci] If not all integrationists were Communists, certainly, according to Ellen Schrecker, the Communist Party itself was integrationist. "Because of its commitment to racial equality, the party pressed its labor activists to fight discrimination in employment . . .

> During World War II, when African Americans broke the color line in previously closed industries, some left-wing unions even pioneered an early form of affirmative action to help these newly hired workers keep their jobs after the war.[ccxcii]

Advocating civil, or equal, rights for African Americans was assumed by many Anti-Communists to be proof of Communist Party membership or sympathies. As Anne Braden wrote in 1963, at the height of the Civil Rights Movement, "This 'feeling' that there is something subversive about the integration movement is widespread.

> Few people can actually define it, but it's there, and it is one of the major factors impeding progress today. Not only does it deter thousands who know that segregation is wrong . . . For many, it is a seal that shuts the mind before they ever begin to think. It is this same "feeling" that enables white Southerners to use

---

landlady for serving coloured customers in her public house [she replied], 'Their money is as good as yours and we prefer their company." K. L. Little in a letter to the *New Statesman and Nation*, August, 1942.

communism as a nebulous scapegoat to which they can shift the guilt for the crimes of their society.[ccxciii]
Braden attributed the linkage of desegregation efforts to Communism directly to the House Committee on Un-American Activities, tracing this back to HUAC's predecessor, the [Hamilton] Fish Committee, which in 1930 "stated ominously that communists were spreading 'revolutionary propaganda among the Negroes' and were 'openly' advocating that 'there must be complete social and racial equality between the whites and Negroes even to the extent of intermarriage.'"[ccxciv]

One motivation for the efforts to maintain an unequal racial structure in the South was sexual, the apprehension that political and social equality would lead to inter-racial sexual relations and (or) mixed race marriages, and children. Virginia Durr remarked a number of times in her autobiography about the obsession of White Southern politicians with inter-racial sexual activities, which they connected with any efforts to temper segregation. She recounts how during the pre-war effort to abolish the poll tax she "had to take some sweet Southern ladies with the Women's Society for Christian Service of the Methodist church to see [Senator] Eastland one day [circa 1940] . . .

> So we walked into Jim Eastland's office, and his secretary saw these nice ladies from Mississippi all dressed up and ushered us right in to Jim Eastland . . . Everything started off very pleasantly until they came to the poll tax . . . He jumped up. His face turned red. He's got these heavy jowls like a turkey and they began to turn purple. And he screamed out, "I know what you women want—black men laying on you!" [ccxcv]

Senator Eastland argued against the anti-poll tax measure in 1944, saying that "The 'driving force behind this measure is the Communist Party, a group of aliens advocating an alien creed, who would attempt to destroy this country' . . .

> Eastland . . . [also] viewed the [UAW] as a Communist front . . . "I am proud that I am slated to be purged by the mongrel radical movement who today attempt to destroy the Constitution and the American way of life . . . the movement which advocates intermarriage and the

amalgamation of the races and socialism in America."[ccxcvi]

The Congressional leaders of resistance to integration, who were also among the most important leaders of both HUAC and the Senate Internal Security Committee, Representative John Rankin and Senator James Eastland, both of Mississippi, held their offices on the basis of extraordinarily small numbers of residents of voting age, almost all of whom were white and few of those were either women or poor. Most of those who could vote were committed to "the Southern Way of life": segregation, Jim Crow, a race- and class-based political system, which "rested on two fundamental beliefs: maintaining the 'integrity' of the white race and maintaining the southern labor system, which depended on a base of underpaid black labor to keep the wages down for all. All else—political repression, segregation, degradation, lynching, a poor educational system— existed to keep those two pillars in place."[ccxcvii] Segregation had not been threatened by the very few Communists in the former Confederate states, nor by the New Deal, which had made an accommodation with the rulers of the southern states. However, it was threatened by the Supreme Court's *Brown v. Board of Education* ruling ordering the desegregation of the schools. Congressional committees held hearings in the South eight times during the Anti-Communist investigations. All but one of these hearings occurred between 1954 and 1958, following the Supreme Court's deliberations leading to the *Brown* decision.[ccxcviii] "By early 1954 . . . Jim Eastland was running for reelection to the Senate in Mississippi on the platform that if the Supreme Court voted to desegregate the public schools, it would show that the court was clearly an arm of the Communist conspiracy."[ccxcix]

The United States Senate's Committee on the Judiciary's Subcommittee to Investigate the Administration of the Internal Security Act and Other Internal Security Laws, held hearings concerning "Subversive Influence in Southern Conference Educational Fund, Inc". on March 18, 19, and 20, 1954, in New Orleans. At that time Senator William Jenner of Indiana was Chairman of the Subcommittee, but the only member of the Subcommittee who attended the New Orleans meeting was Senator Eastland. Lyndon Johnson kept

Democratic senators from going to New Orleans with Eastland; George Bender did that with the Republican senators, both as favors to Virginia Durr.[ccc] (Durr's husband, Clifford Durr, had been a high official in the New Deal and Virginia Durr herself had extensive political and social contacts in Washington, including those through her brother-in-law, Supreme Court Justice Hugo Black.) The New Orleans hearings turned out to be a duel between the segregationist, comparatively *nouveau riche* Eastland and the, in Southern terms, aristocratic civil rights activists, like the Durrs.

The Southern Conference Educational Fund (SCEF) was a civil rights organization, the successor of the Southern Conference for Human Welfare (SCHW), which had been founded in Birmingham, Alabama, in November, 1938.[ccci] The purpose of the SCHW, which had the backing of Frank Graham, President of the University of North Carolina, and Eleanor Roosevelt, among others, was "to support the New Deal program and philosophy for the South.

> To this end it worked actively for removal of all obstacles to freedom of the ballot, for the abolition of discrimination against Southern industry, for protection of the rights of labor and of racial and religious minorities, and for the extension of Federal aid to farmers and to education.[cccii]

Sarah Hart Brown wrote that "SCEF was the only white-led southern organization devoted single-mindedly to ending segregation and disfranchisement."[ccciii] On the other hand, in 1946 "Senator Theodore G. Bilbo of Mississippi called the [SCEF] an 'un-American, negro social equality, communistic, mongrel outfit.'" [ccciv] Perhaps that amounted to the same thing.

During an initial, scene-setting, friendly conversation with the Chairman of the Antisubversive Committee of the Young Men's Business Club of New Orleans, staff member Richard Arens said: "You are conversant with the fact, are you not, that the Un-American Activities Committee of the House has condemned the Southern Conference for Human Welfare as an agency which is designed in devious ways to further the basic Soviet and Communist policy in the United States?"[cccv] By saying this, Arens was asserting that the goals of the Communist Party were also those of the New Deal, or, in the jargon of the day, "it had

111

followed the Communist line." Glenda Elizabeth Gilmore wrote in *Defying Dixie* that Anti-Communist rhetoric and activities in the southern states were in fact not aimed at the very few Communists in the region, but at the civil rights movement: "Anti-Communists and the coming of the Cold War did create a Red Scare that removed white liberal forces from southern politics at the very moment that they were crucial to the extension of meaningful political and civil rights to the vast majority of black Southerners . . .

> Masquerading as Anti-Communist, the Cold War conservative domestic forces were actually anti-liberal. They destroyed the southern Popular Front coalition, along with the groundwork that it had laid for civil rights.[cccvi]

Asserting that the SCHW was not only Communist influenced, but that it was a Communist organization, Senator Eastland asked an ex-Communist, Department of Justice informer, Paul Crouch, whom the Subcommittee had brought to New Orleans, "What was the Communist Party's purpose in setting up the Southern Conference for Human Welfare?" Crouch replied: "It was intended to lead to class hatred, to race hatred, dividing class against class and race against race."[cccvii] The contradiction between the stated aims of the SCHW, to support the New Deal program and philosophy for the South, and those listed by Crouch, could only indicate for Eastland and Arens the "devious" ways in which the Communist Party worked.

Although in British English, "race hatred" reached a single peak in the frequency of its appearance in published work during World War II, in reference to Nazi Germany, in American English there are two frequency peaks, one during the war and one during the civil rights struggle.

Later in the hearing Senator Eastland became involved in discussions of the meaning of asserting Fifth Amendment rights and that of treason, first with attorney Leo Scheiner of Miami and then with James Dombrowski[25] (one of the founders of the SCHW):

Senator Eastland. ". . . if I were accused of belonging to [the Communist Party], and I were not guilty [sic] I certainly would not slink behind the fifth amendment." . . .

Mr. Sheiner. "And we know a witness who uses the fifth amendment is clothed just as much with innocence as he is with guilt, and I resent the interpretation you place upon those patriotic Americans who have used the fifth amendment."[cccviii] . . .

Senator Eastland. ". . . the 11 Communist leaders in this country . . . were convicted of advocating and conspiring with a foreign power to overthrow the Government of the United States by force and violence . . ." . . .

Mr. Dombrowski. "Mr. Chairman, to the best of my knowledge these people were not charged with conspiring to overthrow . . . but . . . with a conspiracy to teach and advocate . . ."[cccix]

In her autobiography, Virginia Durr, commented about the "force and violence" accusation that it was particularly ill-suited to

---

[25] "Dombrowski, an ordained Methodist minister from Florida, graduated from Atlanta's Emory University and then obtained a Ph.D. under Harry Ward and Reinhold Niebuhr at Columbia University, where he became a member of the Socialist Party." Brown, Sarah Hart. Standing Against Dragons: Three Southern Lawyers in an Era of Fear. Baton Rouge: Louisiana State University Press, 1998, p. 15.

investigations in the southern states: "In Montgomery everybody's grandfather had tried to overthrow the government by force and violence in the Civil War."[cccx]

The members of the Internal Security subcommittee and its staff, like those of the House Committee on Un-American Activities, deployed the jargon of the Communist Party itself as an instrument for their interrogations. Communists referred to the Party's policies as its "line." The frequency of the appearance of the phrase "Communist Party line" in American English follows the fortunes of *Anti-Communist* activities:

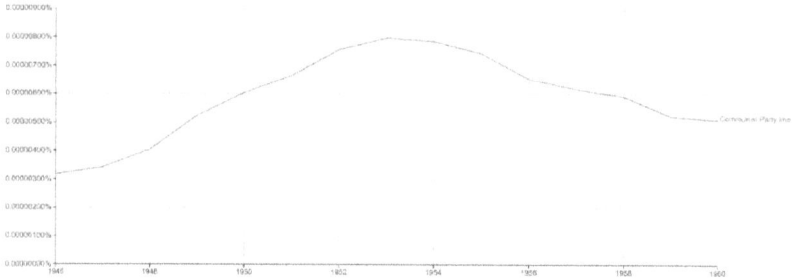

Richard Arens at the New Orleans hearings used that idiom as the equivalent of actual membership in the Party: "The House Un-American Activities Committee . . . says that the decisive key posts [of the Southern Conference for Human Welfare] are in most instances controlled by persons whose record is faithful to the line of the Communist Party and the Soviet Union."[cccxi] Senator Eastland borrowed another Communist Party phrase used about certain front organizations to make his case against the Southern Conference for Human Welfare. According to Eastland, one-time Communist Party leader Earl Browder had said that the organization "was a transmission belt for communism in the South.'"[cccxii]

During the interrogation of Virginia Durr, on March 19, 1954, Senator Eastland declared: "Communism is not a political belief. The Communist Party should be a crime under the statute of the United States."[cccxiii] (It became a crime later that year. The Communist Control Act of August, 1954, declared that, "The Communist Party of the United States, though purportedly a political party, is in fact an instrumentality of a conspiracy to overthrow the Government of the United States.") On March 20th, Richard English, an Anti-Communist screenwriter provided definitions of two key terms: "Communist front" and "fellow traveler."

> Mr. Arens. "Would you first of all describe what is a Communist front and then tell us about the manipulations of various Communist fronts?"
>
> Mr. English. "A front is one of two things: Either a bona fide organization which the Communist Party infiltrates and seeks to control directly through its own members or sympathetic travelers; or, two, a Communist front is an organization created by the party that it may look respectable and attract those who would not normally be attracted to anything associated with communism . . . A fellow traveler is one who stays with the Communist Party through more than one change in party line."[cccxiv]

Later he defined Communism itself: "Communism is an imported malignancy. It is not indigenous to this country."[cccxv]

The public reaction to the New Orleans hearings of the Senate Subcommittee, unusually, favored the witnesses, many of whom were members of longtime landowning families—the group from which state governors and judges were drawn—against Senator Eastland and Richard Arens. A planned follow-up hearing did not occur. Quite literally, Eastland and Arens had been out-classed.

But if Senator Eastland did not purse his investigations against Virginia and Clifford Durr and their colleagues, other Anti-Communists continued similar efforts. Florida, for example, had its own legislative committee investigating Communist and civil rights activists. The network of professional Anti-Communist witnesses was also available to such state and local legislative committees resisting national civil rights legislation and court decisions. "In 1958, J. B. Matthews, habitual professional witness for HUAC and SISS, appeared before the Florida committee . . .

> He told the Florida legislators: "Communists or communist influence were directly involved in every major race incident in the past four years since the Supreme Court 'legislation' on the subject of integration . . ."

He presented to the Florida committee a 99-page list of alleged communist "citations" of 145 national leaders of the NAACP, and he drew on HUAC hearings to document his charge that such people as Mrs. Rosa Parks, who started the Montgomery bus protest, were communist-inspired . . . Matthews again testified about the "subversive" nature of the integration movement before the 1959 hearings of the Mississippi committee, where he labeled not only SCEF [Southern Conference Education Fund] and the NAACP but the Southern Regional Council and its related human relations councils.[cccxvi]

"Subversive" was a key term of the Anti-Communist period. Relatively little used in American English before 1930, it reached a peak in frequency in 1955:

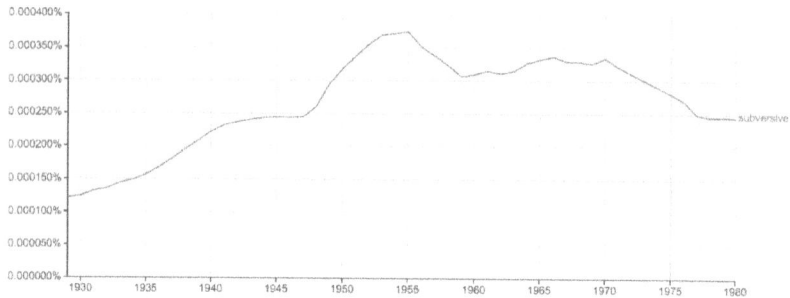

The House Committee on Un-American Activities held hearings on "Communist Infiltration and Activities in the South" beginning on July 20, 1958 in Atlanta. In his opening statement, the Chairman, Francis Walters of Pennsylvania, said: "The hearings in Atlanta are in furtherance of a project of this committee on current techniques of the Communist conspiracy in this Nation.

Today, the Communist Party, though reduced in size as a formal entity, is a greater menace than ever . . . We are engaged in the serious business of tracing the operations in the United States of a world-wide conspiracy which is determined to destroy us.[cccxvii]

His remarks were supplemented by Marvin Griffin, then Governor of the state of Georgia: "The Communist conspiracy in our country . . . would exchange the great American system of States Rights and local self-government for totalitarian dictatorship."ccccxviii "States Rights and local self-government" in Georgia, as elsewhere among the former Confederate states, were understood as code words for the maintenance of Jim Crow. In a direct statement of the purpose of the Hearings, Representative Walters said: "This is a very distasteful task this committee is performing . . . But somebody has to do it . . . I am sure that when the proposals are enacted into law, it will go a great way toward undoing what was done through a decision of the Supreme Court."cccxix Walters was probably talking about *Yates v. United States,* which interpreted the First Amendment as protecting all speech that did not involve a clear and present danger. (In 1951 he had referred to "bleeding hearts and fools, suckers, hard-boiled Communist politicians."cccxx)

The following exchange took place between Richard Arens, at this point Staff Director of HUAC,[26] and Carl Braden, one of the civil rights activist associated with the Southern Conference Education Fund: "Mr. Arens. 'Sir, it is our understanding that you are now a Communist, a member of the Communist Party . . . which is a tentacle of the international Communist conspiracy . . .

[A]s a Communist [you] have been propagating the Communist activity and the Communist line principally in the South; that you have been masquerading behind a façade of humanitarianism; that you have been masquerading behind a façade of emotional appeal to certain segments of our society; that your purpose, objective, your activities, are designed to further the cause of the international Communist conspiracy in the United States.'"

To which Braden responded: "While you are investigating, Mr. Arens, you ought to investigate some of the atrocities against the Jews and Negroes in the South, such as the picketing of the *Atlanta Journal* last Sunday morning."

"Mr. Arens . . . 'We are interested here solely in your participation in an organization which is controlled by a Godless, atheistic conspiracy . . .'"

---

[26] Arens would soon be forced to leave the Committee due to his connections with the racist Pioneer Fund.

"Mr. Braden. 'Are you saying integration is communism like they do in Louisiana? . . . Integration is what you are investigating. All the people subpoenaed here are integrationists.'"[cccxxi]

Arens raised the heat of his rhetoric during his interrogation of Frank Wilkinson, a California-based civil rights activist: "Now, sir, I put it to you as a fact and ask you to affirm or deny . . .

the fact that you are part of an enterprise to destroy the very Constitution of the United States under which we all have protection; that you are the agent of the Communist Party as an arm of the international Communist conspiracy sent into Atlanta for the purpose of engaging in conspiratorial activities on behalf of the Communist Party.[cccxxii]

Wilkinson invoked his free speech rights under the First Amendment, was cited for contempt, and jailed (as he had not invoked his rights under the Fifth Amendment).

Hunter Pitts O'Dell, an African-American, was a some-time member of the National Committee of the Communist Party. He was an advisor to Martin Luther King, Jr., until forced out of the Southern Christian Leadership Conference by the Kennedys. O'Dell was asked by Arens: "Do you honestly feel, and are you trying to make this committee and the people of this country believe, that you, a member of the Communist conspiracy, responsive to the will of the Kremlin, are in truth and in fact concerned about the welfare of the Negro people of this country? . . .

[S]tand up and tell this committee while you are under oath whether or not your activities and this façade that you are throwing around yourself in this aura of so-called respectability are not a front for the conspiratorial activities of yourself as a member of the Communist Party.

O'Dell replied: "You are trying to protect the segregation system."[cccxxiii]

A few months later the Senate Subcommittee to Investigate the Administration of the Internal Security Act and Other Internal Security Laws, chaired by Senator Eastland, opened hearings in Memphis on "Communism in the Mid-South."[cccxxiv] At issue was Kentucky's state sedition statute in relation to the efforts of Carl and Anne Braden to integrate a neighborhood in Louisville by selling their house to a Black family, and the operations of the Highlander School, a key training center for Civil Rights activists. Jo M. Ferguson, Attorney General of the State of Kentucky, testified that "the State of Kentucky could not fail to attempt to defend itself and its people from the type of criminal activity denounced by its sedition statue, which activity had so clearly been engaged in by [Carl] Braden and his cohorts."[cccxxv] The charge was that by selling a house to a Black family, the Bradens were guilty of attempting to overthrow the government of the State of Kentucky as part of "the" Communist conspiracy. A committee staff member said to one of the witnesses, Richard Stauverman: "You know, don't you, that the Communist Party is part of a worldwide conspiracy?" He then informed another witness that "This committee is investigating Communist activity, and Communist activity involves conspiracy."[cccxxvi]

Carl Braden went to jail, but then state sedition laws were declared unconstitutional and he was released. The Durrs and their associates continued to work for civil rights for African-Americans; Senator Eastland, aided by other southern senators, HUAC and such as Richard Arens, continued to defend segregation. While the White civil rights activists worked through the courts with the NAACP, Martin Luther King, Jr., Ralph Abernathy, Rosa Parks and Robert Moses marched. Due in large part to the efforts of President Lyndon Johnson, as well as those of Black and White activists, the law was settled in 1964 and 1965 in favor of civil and voting rights. The struggle took other forms.

*   *   *

The Romans distinguished between power and authority. Power gains its ends through force, authority gains its through prestige. The end, or perhaps, the beginning of the end, of the authority of the House Committee on Un-American Activities was marked by the hearings in May, 1960, in San Francisco. While students, many of whom would soon join the New Left, demonstrated outside San Francisco City Hall, inside many of the witnesses questioned the authority of the committee.

Notable among them was William Mandel, a teacher, journalist and expert on the Soviet Union, who in 1953 had likened Senator McCarthy to Nazi book-burners. He was equally aggressive in 1960:

MR. ARENS: Are you now, or have you ever been, a member of the Communist Party?

MR. MANDEL: Sir, I am 42 years of age, and have never had to face a jury as defendant or grand jury as witness in my life . . . I have committed no crime under any of the laws of this country and am not engaged in subversion. Consequently, I refuse to testify on the grounds that, as a radio and TV public affairs broadcaster, active in those capacities today, the subpoena issued to me interferes with the rights of my stations to schedule informational programs on their merits and is thus a direct violation of the first-amendment guarantee of freedom of speech and of the people's right to hear. Further . . . I also refuse to testify under my right not to be a witness against myself, a right originated to protect the innocent. The guilty can be convicted by the testimony of others if there is any real evidence to present.

MR. ARENS: Do you honestly apprehend that if you told this committee truthfully while you are under oath whether or not you are now, this instant, or ever have been, a member of the Communist Party, you would be supplying information which might be used against you in a criminal proceeding?

This gave Mandel the opportunity for which he had been waiting.

MR. MANDEL: Honorable beaters of children and sadists, uniformed and in plain clothes; distinguished Dixiecrat wearing the clothing of a gentleman; eminent Republican who opposes an accommodation with one country with whom we must live in peace in order for all of us and our children to survive . . . If you think that I am going to cooperate with this collection of Judases, of men who sit there in violation of the United States Constitution, if you think I will cooperate with you in any way, you are insane.

By this time the Communist Party of the United States was little more than an artifact of community nostalgia in a few places around the country, San Francisco among them, but primarily New York City. And with its slow death, so also died Anti-Communism as a force in American life. Anti-Communism remained important in American foreign policy, as long as the Soviet Union remained in existence and then, in that realm also, it disappeared along with its object.

As with the Anti-Communist language of the Catholic Church, in the language of the governmental investigatory committees there was an emphasis on "the conspiracy," often taken as synonymous with the Communist Party. But while with the Church that term stood on its own, for the governmental committees it also carried a legal implication, as conspiracy was a crime. Much else, much characteristic, of the language of the committees was both informal and inflammatory. Communists were called "commies," and they and their sympathizers were characterized as insects and vermin, as diseased and as the vectors of disease, as uniquely dangerous and as "psychologically troubled." This degradation of language was intended to dehumanize its objects, as had similar language been used both in Nazi Germany and Stalinist Russia. Calling people subhuman, alien, diseased, facilitates treating them as such, first marking them out from their fellows, then penalizing them with the loss of livelihoods, then there loom the camps and worse. That was the path pointed out by the language of Anti-Communism in mid-twentieth-century America. The nation was fortunate that it was not followed to its conclusion.

Notes

[cxxix] "There were four [Anti-Communist] investigations during the 79th Congress (1945-47); twenty-two during the Republican 80th Congress (1947-49); thirty-four during the 82nd Congress (1951-53); and fifty-one, an all-time high, during the Republican 83rd Congress (1953-55)." "American Politics and the Origins of 'McCarthyism,'" Griffith, Robert in Griffith, Robert and Athan Teoharis. The Specter: Original Essays on the Cold War and the Origins of McCarthyism. New York: New Viewpoints, 1974, p. 3.
[cxxx] Raumer, Frederich von. America and the American People. Trans. William W. Turner. New York: J. & H. G. Langeley, 1846, p. 148.
[cxxxi] Weeks, Stephen B. Department of the Interior. Bureau of Education. Bulletin, 1918, No. 17. History of Public School Education in Arizona. Washington: Government Printing Office, 1918, p. 84.
[cxxxii] Proceedings of the Union of American Hebrew Congregations, Forty-Seventh Annual Report, November 1, 1919, to October 31, 1920. July, 1921, p. 8893.
[cxxxiii] School & Society, Volume 41. Society for the Advancement of Education. Science Press, 1935, p. 368.
[cxxxiv] http://www.archives.gov/legislative/guide/house/chapter-22-select-propaganda.html. *Guide to the Records of the United States House of Representatives at the National Archives, 1789-1989: Bicentennial Edition* (Doct. No. 100-245). By Charles E. Schamel, Mary Rephlo, Rodney Ross, David Kepley, Robert W. Coren, and James Gregory Bradsher. Washington, DC: National Archives and Records Administration, 1989.
[cxxxv] Hearings Before a Special Committee on Un-American Activities, House of Representatives, Seventy-Fifth Congress, Third Session, p. 96. https://archive.org/stream/investigationofu193801unit#page/180/mode/1up
[cxxxvi] Hearings Before a Special Committee on Un-American Activities, House of Representatives, Seventy-Fifth Congress, Third Session, p. 272. https://archive.org/stream/investigationofu193801unit#page/180/mode/1up
[cxxxvii] Hearings Before a Special Committee on Un-American Activities, House of Representatives, Seventy-Fifth Congress, Third Session, p. 137. https://archive.org/stream/investigationofu193801unit#page/180/mode/1up
[cxxxviii] Hearings Before a Special Committee on Un-American Activities, House of Representatives, Seventy-Fifth Congress, Third Session, p. 278ff. https://archive.org/stream/investigationofu193801unit#page/180/mode/1up
[cxxxix] Hearings Before a Special Committee on Un-American Activities, House of Representatives, Seventy-Fifth Congress, Third Session, p. 411. https://archive.org/stream/investigationofu193801unit#page/180/mode/1up

cxl "Die sogenannte russische Seele," *Das eherne Herz* (Munich: Zentralverlag der NSDAP, 1943), pp. 398-405.
http://research.calvin.edu/german-propaganda-archive/goeb11.htm
cxli Hearings Before a Special Committee on Un-American Activities, House of Representatives, Seventy-Fifth Congress, Third Session, p. 805
https://archive.org/stream/investigationofu193801unit#page/180/mode/1up
cxlii Hearings Before a Special Committee on Un-American Activities, House of Representatives, Seventy-Fifth Congress, Third Session, p. 733; p. 829.
https://archive.org/stream/investigationofu193801unit#page/180/mode/1up
cxliii Hearings Before a Special Committee on Un-American Activities, House of Representatives, Seventy-Fifth Congress, Third Session, p. 857.
https://archive.org/stream/investigationofu193801unit#page/180/mode/1up
cxliv Hearings Before a Special Committee on Un-American Activities, House of Representatives, Seventy-Fifth Congress, Third Session, pp. 1000-1007.
https://archive.org/stream/investigationofu193801unit#page/180/mode/1up
cxlv HUAC 81st Congress, First Session, 1949, Vol. 1, p. 426.
cxlvi Hearings Before a Special Committee on Un-American Activities, House of Representatives, Seventy-Fifth Congress, Third Session, p. 869.
https://archive.org/stream/investigationofu193801unit#page/180/mode/1up
cxlvii Hearings Before a Special Committee on Un-American Activities, House of Representatives, Seventy-Fifth Congress, Third Session, pp. 869-95.
https://archive.org/stream/investigationofu193801unit#page/180/mode/1up
cxlviii Hearings Before a Special Committee on Un-American Activities, House of Representatives, Seventy-Fifth Congress, Third Session, pp. 1239-40.
https://archive.org/stream/investigationofu193801unit#page/180/mode/1up
cxlix Hearings Before a Special Committee on Un-American Activities, House of Representatives, Seventy-Fifth Congress, Third Session, p. 1302.
https://archive.org/stream/investigationofu193801unit#page/180/mode/1up
cl Hearings Before a Special Committee on Un-American Activities, House of Representatives, Seventy-Fifth Congress, Third Session, p. 1316.
https://archive.org/stream/investigationofu193801unit#page/180/mode/1up
cli Hearings Before a Special Committee on Un-American Activities, House of Representatives, Seventy-Fifth Congress, Third Session, pp. 1499; 1503.
https://archive.org/stream/investigationofu193801unit#page/180/mode/1up
clii Hearings Before a Special Committee on Un-American Activities, House

of Representatives, Seventy-Fifth Congress, Third Session, p. 1300-45.
https://archive.org/stream/investigationofu193801unit#page/180/mode/1up
[cliii] Hearings Before a Special Committee on Un-American Activities,
House of Representatives, Seventy-Fifth Congress, Third Session, p. 1509.
https://archive.org/stream/investigationofu193801unit#page/180/mode/1up
[cliv]

https://ia800206.us.archive.org/5/items/investigationofu193905unit/investig
ationofu193905unit.pdf, p. 3505.
[clv]

https://ia800206.us.archive.org/5/items/investigationofu193905unit/investig
ationofu193905unit.pdf, pp. 3579; 3583.
[clvi] Feffer, Andrew. "The Rapp-Coudert Investigation, Liberals, and the
Countersubversive Tradition, 1939-1942.
https://www.academia.edu/29380443/Feffer_The_Rapp-
Coudert_Investigation_Liberals_and_the_Countersubversive_Tradition_19
39-1942_
[clvii] Caute, David. The Great Fear: The Anti-Communist Purge Under
Truman and Eisenhower. New York: Simon and Schuster, 1978, pp. 438;
445.
[clviii] Taylor, Clarence. Reds at the Blackboard: Communism, Civil Rights,
and the New York City Teachers Union. New York: Columbia University
Press, 2011, p. 7.
[clix] Jenkins, Philip. The Cold War at Home: The Red Scare in Pennsylvania,
1945-1960. Chapel Hill: University of North Carolina Press, 1999, Platform
of the Republican Party of Pennsylvania, 1946, p. 50.
[clx] Caute, p. 26.
[clxi] Jenkins, Philip. The Cold War at Home: The Red Scare in Pennsylvania,
1945-1960. Chapel Hill: University of North Carolina Press, 1999, p. 50.
[clxii] Jenkins, p. 61.
[clxiii] Hearings Before a Special Committee on Un-American Activities,
House of Representatives, Seventy-Fifth Congress, Third Session, p. 39.
https://archive.org/stream/investigationofu193801unit#page/180/mode/1up
[clxiv] Hearings Before a Special Committee on Un-American Activities,
House of Representatives, Seventy-Fifth Congress, Third Session, p. 50.
https://archive.org/stream/investigationofu193801unit#page/180/mode/1up
[clxv] Hearings Before a Special Committee on Un-American Activities,
House of Representatives, Seventy-Fifth Congress, Third Session, pp. 168-9.
https://archive.org/stream/investigationofu193801unit#page/180/mode/1up
[clxvi] Hearings Before a Special Committee on Un-American Activities,
House of Representatives, Seventy-Fifth Congress, Third Session, pp. 3; 14.

https://archive.org/stream/investigationofu193801unit#page/180/mode/1up
clxvii Hearings Before a Special Committee on Un-American Activities, House of Representatives, Seventy-Fifth Congress, Third Session, p.24. https://archive.org/stream/investigationofu193801unit#page/180/mode/1up
clxviii Hearings Before a Special Committee on Un-American Activities, House of Representatives, Seventy-Fifth Congress, Third Session, p. 40. https://archive.org/stream/investigationofu193801unit#page/180/mode/1up
clxix Oshinsky, David M. A Conspiracy So Immense: The World of Joe McCarthy. New York: The Free Press, 1983. p. 97.
clxx Hearings Before a Special Committee on Un-American Activities, House of Representatives, Seventy-Fifth Congress, Third Session, p. 159. https://archive.org/stream/investigationofu193801unit#page/180/mode/1up
clxxi Hearings Before The Committee on Un-American Activities House of Representatives Eightieth Congress First Session on H. R. 1884 And H. R. 2122 Bills to Curb or Outlaw The Communist Party of The United States Washington, D. C. March 24, 25, 26, 27, 28, 1947; p. 3;14. https://ia902607.us.archive.org/10/items/investigatonofun1947unit/investigatonofun1947unit.pdf
clxxii Hearings Before The Committee on Un-American Activities House of Representatives Eightieth Congress First Session on H. R. 1884 And H. R. 2122 Bills to Curb or Outlaw The Communist Party of The United States Washington, D. C. March 24, 25, 26, 27, 28, 1947; p. 40. https://ia902607.us.archive.org/10/items/investigatonofun1947unit/investigatonofun1947unit.pdf
clxxiii Hearings Before The Committee on Un-American Activities House of Representatives Eightieth Congress First Session on H. R. 1884 And H. R. 2122 Bills to Curb or Outlaw The Communist Party of The United States Washington, D. C. March 24, 25, 26, 27, 28, 1947; p. 223, 225. https://ia902607.us.archive.org/10/items/investigatonofun1947unit/investigatonofun1947unit.pdf
clxxiv Hearings Before The Committee on Un-American Activities House of Representatives Eightieth Congress First Session on H. R. 1884 And H. R. 2122 Bills to Curb or Outlaw The Communist Party of The United States Washington, D. C. March 24, 25, 26, 27, 28, 1947; p. 249. https://ia902607.us.archive.org/10/items/investigatonofun1947unit/investigatonofun1947unit.pdf
clxxv Hearings Before The Committee on Un-American Activities House of Representatives Eightieth Congress First Session on H. R. 1884 And H. R. 2122 Bills to Curb or Outlaw The Communist Party of The United States

Washington, D. C. March 24, 25, 26, 27, 28, 1947; p. 275.
https://ia902607.us.archive.org/10/items/investigatonofun1947unit/investiga
tonofun1947unit.pdf

clxxvi Hearings Before The Committee on Un-American Activities House of Representatives Eightieth Congress First Session on H. R. 1884 And H. R. 2122 Bills to Curb or Outlaw The Communist Party of The United States Washington, D. C. March 24, 25, 26, 27, 28, 1947; p. 3.
https://ia902607.us.archive.org/10/items/investigatonofun1947unit/investiga
tonofun1947unit.pdf

clxxvii Hearings Before The Committee on Un-American Activities House of Representatives Eightieth Congress First Session on H. R. 1884 And H. R. 2122 Bills to Curb or Outlaw The Communist Party of The United States Washington, D. C. March 24, 25, 26, 27, 28, 1947; p. 5.
https://ia902607.us.archive.org/10/items/investigatonofun1947unit/investiga
tonofun1947unit.pdf

clxxviii Hearings Before The Committee on Un-American Activities House of Representatives Eightieth Congress First Session on H. R. 1884 And H. R. 2122 Bills to Curb or Outlaw The Communist Party of The United States Washington, D. C. March 24, 25, 26, 27, 28, 1947; pp. 8;13.
https://ia902607.us.archive.org/10/items/investigatonofun1947unit/investiga
tonofun1947unit.pdf

clxxix Hearings Before The Committee on Un-American Activities House of Representatives Eightieth Congress First Session on H. R. 1884 And H. R. 2122 Bills to Curb or Outlaw The Communist Party of The United States Washington, D. C. March 24, 25, 26, 27, 28, 1947; p. 15.
https://ia902607.us.archive.org/10/items/investigatonofun1947unit/investiga
tonofun1947unit.pdf

clxxx Hearings Before The Committee on Un-American Activities House of Representatives Eightieth Congress First Session on H. R. 1884 And H. R. 2122 Bills to Curb or Outlaw The Communist Party of The United States Washington, D. C. March 24, 25, 26, 27, 28, 1947; pp. 19; 21; 97 and 147.
https://ia902607.us.archive.org/10/items/investigatonofun1947unit/investiga
tonofun1947unit.pdf

clxxxi Sartre, Jean-Paul. Anti-Semite and Jew. New York: Schocken Books, 1995 (1948), p. 54.

clxxxii Hearings Before The Committee on Un-American Activities House of Representatives Eightieth Congress First Session on H. R. 1884 And H. R. 2122 Bills To Curb Or Outlaw The Communist Party of The United States Washington, D. C. March 24, 25, 26, 27, 28, 1947; p. 44.
https://ia902607.us.archive.org/10/items/investigatonofun1947unit/investiga

tonofun1947unit.pdf

clxxxiii Report of the Committee on Un-American Activities to the United States House of Representatives, Eightieth Congress. Investigation of Un-American Activities in the United States. Committee on Un-American Activities, House of Representatives, Eightieth Congress, Second Session, Public Law 201, December 31, 1948, pp. 22-3.

clxxxiv Report of the Committee on Un-American Activities to the United States House of Representatives, Eightieth Congress. Investigation of Un-American Activities in the United States. Committee on Un-American Activities, House of Representatives, Eightieth Congress, Second Session, Public Law 201, December 31, 1948, p .25.

clxxxv Hearings Regarding The Communist Infiltration of The Motion Picture Industry Hearings Before The Committee on Un-American Activities House of Representatives Eightieth Congress First Session Public Law 601 (Section 121, Subsection Q (2)) October 20, 21, 22, 23, 24, 27, 28, 29, and 30, 1947.
https://ia802607.us.archive.org/23/items/hearingsregardin1947aunit/hearingsregardin1947aunit.pdf

clxxxvi Hearings Regarding The Communist Infiltration of The Motion Picture Industry Hearings Before The Committee on Un-American Activities House of Representatives Eightieth Congress First Session Public Law 601 (Section 121, Subsection Q (2)) October 20, 21, 22, 23, 24, 27, 28, 29, and 30, 1947, pp. 9-11.
https://ia802607.us.archive.org/23/items/hearingsregardin1947aunit/hearingsregardin1947aunit.pdf

clxxxvii Hearings Regarding The Communist Infiltration of The Motion Picture Industry Hearings Before The Committee on Un-American Activities House of Representatives Eightieth Congress First Session Public Law 601 (Section 121, Subsection Q (2)) October 20, 21, 22, 23, 24, 27, 28, 29, and 30, 1947, p. 20.
https://ia802607.us.archive.org/23/items/hearingsregardin1947aunit/hearingsregardin1947aunit.pdf

clxxxviii Hearings Regarding The Communist Infiltration of The Motion Picture Industry Hearings Before The Committee on Un-American Activities House of Representatives Eightieth Congress First Session Public Law 601 (Section 121, Subsection Q (2)) October 20, 21, 22, 23, 24, 27, 28, 29, and 30, 1947, p. 94.
https://ia802607.us.archive.org/23/items/hearingsregardin1947aunit/hearingsregardin1947aunit.pdf

clxxxix Navasky, Victor S. Naming Names. New York: Hill and Wang, 2003 (Viking, 1991), p. 109.

cxc Navasky, p. 112.

cxci Hearings Regarding The Communist Infiltration of The Motion Picture Industry Hearings Before The Committee on Un-American Activities House of Representatives Eightieth Congress First Session Public Law 601 (Section 121, Subsection Q (2)) October 20, 21, 22, 23, 24, 27, 28, 29, and 30, 1947, p. 130.
https://ia802607.us.archive.org/23/items/hearingsregardin1947aunit/hearing sregardin1947aunit.pdf

cxcii Hearings Regarding The Communist Infiltration of The Motion Picture Industry Hearings Before The Committee on Un-American Activities House of Representatives Eightieth Congress First Session Public Law 601 (Section 121, Subsection Q (2)) October 20, 21, 22, 23, 24, 27, 28, 29, and 30, 1947, p. 141.
https://ia802607.us.archive.org/23/items/hearingsregardin1947aunit/hearing sregardin1947aunit.pdf

cxciii Hearings Regarding The Communist Infiltration of The Motion Picture Industry Hearings Before The Committee on Un-American Activities House of Representatives Eightieth Congress First Session Public Law 601 (Section 121, Subsection Q (2)) October 20, 21, 22, 23, 24, 27, 28, 29, and 30, 1947, p. 283.
https://ia802607.us.archive.org/23/items/hearingsregardin1947aunit/hearing sregardin1947aunit.pdf

cxciv Report on The Communist Party of The United States As An Advocate of Overthrow of Government By Force And Violence Investigation of Un-American Activities In The United States Committee on Un-American Activities House of Representatives Eightieth Congress Second Session Public Law 601 (Section 121, Subsection Q (2)) Printed For The Use of The Committee on Un-American Activities MAY 10, 1948.
https://ia600201.us.archive.org/25/items/reportoncommunis1948unit/report oncommunis1948unit.pdf

cxcv Report on The Communist Party of The United States As An Advocate of Overthrow of Government By Force And Violence Investigation of Un-American Activities In The United States Committee on Un-American Activities House of Representatives Eightieth Congress Second Session Public Law 601 (Section 121, Subsection Q (2)) Printed For The Use of The Committee on Un-American Activities MAY 10, 1948, pp. 2; 76.
https://ia600201.us.archive.org/25/items/reportoncommunis1948unit/report oncommunis1948unit.pdf

[cxcvi] Hearings Regarding Communist Espionage in the United States Government; Hearings Before the Committee on Un-American Activities, House of Representatives, Eightieth Congress, Second Session, Public Law 601, July 31; August 3, 4, 5, 7, 9, 10, 11, 12, 13, 16, 17, 18, 20, 24, 25, 26, 27, 30; September 8 and 9, 1948, p. 502.

[cxcvii] Hearings Regarding Communist Espionage in the United States Government; Hearings Before the Committee on Un-American Activities, House of Representatives, Eightieth Congress, Second Session, Public Law 601, July 31; August 3, 4, 5, 7, 9, 10, 11, 12, 13, 16, 17, 18, 20, 24, 25, 26, 27, 30; September 8 and 9, 1948, p. 544.

[cxcviii] Hearings Regarding Communist Espionage in the United States Government; Hearings Before the Committee on Un-American Activities, House of Representatives, Eightieth Congress, Second Session, Public Law 601, July 31; August 3, 4, 5, 7, 9, 10, 11, 12, 13, 16, 17, 18, 20, 24, 25, 26, 27, 30; September 8 and 9, 1948, p. 548.

[cxcix] Hearings Regarding Communist Espionage in the United States Government; Hearings Before the Committee on Un-American Activities, House of Representatives, Eightieth Congress, Second Session, Public Law 601, July 31; August 3, 4, 5, 7, 9, 10, 11, 12, 13, 16, 17, 18, 20, 24, 25, 26, 27, 30; September 8 and 9, 1948, p. 667; 668.

[cc] Hearings Regarding Communist Espionage in the United States Government; Hearings Before the Committee on Un-American Activities, House of Representatives, Eightieth Congress, Second Session, Public Law 601, July 31; August 3, 4, 5, 7, 9, 10, 11, 12, 13, 16, 17, 18, 20, 24, 25, 26, 27, 30; September 8 and 9, 1948, p. 1040.

[cci] Theoharis, Athan. The F.B.I. & American Democracy: A Brief Critical History. Lawrence, Kansas: The University Press of Kansas, 2004, p. 77.

[ccii] Hearings Regarding Communist Infiltration of Radiation Laboratory and Atomic Bomb Project at the University of California, Berkeley, California, Volume I, Hearings Before the Committee on Un-American Activities, House of Representatives, Eighty-First Congress, First Session, April 22, 26, May 25, June 10 and 14, 1949.

[cciii] In the 1950s, after the loyalty oath controversy, "The chairman of the Physics Department, which lost five people as a result of the controversy, claimed, 'We cannot now induce a single first class theoretical physicist to accept a position at Berkeley.'" Schrecker, Ellen W. No Ivory Tower: McCarthyism and the Universities. New York: Oxford University Press, 1986, p. 123.

[cciv] "Though a Democrat, McCarran, the powerful chairman of the Senate

Judiciary Committee, was a staunch Catholic cold warrior and a long-time supporter of Chiang. The hearings he conducted [concerning IPR] were his contribution to the China Lobby's campaign. They turned what was originally a matter of policy into one of subversion and force the American government and the American public to accept the conspiracy theory of the loss of China and its corollary policy, the continued support of Chiang Kai-shek." Schrecker, Ellen W. No Ivory Tower: McCarthyism and the Universities. New York: Oxford University Press, 1986, pp. 162-3.

[ccv] Section 4, SS. 1194, McCarran Internal Security Act, September 23, 1950, Public Law 831, 81st Congress, "Control of Subversive Activities." Hearings Before a Subcommittee of the Committee on the Judiciary, United States Senate, Eighty-First Congress, First Session, pp. 28-9

[ccvi] "Control of Subversive Activities." Hearings Before a Subcommittee of the Committee on the Judiciary, United States Senate, Eighty-First Congress, First Session, p. 1.

[ccvii] "Control of Subversive Activities." Hearings Before a Subcommittee of the Committee on the Judiciary, United States Senate, Eighty-First Congress, First Session, p. 22.

[ccviii] "Control of Subversive Activities." Hearings Before a Subcommittee of the Committee on the Judiciary, United States Senate, Eighty-First Congress, First Session, p. 29.

[ccix] "Control of Subversive Activities." Hearings Before a Subcommittee of the Committee on the Judiciary, United States Senate, Eighty-First Congress, First Session, p. 53.

[ccx] "Control of Subversive Activities." Hearings Before a Subcommittee of the Committee on the Judiciary, United States Senate, Eighty-First Congress, First Session, p. 116.

[ccxi] "Control of Subversive Activities." Hearings Before a Subcommittee of the Committee on the Judiciary, United States Senate, Eighty-First Congress, First Session, p. 151.

[ccxii] "Control of Subversive Activities." Hearings Before a Subcommittee of the Committee on the Judiciary, United States Senate, Eighty-First Congress, First Session, p. 127.

[ccxiii] "Control of Subversive Activities." Hearings Before a Subcommittee of the Committee on the Judiciary, United States Senate, Eighty-First Congress, First Session, p. 209.

[ccxiv] "Control of Subversive Activities." Hearings Before a Subcommittee of the Committee on the Judiciary, United States Senate, Eighty-First Congress, First Session, p. 218.

[ccxv] http://www.presidency.ucsb.edu/ws/index.php?pid=25837

ccxvi See, for example: https://www.cia.gov/library/readingroom/docs/CIA, which is a collection of letters between Senator McCarthy and Allen Dulles, then Director of Central Intelligence.

ccxvii Oshinsky, David M. A Conspiracy So Immense: The World of Joe McCarthy. New York: The Free Press, 1983, p. 157, May, 1950.

ccxviii Executive Sessions of the Senate Permanent Subcommittee on Investigations
of the Committee on Government Operation, 83rd Congress, First Session, 1953, Volume I, File Destruction in the Department of State, January, 1953, p. 166.

ccxix Executive Sessions of the Senate Permanent Subcommittee on Investigations
of the Committee on Government Operation, 83rd Congress, First Session, 1953, Volume I, File Destruction in the Department of State, January, 1953, p. 306.

ccxx Executive Sessions of the Senate Permanent Subcommittee on Investigations
of the Committee on Government Operation, 83rd Congress, First Session, 1953, Volume I, File Destruction in the Department of State, January, 1953, p. 427.

ccxxi U.S. Senate, Senate Permanent Subcommittee on Investigations of The Committee on Government Operations, Washington, Dc. Testimony of Charles P. Arnot, Director, International Press Service, International Information Administration, Department of State, Monday, March 16, 1953, P. 894.

ccxxii State Department Information Program—Information Centers Wednesday, March 25, 1953, U.S. Senate, Senate Permanent Subcommittee on Investigations of The Committee on Government Operations, Testimony off Mary Van Kleeck, p. 1006

ccxxiii Executive Sessions of the Senate Permanent Subcommittee on Investigations
of the Committee on Government Operation, 83rd Congress, First Session, 1953, Volume I, File Destruction in the Department of State, January, 1953, p. 478.

ccxxiv Executive Sessions of the Senate Permanent Subcommittee on Investigations
of the Committee on Government Operation, 83rd Congress, First Session, 1953, Volume I, File Destruction in the Department of State, January, 1953, p. 555.

ccxxv Executive Sessions of the Senate Permanent Subcommittee on Investigations
of the Committee on Government Operation, 83rd Congress, First Session,
1953, Volume I, File Destruction in the Department of State, January, 1953,
p. 649.
ccxxvi Executive Sessions of the Senate Permanent Subcommittee on Investigations
of the Committee on Government Operation, 83rd Congress, First Session,
1953, Volume I, State Department Information Program—Information
Centers, Tuesday, March 31, 1953, p. 1030.
ccxxvii Executive Sessions of the Senate Permanent Subcommittee on Investigations
of the Committee on Government Operation, 83rd Congress, First Session,
1953, Volume I, State Department Information Program—Information
Centers, February 28, 1953, p. 754.
ccxxviii Executive Sessions of the Senate Permanent Subcommittee on Investigations
of the Committee on Government Operation, 83rd Congress, First Session,
1953, Volume I, State Department Information Program—Information
Centers, March 10, 1953, p. 819.
ccxxix Executive Sessions of the Senate Permanent Subcommittee on Investigations
of the Committee on Government Operation, 83rd Congress, First Session,
1953, Volume I, State Department Information Program—Information
Centers, February 28, 1953, p. 763.
ccxxx Executive Sessions of the Senate Permanent Subcommittee on Investigations
of the Committee on Government Operation, 83rd Congress, First Session,
1953, Volume I, State Department Information Program—Information
Centers, Tuesday, April 28, 1953, p. 1083.
ccxxxi Executive Sessions of the Senate Permanent Subcommittee on Investigations
of the Committee on Government Operation, 83rd Congress, First Session,
1953, Volume I, State Department Information Program—Information
Centers, Wednesday, July 1, 1953, p. 1201.
ccxxxii Executive Sessions of the Senate Permanent Subcommittee on Investigations
of the Committee on Government Operation, 83rd Congress, First Session,
1953, Volume I, State Department Information Program—Information
Centers, March 26, 1953, p. 995.

ccxxxiii Executive Sessions of the Senate Permanent Subcommittee on Investigations
of the Committee on Government Operation, 83rd Congress, First Session, 1953, Volume I, State Department Information Program—Information Centers, May 25, 1953, p. 1252.
ccxxxiv "McCarthy Hits 'Comrade Attlee'—Briton Denies Any Slur at U.S.," by William S. White, *The New York Times*, May 15, 1953.
ccxxxv Executive Sessions of the Senate Permanent Subcommittee on Investigations
of the Committee on Government Operation, 83rd Congress, First Session, 1953, Volume I, State Department Information Program—Information Centers, August 21, 1953, p. 1597.
ccxxxvi Hofstadter, Richard. Anti-Intellectualism in American Life. New York: Vintage Books, 1963.
p.1, citing Immanuel Wallerstein, unpublished M.A. essay: "McCarthy and the Conservative," Columbia University, 1954, pp. 46ff.
ccxxxvii State Department Teacher-Student Exchange Program Monday, May 25, 1953 U.S. Senate, Senate Permanent Subcommittee on Investigations of The Committee on Government Operations, Washington, DC. Testimony of Helen B. Lewis, p. 1248.
ccxxxviii "M'Carthy Asserts Silence Convicts: Senator Says in TV Debate if Witness Invokes Constitution He Proves He is a Red," *The New York Times,* June 22, 1953.
ccxxxix State Department Teacher-Student Exchange Program Monday, June 19, 1953 U.S. Senate, Senate Permanent Subcommittee on Investigations of The Committee on Government Operations, Washington, DC. Testimony of Clarence Francis Hiskey, p. 1309.
ccxl Executive Sessions of the Senate Permanent Subcommittee on Investigations
of the Committee on Government Operation, 83rd Congress, First Session, 1953, Volume I, September 1, 1953, p. 1684.
ccxli U.S. Senate Committee on Government Operations, Hearings before the Permanent Subcommittee on Investigations, Communist Infiltration in the Army, 1953, p. 2722.
ccxlii Weingarten, Aviva. Jewish Organizations' Response to Communism and Senator McCarthy. London. Vallentine Mitchell, 2008, pp. 68; 119.
ccxliii Weingarten, pp. 68; 119.
ccxliv U.S. Senate Committee on Government Operations, Hearings before the Permanent Subcommittee on Investigations, Communist Infiltration in

the Army, 1953, p. 2886.

ccxlv U.S. Senate Committee on Government Operations, Hearings before the Permanent Subcommittee on Investigations, Communist Infiltration in the Army, 1953, p. 2309.

ccxlvi U.S. Senate Committee on Government Operations, Hearings before the Permanent Subcommittee on Investigations, Communist Infiltration in the Army, 1953, p. 2348.

ccxlvii U.S. Senate Committee on Government Operations, Hearings before the Permanent Subcommittee on Investigations, Communist Infiltration in the Army, 1953, p. 2540.

ccxlviii U.S. Senate Committee on Government Operations, Hearings before the Permanent Subcommittee on Investigations, Communist Infiltration in the Army, 1953, p. 2666.

ccxlix "M'Carthy Attacks 'Bleeding Hearts,'" *The New York Times*, October 29, 1953.

ccl "M'Carthy Charges 'Mess' at Harvard: Asserts Students are Exposed to Communist Philosophy—Asks Professor's Ouster,'" *The New York Times*, November 6, 1953.

ccli Hofstadter, p. 41.

cclii https://archive.org/details/InfoAge_Senator_Joseph_McCarthy

ccliii "M'Carthy Charges Betrayal on Reds: Says Democrats Put Them in Office—Accuses M'Cloy Who Denies Allegations," *The New York Times*, February 8, 1954.

ccliv *The New York Times*, March 18, 1954.

cclv "The Politics of Civil Liberties: The American Civil Liberties Union During the McCarthy Years." McAuliffe, Mary S. in Griffith, Robert and Athan Teoharis. The Specter: Original Essays on the Cold War and the Origins of McCarthyism. New York: New Viewpoints, 1974, p. 170. In September, 1950 "a handful of Senate liberals led by Paul H. Douglas and Harley M. Kilgore introduced an emergency detention bill (S.4130) authorizing the President to declare, either under specific conditions or at his discretion, an 'internal security emergency' during which the Attorney General would be authorized to round up and detain persons who he had 'reason to believe' might engage in sabotage, espionage, or other subversive activities. This new bill, which a White House aide privately labeled 'a concentration camp bill,' had been first proposed by Senator Magnuson in early July and was co-sponsored by Senators Kilgore, Douglas, Hubert H. Humphrey . . .Lehman, Frank P. Graham . . . Estes Kefauver . . . and William Benton . . . It had been drafted by Douglas's staff in consultation with the staffs of the other Senate sponsors and with *attorneys from the*

American Civil Liberties Union." "Legislative Politics and 'McCarthyism': The Internal Security Act of 1950." Tanner, William R. and Robert Griffith, in Griffith and Teoharis, p. 183. (Emphasis added.)

cclvi "See It Now," CBS television, April 6, 1954,

cclvii Communist Methods of Infiltration (Education). Hearings Before the Committee on Un-American Activities, House of Representatives, Eighty-Third Congress, First Session, February 25, 26, and 27, p. 3.

cclviii Communist Methods of Infiltration (Education). Hearings Before the Committee on Un-American Activities, House of Representatives, Eighty-Third Congress, First Session, February 25, 26, and 27, p. 58.

cclix Communist Methods of Infiltration (Education). Hearings Before the Committee on Un-American Activities, House of Representatives, Eighty-Third Congress, First Session, February 25, 26, and 27, p. 60.

cclx Communist Methods of Infiltration (Education). Hearings Before the Committee on Un-American Activities, House of Representatives, Eighty-Third Congress, First Session, February 25, 26, and 27, p. 88.

cclxi Communist Methods of Infiltration (Education). Hearings Before the Committee on Un-American Activities, House of Representatives, Eighty-Third Congress, First Session, February 25, 26, and 27, p. 94.

cclxii Communist Methods of Infiltration (Education). Hearings Before the Committee on Un-American Activities, House of Representatives, Eighty-Third Congress, First Session, February 25, 26, and 27, p. 172.

cclxiii Communist Methods of Infiltration (Education). Hearings Before the Committee on Un-American Activities, House of Representatives, Eighty-Third Congress, First Session, February 25, 26, and 27, p. 177.

cclxiv Communist Methods of Infiltration (Education). Hearings Before the Committee on Un-American Activities, House of Representatives, Eighty-Third Congress, First Session, February 25, 26, and 27, p. 173.

cclxv Communist Methods of Infiltration (Education). Hearings Before the Committee on Un-American Activities, House of Representatives, Eighty-Third Congress, First Session, February 25, 26, and 27, p. 215.

cclxvi Durr, Virginia Foster. Outside the Magic Circle. Ed. Hollinger F. Barnard. The Autobiography of Virginia Foster Durr. University of Alabama Press, 1985, p. 124.

cclxvii Communist Methods of Infiltration (Education). Hearings Before the Committee on Un-American Activities, House of Representatives, Eighty-Third Congress, First Session, February 25, 26, and 27, p. 993.

cclxviii Communist Methods of Infiltration (Education). Hearings Before the Committee on Un-American Activities, House of Representatives, Eighty-

Third Congress, First Session, February 25, 26, and 27, p. 1007.

cclxix Communist Methods of Infiltration (Education). Hearings Before the Committee on Un-American Activities, House of Representatives, Eighty-Third Congress, First Session, February 25, 26, and 27, p. 1030.

cclxx Communist Methods of Infiltration (Education). Hearings Before the Committee on Un-American Activities, House of Representatives, Eighty-Third Congress, First Session, February 25, 26, and 27, p. 1045.

cclxxi Communist Methods of Infiltration (Education). Hearings Before the Committee on Un-American Activities, House of Representatives, Eighty-Third Congress, First Session, February 25, 26, and 27, pp. 1051; 1054; 1059.

cclxxii Communist Methods of Infiltration (Education). Hearings Before the Committee on Un-American Activities, House of Representatives, Eighty-Third Congress, First Session, February 25, 26, and 27, p. 1558.

cclxxiii Communist Methods of Infiltration (Education). Hearings Before the Committee on Un-American Activities, House of Representatives, Eighty-Third Congress, First Session, February 25, 26, and 27, pp. 1084; 1087. https://babel.hathitrust.org/cgi/pt?id=umn.31951d03564113z;view=1up;seq =708

cclxxiv Communist Methods of Infiltration (Education). Hearings Before the Committee on Un-American Activities, House of Representatives, Eighty-Third Congress, First Session, June 28, 1954, p. 5764.

cclxxv Communist Methods of Infiltration (Education). Hearings Before the Committee on Un-American Activities, House of Representatives, Eighty-Third Congress, First Session, June 28, 1954, p. 5788.

cclxxvi Communist Methods of Infiltration (Education). Hearings Before the Committee on Un-American Activities, House of Representatives, Eighty-Third Congress, First Session, June 28, 1954, p. 5825.

cclxxvii "School Red Drive Held Incomplete," C. P. Trussell, *The New York Times,* March 26, 1953.

cclxxviii Hearings on "Communist Political Subversion" Hearings Before the Committee on Un-American Activities, House of Representatives, Second Session, Eighty-Fourth Congress, November and December, 1956.

cclxxix Hearings on "Communist Political Subversion" Hearings Before the Committee on Un-American Activities, House of Representatives, Second Session, Eighty-Fourth Congress, November and December, 1956, p. 6144-52.

cclxxx For example, November 12, 1956, pp. 6159, 6163, 6165.

cclxxxi Hearings on "Communist Political Subversion" Hearings Before the Committee on Un-American Activities, House of Representatives, Second

Session, Eighty-Fourth Congress, November and December, 1956, p. 6352.
cclxxxii Hearings on "Communist Political Subversion" Hearings Before the Committee on Un-American Activities, House of Representatives, Second Session, Eighty-Fourth Congress, November and December, 1956, p. 6352.
cclxxxiii Hearings on "Communist Political Subversion" Hearings Before the Committee on Un-American Activities, House of Representatives, Second Session, Eighty-Fourth Congress, November and December, 1956, p. 6527.
cclxxxiv Hearings on "Communist Political Subversion" Hearings Before the Committee on Un-American Activities, House of Representatives, Second Session, Eighty-Fourth Congress, November and December, 1956, p. 6602.
cclxxxv Hearings on "Communist Political Subversion" Hearings Before the Committee on Un-American Activities, House of Representatives, Second Session, Eighty-Fourth Congress, November and December, 1956, p. 6677.
cclxxxvi Hearings on "Communist Political Subversion" Hearings Before the Committee on Un-American Activities, House of Representatives, Second Session, Eighty-Fourth Congress, November and December, 1956, p. 6776.
cclxxxvii Hearings on "Communist Political Subversion" Hearings Before the Committee on Un-American Activities, House of Representatives, Second Session, Eighty-Fourth Congress, November and December, 1956, p. 6809.
cclxxxviii Communist Infiltration and Activities in the South. Hearings Before the Committee on Un-American Activities, House of Representatives, Eighty-Fifth Congress, Second Session. p. 2714-5
cclxxxix Brown, Sarah Hart. Standing Against Dragons: Three Southern Lawyers in an Era of Fear. Baton Rouge: Louisiana State University Press, 1998, p. 7.
ccxc Brown, p. 141.
ccxci Caute, p. 168.
ccxcii Schrecker, Ellen. Many Are the Crimes, pp. 31-32.
ccxciii Braden, Anne. House Un-American Activities Committee: Bulwark of Segregation. National Committee to Abolish the House Un-American Activities Committee; 1St Edition (1963), pp. 6-7.
http://www.crmvet.org/info/64_braden_huac-r.pdf
ccxciv Braden, p. 17. http://www.crmvet.org/info/64_braden_huac-r.pdf
ccxcv Durr, p. 172.
ccxcvi Finley, Keith M. Delaying the Dream: Southern Senators and the Fight Against Civil Rights, 1983-1965. Baton Rouge: Louisiana University Press, 2008, p. 77.
ccxcvii Glenda Elizabeth Gilmore. Defying Dixie: The Radical Roots of Civil Rights, 1919-1950. New York: Norton, 2008, p. 361.

[ccxcviii] Brown, p. 142.

[ccxcix] Durr, p. 254.

[ccc] Durr, pp. 236-7.

[ccci] Durr, p. 120.

[cccii] Southern Conference for Human Welfare collection. Archives Research Center. Atlanta University Center Robert W. Woodruff Library. [http://findingaid.auctr.edu/arc/view?docId=ead/auctr.edu/southern_confere nce_for_human_welfare.xml]

[ccciii] Brown, p. 13.

[ccciv] Brown, p. 14.

[cccv] Hearings Before the Subcommittee to Investigate the Administration of the Internal Security Act and Other Internal Security Laws of the Committee on the Judiciary, United States Senate, Eighty-Third Congress, Second Session on Subversive Influence in Southern Conference Educational Fund, Inc. March 18, 19, and 20, 1954. New Orleans, p. 4. https://babel.hathitrust.org/cgi/pt?id=umn.31951d02120634f;view=1up;seq =4

[cccvi] Gilmore, p. 414; 417.

[cccvii] Hearings Before the Subcommittee to Investigate the Administration of the Internal Security Act and Other Internal Security Laws of the Committee on the Judiciary, United States Senate, Eighty-Third Congress, Second Session on Subversive Influence in Southern Conference Educational Fund, Inc. March 18, 19, and 20, 1954. New Orleans, p. 15. https://babel.hathitrust.org/cgi/pt?id=umn.31951d02120634f;view=1up;seq =4

[cccviii] Hearings Before the Subcommittee to Investigate the Administration of the Internal Security Act and Other Internal Security Laws of the Committee on the Judiciary, United States Senate, Eighty-Third Congress, Second Session on Subversive Influence in Southern Conference Educational Fund, Inc. March 18, 19, and 20, 1954. New Orleans, pp. 16-7. https://babel.hathitrust.org/cgi/pt?id=umn.31951d02120634f;view=1up;seq =4. 1954 "In Florida, when the lawyer Leo Sheiner refused to disclose whether he had ever been a Party member, Judge Vincent Giblin promptly disbarred him . . . 'no need to depend on the advice of college professors . . . in devising effective ways and means of exterminating the vermin gnawing at the foundations of our governmental structure . . .'" p. 142. Giblin was Al Capone's lawyer in Florida. Sheiner disbarment was overturned in 1959.

[cccix] Hearings Before the Subcommittee to Investigate the Administration of the Internal Security Act and Other Internal Security Laws of the Committee on the Judiciary, United States Senate, Eighty-Third Congress,

Second Session on Subversive Influence in Southern Conference
Educational Fund, Inc. March 18, 19, and 20, 1954. New Orleans, p. 56.
https://babel.hathitrust.org/cgi/pt?id=umn.31951d02120634f;view=1up;seq
=4

cccx Durr, p. 266.

cccxi Hearings Before the Subcommittee to Investigate the Administration of
the Internal Security Act and Other Internal Security Laws of the
Committee on the Judiciary, United States Senate, Eighty-Third Congress,
Second Session on Subversive Influence in Southern Conference
Educational Fund, Inc. March 18, 19, and 20, 1954. New Orleans, p. 59.
https://babel.hathitrust.org/cgi/pt?id=umn.31951d02120634f;view=1up;seq
=4

cccxii Hearings Before the Subcommittee to Investigate the Administration of
the Internal Security Act and Other Internal Security Laws of the
Committee on the Judiciary, United States Senate, Eighty-Third Congress,
Second Session on Subversive Influence in Southern Conference
Educational Fund, Inc. March 18, 19, and 20, 1954. New Orleans, p. 61.
https://babel.hathitrust.org/cgi/pt?id=umn.31951d02120634f;view=1up;seq
=4

cccxiii Hearings Before the Subcommittee to Investigate the Administration of
the Internal Security Act and Other Internal Security Laws of the
Committee on the Judiciary, United States Senate, Eighty-Third Congress,
Second Session on Subversive Influence in Southern Conference
Educational Fund, Inc. March 18, 19, and 20, 1954. New Orleans, p. 89.
https://babel.hathitrust.org/cgi/pt?id=umn.31951d02120634f;view=1up;seq
=4

cccxiv Hearings Before the Subcommittee to Investigate the Administration of
the Internal Security Act and Other Internal Security Laws of the
Committee on the Judiciary, United States Senate, Eighty-Third Congress,
Second Session on Subversive Influence in Southern Conference
Educational Fund, Inc. March 18, 19, and 20, 1954. New Orleans, p. 156-7.
https://babel.hathitrust.org/cgi/pt?id=umn.31951d02120634f;view=1up;seq
=4

cccxv Hearings Before the Subcommittee to Investigate the Administration of
the Internal Security Act and Other Internal Security Laws of the
Committee on the Judiciary, United States Senate, Eighty-Third Congress,
Second Session on Subversive Influence in Southern Conference
Educational Fund, Inc. March 18, 19, and 20, 1954. New Orleans, p. 160.
Communism was "an imported malignancy, in contrast to, say, Jim Crow,

which was indigenous.
https://babel.hathitrust.org/cgi/pt?id=umn.31951d02120634f;view=1up;seq
=4

cccxvi Braden, pp. 25-6. http://www.crmvet.org/info/64_braden_huac-r.pdf

cccxvii Communist Infiltration and Activities in the South : hearings before
the Committee on Un-American Activities, House of Representatives,
Eighty-fifth Congress, second session. July 29, 30, and 31, 1958, pp. 2606-7.
https://babel.hathitrust.org/cgi/pt?id=umn.31951d035643755;view=1up;seq
=3;size=125

cccxviii Communist Infiltration and Activities in the South : hearings before
the Committee on Un-American Activities, House of Representatives,
Eighty-fifth Congress, second session. July 29, 30, and 31, 1958, p. 2608.
https://babel.hathitrust.org/cgi/pt?id=umn.31951d035643755;view=1up;seq
=3;size=125

cccxix Communist Infiltration and Activities in the South : hearings before the
Committee on Un-American Activities, House of Representatives, Eighty-
fifth Congress, second session. July 29, 30, and 31, 1958, p. 2628.
https://babel.hathitrust.org/cgi/pt?id=umn.31951d035643755;view=1up;seq
=3;size=125

cccxx Navasky, p. ix.

cccxxi Communist Infiltration and Activities in the South : hearings before the
Committee on Un-American Activities, House of Representatives, Eighty-
fifth Congress, second session. July 29, 30, and 31, 1958, p. 2669-71.
https://babel.hathitrust.org/cgi/pt?id=umn.31951d035643755;view=1up;seq
=3;size=125

cccxxii Communist Infiltration and Activities in the South : hearings before
the Committee on Un-American Activities, House of Representatives,
Eighty-fifth Congress, second session. July 29, 30, and 31, 1958, p. 2687.
https://babel.hathitrust.org/cgi/pt?id=umn.31951d035643755;view=1up;seq
=3;size=125

cccxxiii Communist Infiltration and Activities in the South : hearings before
the Committee on Un-American Activities, House of Representatives,
Eighty-fifth Congress, second session. July 29, 30, and 31, 1958, p. 2716-8.
https://babel.hathitrust.org/cgi/pt?id=umn.31951d035643755;view=1up;seq
=3;size=125

cccxxiv "Communism in the Mid-South, Hearings Before the Subcommittee to
Investigate the Administration of the Internal Security Act and other
Internal Security Laws of the Committee on the Judiciary, United States
Senate, Eighty-Fifth Congress, First Session, October 28 and 29, 1957.

https://babel.hathitrust.org/cgi/pt?id=uc1.$b643277;view=1up;seq=5

cccxxv "Communism in the Mid-South, Hearings Before the Subcommittee to Investigate the Administration of the Internal Security Act and other Internal Security Laws of the Committee on the Judiciary, United States Senate, Eighty-Fifth Congress, First Session, October 28 and 29, 1957, p. 3. https://babel.hathitrust.org/cgi/pt?id=uc1.$b643277;view=1up;seq=5

cccxxvi "Communism in the Mid-South, Hearings Before the Subcommittee to Investigate the Administration of the Internal Security Act and other Internal Security Laws of the Committee on the Judiciary, United States Senate, Eighty-Fifth Congress, First Session, October 28 and 29, 1957, pp. 50; 60. https://babel.hathitrust.org/cgi/pt?id=uc1.$b643277;view=1up;seq=5

The Non-Communist Left

The Illegitimate Children of Willi Münzenberg

The entry of the United States into the Second World War was fatal to the nation's authoritarian far right of the day, hopelessly compromised as it was by its association with the enemy regimes. The ideologically neighboring groups, closer to and sometimes within the traditional political parties—those groups supported by such as Henry Ford and DuPont, Hearst and Marshall Field—were more temporarily quieted. And within the tent, as it were, the segregationist politicians of the old Confederacy and the isolationists of the Midwest agreed over afternoon whiskeys with the President's men that there was a war to be won. There was a certain symmetry with this on the left. In 1941 two dozen members of the Socialist Workers Party (SWP), followers of Leon Trotsky, were convicted under the Alien Registration Act of 1940 (the Smith Act). The Socialist Party of perennial presidential candidate Norman Thomas fragmented. The Communist Party of the United States (which had supported the prosecutions of the SWP) called for all-out support of the war and the administration. In 1944 the CPUSA went further, dissolving itself into the Communist Political Association, seemingly on the verge of becoming nothing more than the left wing of the Democratic Party.

But with the death of President Roosevelt, his foreign policy—anti-imperialist and attempting to maintain the wartime Grand Alliance with the Soviet Union—collapsed, replaced by support for the restitution of the colonial empires of the U.S.'s Western European allies and first the "containment," then the "rollback" of Soviet power. The Central Intelligence Agency (CIA), the nation's first permanent peacetime foreign intelligence organization, was an instrument created, in part, for this latter purpose.[27] The CIA, particularly in its early days, created and encouraged "resistance" groups in those areas occupied by the Red Army and in the Soviet Union itself, particularly in Poland on the one hand and in the Ukraine on the other. Alongside these dreams of Special Operations Executive adventure, the CIA also followed the British Second World War pattern in the creation of a wide range of propaganda activities: "white," "grey" and "black": truth, mixed, and lies. A particular focus of attention were the fragile post-war regimes in Western Europe, especially France, where large Communist Parties seemed to some to be on the verge of coming to power in elections in which (except for the Gaullists) there was no remaining effective right-wing opposition. The CIA, therefore, concentrated on supporting or creating center-left opposition parties (and other non- or Anti-Communist organizations, such as "free" labor unions and cultural institutions). The CIA called this propaganda effort "the Non-Communist Left."

The CIA's propaganda machine was modeled on Willi Münzenberg's enterprises on behalf of the Communist Party between the wars. After the Red Army had been defeated in the Polish-Soviet War and the various revolts in Germany, Hungary and elsewhere were crushed, Lenin, who believed that Communism would fail if confined to the relatively backward former Russian Empire, turned to revolution by other means. Münzenberg, a member of the German Communist Party, invented the idea of "fronts": organizations that appeared independent, but which were actually controlled by the Communist Party. These included International Worker's Relief and the World Committee Against War and Fascism. In addition to the organizations (of which there were many), there were newspapers, magazines, conferences and other activities: an entire ecosystem for those believers hoping for a better world and those merely looking for hope. Arthur Koestler, who had worked for Münzenberg, was the

---

[27] In the mid- to late-1940s U.S. secret intelligence went through a number of changes of name and organizational structure. It is convenient, although anachronistic, to refer to them all by the name of the eventual consolidated entity.

direct link between these Communist front activities and those of the British and American secret intelligence agencies in the post-war period.[28]

The emergence of the Anti-Communist fronts of the Non-Communist Left can be traced to New York City, shortly after the re-election of President Truman and the failure of the Communist Party's effort at electoral politics on behalf of Henry Wallace. The March, 1949, Scientific and Cultural Conference for World Peace (usually called the "Waldorf Conference") was one of a "series of Soviet-sponsored cultural conferences beginning in September 1948 [which] called for world peace and denounced the policies of the Truman administration . . ."[cccxxvii] It was a typical Münzenberg-type event (even though Münzenberg himself had been dead for nearly a decade), this time rather brazenly taking place in the United States itself. There were delegations from the Soviet Union, Poland and Czechoslovakia, and sponsorship and participation from many of the organizations that would be included in Attorney General Biddle's list of subversive organizations and in later House Committee on Un-American Activities hearings. The more than 500 sponsors of the conference ran from theatrical figure Stella Adler to Albert Einstein, the painter Ad Reinhardt, the photographer Edward Weston and mathematician Norbert Wiener. The group of American composer and musician sponsors was particularly distinguished, including Aaron Copland, Morton Gould, Leonard Bernstein, Marc Blitzstein, Alan Lomax and Artur Schnabel. That the conference took place during the early stages of the trial of the U.S. Communist Party leaders, *Dennis v. United States,* added a certain edge to the proceedings.

With Nicolas Nabokov, a Russian refugee composer and cousin of the novelist, fellow left-wing Anti-Communist writers Dwight MacDonald and Mary McCarthy, and others, New York University philosophy professor Sidney Hook created a group he called "Americans for Intellectual Freedom," and, with funding from Anti-Communist trade unions,[cccxxviii] set about disrupting the Waldorf

---

[28] Koestler's reputation was later affected when his habit of raping women became known.

Conference. Hook acted as the "self-appointed field marshal of the 'little Anti-Communist suite"[cccxxix] in the Waldorf, rooms provided to them rent-free courtesy of their Anti-Communist trade union allies. A typical, and the best-known, action of the group occurred when Nabokov attended a panel where the composer Dmitri Shostakovich was one of the speakers. Nabokov demanded of Shostakovich, who was flanked by his KGB minders, that he denounce *Pravda:* "On such-and-such a date in No. X of *Pravda* appeared an unsigned article that had all the looks of an editorial" Nabokov declared.

> It concerned three western composers: Paul Hindemith, Arnold Schoenberg, and Igor Stravinsky. In this article, they were branded, all three of them, as "obscurantists", "decadent bourgeois formalists" and "lackeys of imperialist capitalism". The performance of their music should "therefore be prohibited in the U.S.S.R." Does Mr Shostakovich personally agree with this official view as printed in *Pravda?*

Frances Stonor Saunders takes up the story at that point: "Shostakovich received whispered instructions from his KGB 'nurse'.

> The composer then stood up, was handed a microphone and, his ashen face turned down to study the floorboards, murmured in Russian, 'I fully agree with the statements made in *Pravda.*' . . . He was the sacrificial lamb . . . Any display of independent spirit on his part was a life or death matter . . . Nicolas Nabokov was throwing punches at a man whose arms were tied behind his back.[cccxxx]

The Conference and the role of Hook's group received much press attention. It also favorably impressed secret intelligence leader Frank Wisner, who may have played a more direct role in support of the Hook group than solely that of an interested observer. In any case, Wisner directed his aide Carmel Offie (who deserves a biography of his own) to set about organizing a similar effort for the next Communist international conference, which was to take place in Paris in the spring of 1949. This was part of the "National Psychological Effort" of anti-Soviet propaganda.[cccxxxi] Offie, who took care of the OPC's National Committee for Free Europe, labor union matters and émigré affairs, contacted the State Department and activated his own networks. Wisner, for his part, asked Averell Harriman of the Economic Cooperation Administration (of the Marshall Plan) for five million francs in counterpart funds to finance the operation.[29]"Working with [Irving] Brown, [an OPC representative] contacted French socialist David Rousset[cccxxxii] and his allies at the breakaway leftist newspaper Franc-Tireur, which in turn organized a meeting called the International Day of Resistance to Dictatorship and War, inviting Sidney Hook and other prominent Anti-Communists" (including Ignazio Silone and Carlo Levi), for that Anti-Communist counter-demonstration in Paris on April 30, 1949, a week after the World Congress for Peace. OPC paid for the travel of many of the attendees, including Hook, although, not for the last time, it was not clear which of the recipients knew the source of the funds. As it turned out, the Paris meeting was primarily an event of the civil war on the French left, this marking the break between Rousset and the Sartre group. The former increasingly concentrated on publicizing, and denouncing, the Soviet gulag system, the latter taking up a position of "a plague on both their houses" neutralism. It was the "explicit purpose of the [Congress for Cultural Freedom]'s founders . . . to combat the idea that morally serious writers could be neutral in the Cold War."[cccxxxiii]

Sidney Hook wrote in a report on the Paris conference published in *The Partisan Review* that: "The French public, by and large, is shockingly ignorant of American life and culture,

> Its picture of America is a composite of impressions derived from reading the novels of social protest and revolt . . . from seeing American movies, and from exposure to an incessant Communist barrage which seeps into the non-Communist press. *The informational re-education of the French public seems to me to be the most fundamental as well as most pressing task of American democratic policy in France, towards which almost nothing along effective lines has been done.*"[cccxxxiv]

---

[29] "Counterpart funds," were a matching requirement in local currency to Marshall Plan grants and appear to have been extensively used for American secret intelligence operations.

According to the CIA's in-house history of the event, "The Paris counter-conference on 30 April 1949 disappointed its American backers. . . .

The main problem, Offie noted [in an after-action memorandum], was the barely concealed anti-Americanism of the Franc-Tireur group and many of the intellectuals it had invited. This flaw was aggravated by the loose organization of the meeting itself . . . Wisner added a pointed postscript to Offie's memo: "We are concerned lest this type of leadership for a continuing organization would result in the degeneration of the entire idea (of having a little DEMINFORM[30]) into a nuts folly of miscellaneous goats and monkeys whose antics would completely discredit the work and statements of the serious and responsible liberals." [cccxxxv]

As early, then, as 1949, Frank Wisner and his circle were thinking about creating a United States-sponsored analogue to the COMINFORM, which would be a world-wide alliance of political parties and cultural organizations promoting America's image and policies. The CIA historian commented that: "One small forward step was taken in Paris, however. Hook had chatted with a former editor of *The New Leader* named Melvin Lasky about the prospects for a permanent committee of Anti-Communist intellectuals from Europe and America. This idea would soon take on a life of its own."[cccxxxvi] It marked the beginning of American secret intelligence's construction of what became the Congress for Cultural Freedom.

In August, 1949, shortly after the Paris conference, Melvin Lasky, then working as a journalist for the American Occupation government in Germany, met in Frankfort with ex-Communists Franz Borkenau and Ruth Eisler Fischer. According to Fischer, they discussed "the idea of organizing a big Anti-Waldorf-Astoria Congress in Berlin itself.

It should be a gathering of all ex-Communists, plus a good

---

[30] "DEMINFORM" was Wisner's coinage based on the Communist COMINFORM abbreviation for the international Communist Party coordination group that succeeded the COMINTERN.

representative group of anti-Stalinist American, English, and European intellectuals, declaring its sympathy for Tito and Yugoslavia and the silent opposition in Russia and the satellite states, and giving the Politburo hell right at the gate of their own hell. All my friends agree that it would be of enormous effect and radiate to Moscow, if properly organized. It would create great possibilities for better co-ordination afterwards and would also lift the spirits of Berlin anti-Stalinists, which are somewhat fallen at present.

The idea was communicated to some of Fischer's "friends in Washington." Some liked it, some did not. Carmel Offie liked it, which sufficed. Responsibility for the project was handed off to Michael Josselson, who would be the longtime OPC, then CIA, officer responsible for the Congress for Cultural Freedom. Funding from OPC came through Josselson, who encouraged Lasky to set about organizing the meeting. Lasky brought in Sidney Hook, among others. Hook, again with Burnham, organized the American delegation, which included novelist James T. Farrell, playwright Tennessee Williams, Arthur M. Schlesinger, Jr., actor Robert Montgomery and David Lilienthal, chairman of the Atomic Energy Commission.[cccxxxvii] Schlesinger recalled that while he and Hook were traveling to Berlin, Hook was "apparently intoxicated by the idea of how dangerous it was going to be to go to Berlin.

> "He had this fantasy about Communist attacks from all sides," Schlesinger recalled. "He was quite excited about it all . . ."
> After his first taste of blood at the Waldorf Astoria, Hook was chafing for a full-scale campaign.[cccxxxviii]

The Berlin Conference was a success for the OPC. There were nearly two hundred delegates and 4,000 attendees at the conference, while the closing rally was attended by 15,000 Berliners, who were accustomed to large rallies with emotional anti-Communist speakers. They responded with practiced enthusiasm when Koestler shouted the OPC-branded battle-cry: "Friends, freedom has seized the offensive!"[31] Greg Barnhisel comments in this regard that "In fact,

---

[31] The Berliners heard: *"Freunde, die Freiheithat die Offensive ergriffen!*

the White House committee overseeing the ideological programs of the Cold War resolved that 'freedom' was to be the USIA's 'single, dominant propaganda line,' with the primary objective being to 'create in the minds of our audience acceptance of the concept that the free peoples and nations are united by basic common interests' diametrically opposed to the 'Soviet-Communist efforts to destroy free world unity.'"cccxxxix

OPC and those cooperating with it immediately began planning Wisner's "DEMIFORM" front organization: the Congress for Cultural Freedom.

* * *

Others, such as Frances Stonor Saunders and Hugh Wilford, have written exhaustively about the Congress for Cultural Freedom. However, this brief account of the beginnings of the CCF should suffice as background for this chapter's consideration of books by three members of the CIA's American Committee for Cultural Freedom (ACCF): *The Vital Center* (1949) by the historian Arthur M. Schlesinger, Jr., *The Irony of American History* (1952), by the theologian Reinhold Niebuhr and *Heresy, Yes; Conspiracy, No* (1953), by the philosopher Sidney Hook. These accounts are followed by a reading of *Encounter,* which, although published in London, was edited at various times by two other members of the ACCF, Irving Kristol and CIA agent Melvin Lasky and included articles by Schlesinger, Hook and Niebuhr. Schlesinger, Hook and Niebuhr were crucial figures in American "liberal" Anti-Communism. Hook, as we have seen, was an Anti-Communist organizer, both in public and behind the scenes. His publications provided a non-Communist, quasi-Marxist imprimatur to the

---

"The seventh Nazi Party Congress was called the *Reichsparteitag der Freiheit,* National party day of freedom, introducing conscription. See the Leni Riefenstahl film "Day of Freedom (Tag der Freiheit): Our Armed Forces," 1935.

movement. Schlesinger, a twentieth-century version of the Vicar of Bray, brought the prestige of Harvard. And Niebuhr, moving steadily to the right, brought a theological gravitas, an example that the United States was not only the country of Madison Avenue and Wall Street. Each had Socialist backgrounds, were later involved with the Anti-Communist Americans for Democratic Action, and were familiars of the CIA and the State Department's Policy Planning Office, which under George Kennan guided American secret intelligence in this period. Their books, and *Encounter,* are related to one another through those connections and by the peculiar Cold War vocabulary that characterized each. We will begin with the work of the youngest of these men, Arthur M. Schlesinger, Jr.

Notes

cccxxvii https://www.cia.gov/library/center-for-the-study-of-intelligence/csi-publications/csi-studies/studies/95unclass/Warner.html]

cccxxviii And from the CIA [OPC] according to Saunders. Saunders, Frances Stonor. Who Paid the Piper? The CIA and the Cultural Cold War. London: Granta Books, 1999, p. 54.

cccxxix Saunders, p. 49.

cccxxx Saunders, p. 50.

cccxxxi See, for example, "Memorandum to the Director of the Psychological Strategy Board – Status of United States Programs for National Security," May 29, 1952. https://www.cia.gov/library/readingroom/docs/CIA-RDP80-01065A000500090001-3.pdf

cccxxxii Rousset had been a Trotskyite in the 1930s, participated in the Resistance, captured and sent to Buchenwald, which he survived. At the time of the conference he was allied to Sartre, but broke with him over the issue of the gulags a short time later.

cccxxxiii Gleason, Abbott. Totalitarianism: The Inner History of the Cold War. New York: Oxford University Press, 1995, p. 89.

cccxxxiv Saunders, pp. 69-70. Citing Sidney Hook, "Report on the International Day of Resistance to Dictatorship and War," *Partisan Review,* vol. 16/7, Fall 1949.

cccxxxv https://www.cia.gov/library/center-for-the-study-of-intelligence/csi-publications/csi-studies/studies/95unclass/Warner.html]

cccxxxvi https://www.cia.gov/library/center-for-the-study-of-intelligence/csi-publications/csi-studies/studies/95unclass/Warner.html]

cccxxxvii Warner, Michael. Origins of the Congress for Cultural Freedom, 1949-50. Center for the Study of Intelligence, Central Intelligence Agency, https://www.cia.gov/library/center-for-the-study-of-intelligence/csi-publications/csi-studies/studies/95unclass/Warner.html

cccxxxviii Saunders, p. 74.

cccxxxix Barnhisel, Greg, Cold War Modernists: Art, Literature, and American Cultural Diplomacy, 1946-1959, New York: Columbia University Press, 2015, p. 40.

The Non-Communist Left

A Cold War Historian: Arthur Schlesinger, Jr.

The Vital Center

Arthur M. Schlesinger, Jr., was at the very center of a certain American Establishment: schooled at Phillips Exeter Academy; traveling first-class around the world with his parents, meeting a governor general here, a future prime minister there; Harvard College; Peterhouse College, Cambridge; Harvard Society of Fellows; a research position in the Office of Strategic Services (O.S.S., predecessor of the CIA); Harvard professor; advisor and speech writer for presidential candidate Adlai Stevenson; Special Assistant to President Kennedy; historian of the New Deal and polka-dot-bow-tie-wearing socialite. Just as the natural habitat of Sartre and De Beauvoir was the café and the editorial office, so that of Schlesinger was the Harvard Faculty Club and similar all-male venues in New York City and Washington; the large houses of colleagues and family (often the same) along the streets leading to Harvard Yard and in Georgetown; the apartments of intellectuals on the Upper West Side of Manhattan, of the wealthy and fashionable on the Upper East Side.

Schlesinger's academic career was built on that of his father, Arthur M. Schlesinger, something that he himself marked by changing his name early on from Arthur Bancroft to Arthur M., Jr. Following a family tradition of interest in the presidency of Andrew Jackson, his first major publication was *The Age of Jackson* (with notes and bibliography said to have been provided by his father), which won the Pulitzer Prize for History in 1946. The political orientation and sensibility of that book were those of a historian of ideas. It was curiously insensitive to matters that would seem to define the liberalism with which Schlesinger claimed to sympathize. According to a 1986 retrospective review, Schlesinger in *The Age of*

Jackson "gives almost no attention to women, blacks, and American Indians . . . Although there is a lengthy discussion of the political issue of slavery, there is little concern for the social issue of race." This despite the fact that Jackson had been a major slave-holder. Further, "Indians are omitted completely; even the [Jacksonian] Indian Removal Act fails to make it" into this account of a person famous for genocidal campaigns against Indians. It is also noticeable, in this first major work by a protégée of Eleanor Roosevelt, that in "an index of some 1,100 citation, only ten are to women, eight of which are brief references in which the woman is used to describe a male politician."cccxl

Those omissions, one might say prejudices, as admitted by Schlesinger himself many decades later, delimited the political view of the young Schlesinger and with him what Sidney Hook called the "realistic" liberalism for which he and Schlesinger claimed to speak. It was the politics of the White Protestant male ascendency, respectful of authority, both in institutions and in persons; confident that the views of his class required no examination, that they could hardly be differentiated from truth itself. That class was an American version of the English clerisy: if unbelieving, yet interested in the contestation of belief; possessing comfortable incomes and yet contemptuous of business; well-educated, only slightly prejudiced against those who did not have a background of private schools, New England colleges, private clubs—those unassimilated Jews, Italians, Irish Catholics, foreigners who were not English, French or German, and, of course, the American descendants of enslaved Africans. These heirs of John Quincy Adams, who had thought that the administration of Theodore Roosevelt marked the beginning of the end to the corruption of the Republic by big business, had first tasted power in the administration of Woodrow Wilson and then become accustomed to it in that of Franklin Roosevelt, believing, as many often do, that the political situation of the moment would continue indefinitely. If being the son of Arthur M. Schlesinger connected him with everyone who mattered at Harvard, his relatively brief tour of duty in O.S.S. London and Paris widened his network, what Schlesinger called the circularity of life, to include the permanent government of advisors and occasional members of the administration in Washington and the journalists who wrote about and drank with them. By some time in the mid-1940s Schlesinger had drifted away from his father's left-liberal views to a politics that had as its touchstone the insistent Anti-Communism that came to color his writing. It was natural, then, that in Washington after the war, he became part of the circle of Joseph Alsop, that very conservative journalist.

"It is absolutely essential to give the Commies no quarter," Schlesinger wrote to his parents from Paris in November, 1944, six months before the Red Army took Berlin, branding himself on the tongue with this verbal indicator of the witch-hunt to come. American English had hitherto made relatively little use of the Anti-Communist slang term for Communist Party members and governments. Schlesinger in 1944 might have been called a premature Anti-Communist, on the model of the premature anti-Fascists of the Abraham Lincoln Brigade in the Spanish Civil War. Schlesinger went on in the same letter to predict that "the liberal movement in the USA will be injured by every form of collaboration with Communists. I cannot say too strongly how I feel about this."[cccxli] It was around this time that Schlesinger's social circle expanded from the neighborhood around Harvard Yard to include wealthier and more conservative people, men like Frank Wisner.[cccxlii]

But if the "Commies" were the enemy, who among the fragile governments in Europe were to be allies? Over dinners in London, Schlesinger later wrote, "Nye [Aneurin Bevan] and Jennie [Lee] reinforced my conviction that the best hope for postwar Europe lay in the non-Communist left[32]—in American terms, the extension of the New Deal . . ."[cccxliii] In British terms, the left wing of the Labour Party represented by Bevan (and the extreme, fellow-traveling left to which Lee belonged), was not an extension of the New Deal, but full European social democracy, pledged to nationalization of the means of production and distribution, socialized medicine and government-

---

[32] This seems anachronistic on Schlesinger's part. Bevan and Lee probably used the term "Socialism," or "Social Democracy." There are no instances of the use of the term "non-Communist left" in British publications before 1947.

owned housing for the vast majority of the population. Nonetheless, for a few years, from late-1944, say, to the end of the Attlee Government, British social democracy was a workable rhetorical counterweight to Soviet people's democracies for surviving sympathizers with the New Deal.

A couple of years later Schlesinger learned that the "non-Communist Left," was becoming a U.S. governmental acronym: "In March 1946 . . . I found myself seated at dinner [at Joseph Alsop's, of course] next to Charles W. Thayer, a foreign service officer whom I had known a bit in the O.S.S. We discussed foreign policy. I ventured the thought that the postwar struggle for Europe would be between democratic socialism and communism. 'Oh, so you're NCL,' Charlie said. 'NCL?' 'Yes, non-Communist left.'"[cccxliv] In other words, it seems that Schlesinger's key term was a U.S. State Department coinage. (Or perhaps it came from the earliest days of the CIA itself: Thayer helped found the CIA's predecessor organization the Office for Policy Coordination.) In any case, the term at first did not gain much currency outside of government circles and Schlesinger's own writing.[33] The frequency pattern from the Ngram Viewer shows its increasing usage during the early Cold War, and then a higher peak with the rise of the New Left, followed by a falling away as the international Cold War came to an end:

---

[33] Schlesinger's friends would soon divide into the hunters and the hunted. Thayer, brother-in-law of the extreme Anti-Communist Charles "Chip" Bohlen, would be forced to resign from the State Department in 1953 and was then driven into exile by McCarthy and Hoover, both as a security risk and for rumors of "sexual immorality" with persons of both sexes.

Henry Luce's *Life* magazine published Schlesinger's article, "The U.S. Communist Party" in its July 29, 1946 issue. "To understand the Communists," he wrote, in what would become a common psychologizing move, "You must think of them in terms, not of a normal political party, but in terms of the Jesuits, the Mormons or Jehovah's Witnesses . . . The appeal is essentially the appeal of a religious sect . . ." This chart shows that the phrase, "Communist religion," increases in frequency in American English from virtually nothing in 1940 to a plateau in the years of the Anti-Communist witch-hunts. It was a favorite way in which Anti-Communists could justify disregarding the political aspects of Communist writing and actions.

Communists, Schlesinger continued, changing to a common disease metaphor for the movement, popularized by the Nazis, among others, carry "their infection of intrigue and deceit wherever they go." Echoing his comments to his father two years earlier, Schlesinger framed his Anti-Communism as a defense of liberalism: "The

Communist party is no menace to the right in the U.S. . . . . It is to the American left that Communism presents the most serious danger."[cccxlv] As it turned out, it was to the American left that *Anti-Communism* presented the most serious danger.

The death of Roosevelt, the succession of Truman, and the Republican victory in the 1946 congressional elections brought Schlesinger's hopes for a seamless continuation of the New Deal to an end. At this point, Schlesinger's political sentiments were still inclined to the left wing of the Democratic Party. He wrote at the time that the death of Roosevelt "plunged me into a bad depression . . . His death leaves a kind of awful vacancy . . . Any others of the Big Three could have been much better spared . . . What a shame Henry Wallace is not in there. Poor Harry Truman."[cccxlvi] The business of the United States was once more business and it would become evident in a few years that the New Deal was not the future but the past. It was to defend that past against attacks from those whom it had marginalized and enraged, on the right, and those on the left, such as Wallace and the Communist Party, whose embrace now brought with it a mortal taint, that in January, 1947 Eleanor Roosevelt and a group "associated with the administration of the late President Roosevelt," joined with some others in the Democratic Party and with civil rights and union leaders, notably among the latter United Auto Workers union leader Walter Reuther, in founding the Americans for Democratic Action (ADA). The ADA was equally against "concentrated wealth and over-centralized government," they said, as if those were necessarily incompatible opposites. Two former members of the Roosevelt administration, Leon Henderson and Wilson W. Wyatt, were named as leaders of the organization. Schlesinger, still junior in this group, was part of the "Committee of the Whole," but not a member of the organizing committee.[cccxlvii] Remembering his conversations with Bevan, Schlesinger later claimed that "We ADA types held the British experiment in socialism to be of far greater value to Americans than the Russian experiment in communism."[cccxlviii] Their erstwhile enemies on the right saw little difference between the two. Soon enough, Schlesinger and his friends agreed.

The Republican Congress

had made clear its intentions to use charges of Communist infiltration of the government as a lever to dismantle the New Deal. The founding discussions of the ADA therefore defensively focused on explicit opposition to the Communist Party and, in part because of his Communist support, opposition to former Vice President Henry Wallace's third party bid for the presidency in the 1948 election. Similarly, seeking to immunize the administration from Republican charges that it was insufficiently Anti-Communist, President Truman, who had the de facto support of the ADA, signed his Executive Order 9835 on March 22, 1947, instituting "loyalty" screenings in the federal government, thereby moving the debate from actions— espionage—to beliefs: loyalty. For civil rights activist Virginia Durr, "As long as it was Joe McCarthy or crazy Dies or some other idiot doing these things, it didn't carry so much weight. But when the government, when . . . [President Truman] inaugurated the loyalty program and had people called up and accused by informants, faceless informants, at that point . . . things were getting bad."cccxlix

It was in this context that near the end of 1947 Schlesinger published an article in *The New York Times Magazine,* entitled "What is Loyalty? A Difficult Question."cccl Schlesinger began his article by granting the central thesis of the far right: "Civil libertarians who honestly fear a witch-hunt must be reminded that in an imperfect world of spies and traitors a Government must be conceded the right of self-protection." As we now know, and was clear even then, the Government most faced with spies (if not "traitors") had been that of the Roosevelt administration, then rapidly fading into history, not the increasingly right-wing Truman administration with its loyalty investigations and persecution of homosexuals and consumer advocates. But Schlesinger, agreeing with his putative opponents in the American Legion and Congress, saw "an inescapable conflict between civil liberty" and "national security," and concluded that "we must face up to the problem of resolving the conflict." As the following chart shows, "National Security" was (and is) a key term in American politics, its use increasing from the end of the Second World War throughout the Cold War years:

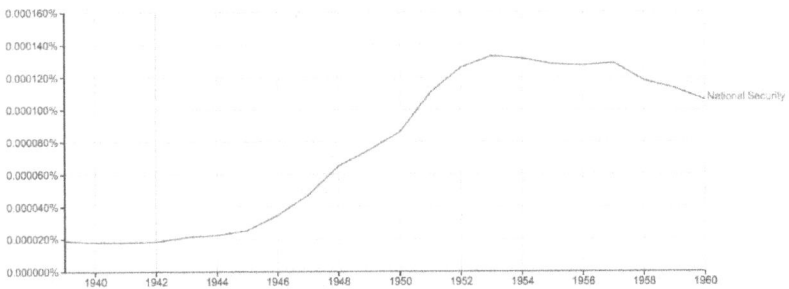

"Civil liberty" is a relatively definite term, pointing to matters protected by the Bill of Rights and similar documents and traditions. "National Security," on the other hand, is, perhaps purposefully, indefinite. It can refer to military power, to the activities of the F.B.I., or to economic policy. It is often the rationale for violations of civil liberty. Schlesinger illustrates his views of what he proposes as the conflict between civil liberty and national security with examples drawn from the activities in 1947 by two branches of the government. First, he considers the House Committee on Un-American Activities' widely publicized investigations of Hollywood with its famous demands for the "naming of names." Schlesinger's opinion of this was that "The private political views of a Hollywood writer, for example, hardly seem to be the proper consideration of the United States Government or a committee of Congress." But then, there is the staffing of departments of the Executive Branch of the American government. Although an "American citizen clearly must be protected in his right to think and speak freely - as a Communist, a Fascist or whatever he wants; but no rule of the Constitution or of common sense requires the State Department to employ him." Of course that was not the question. The State Department is not required to employ anyone in particular. The question, which Schlesinger avoided, was whether the State Department was required to *fire* anyone who exercises his (or her) Constitutional right to free speech. It was a slippery slope from Schlesinger's position to the requirement that the State Department investigate and then terminate the employment of those of its officials who exercised their right to free speech, thought or belief, past or present. Defining a "right to think," with a proviso that there are political limits on thought itself, would be a task undertaken by HUAC, McCarthy and their allies. In the Lattimore case, in 1954, "the Justice Department argued to the Court of Appeals that a state of mind is a fact even when hard to prove, and that misrepresenting a state of mind is perjury." It argued that "Lattimore's views paralleled 'the Communist line.'"[ccccli] The theory proposed was that if the Communist Party supported, say, the right to form a union, and an individual under suspicion also thought that the right to form a union was a good thing, that individual was evidently a Communist.

As it happened, the loyalty investigators were particularly concerned not so much with *present* political affiliations as with *past* speech, thought, and belief. Past thoughts, beliefs and associations were important, because what was at issue in these matters was the criminalization of the immediate past, of the New Deal, its policies, officials and sympathizers. Accepting loyalty investigations in government, investigations of beliefs, thought, speech and the past, opened a door through which the enemies of the New Deal, which Schlesinger and his colleagues in the ADA sought to defend, would rush.

Schlesinger, with the remnants of the ideology of the clerisy in mind, included in "What is Loyalty? A Difficult Question" a declaration that would become quite unthinkable a year or two later, identifying as one of the central issues of the campaign against New Deal liberalism the belief that the Constitution mandated what the McCarthyites would call "a capitalist form of government." Schlesinger pointed out that "The Constitution of the United States does not ordain the economic status quo . . . This insistence on the infallibility of capitalism and on the heresy of change finds no sanction in the usages of the American democratic tradition." However, HUAC and others would in fact insist on just that, its members repeatedly asking witnesses if they believed in "our capitalist form of government." For example, in 1946 a Canoga Park (Los Angeles) High School teacher was investigated because "she had taught 'disrespect for the capitalist system of government of the United States.'" And at the

University of Washington in 1948 Professor Melvin Rader was asked "Do you believe in the capitalist form of government [sic] as it exists in the United States today?"[ccclii]

Schlesinger also asked: "Have we, in fact, a witch-hunt today?[34]" "Witch-hunt" had been an uncommon term in American publications before 1930. It became gradually more frequent until the late 1930s, after which it was used with steeply increasing frequency, reaching a peak in the McCarthyite years between 1950 and 1955.

Schlesinger points to evidence that in fact a witch-hunt was indeed taking place as early as 1947 and that it was causing problems for the proper functioning of government: "the President's executive order, the State Department's loyalty code and some of the recent firings - have doubtless been motivated in great part by a desire to head off more extreme action from Congress.

Yet, this very process of appeasing the worst element in Congress has led to the compromise of principles which cannot be properly compromised in a democracy. Appeasement has produced throughout the Executive Branch an atmosphere of apprehension and anxiety that is fatal to boldness in government. Bureaucratic efficiency is a rather odd argument to bring into play in defense of civil liberties and democracy, but in that climate of rising hysteria, it may have seemed to Schlesinger the only one that could

---

[34] The Merriam-Webster dictionary has as its second definition of "witch-hunt" "the searching out and deliberate harassment of those (such as political opponents) with unpopular views."

be safely deployed. It would soon be apparent that the witch-hunts in the U.S., like "everyday Stalinism" in the U.S.S.R., were propelled from the bottom up as much as from the top down, departmental, institutional and corporate security officers—ex-policemen and ex-F.B.I. employees—wielding more power than the executives of their organizations; denunciations, in both systems, becoming instruments for career advancement or of the satisfaction of grudges and resentment, as well as for more sinister ends.

Schlesinger concludes the article by confessing that for him, defining matters as he has done, "There is no easy answer to this conflict of principles between civil liberty and national security. The practical results thus must depend too much for comfort upon the restraint and wisdom of individuals." Having already conceded the game to those on the right who would limit civil liberty in the name of slight and increasingly non-existent internal threats to national security, Schlesinger is left to despair of the rule of law and the institutions of constitutional government, relying, as was the custom of his caste, on deference to "the restraint and wisdom of individuals," almost always male, usually from Harvard.

As if to reinforce both his doubts about the government's loyalty program and the importance of "the restraint and wisdom of individuals," in the summer of 1948 Schlesinger had his own encounter with the witch-hunt. Schlesinger had been asked by Averell Harriman to help with the Marshall Plan (ECA). His appointment was held up by the F.B.I., which, he found, had confused him with another Arthur Schlesinger, whom rumor had it, was a Communist Party member in New England, and with his own father, who had associated with groups in the 1930s that were *ex post facto* suspect. Eventually, one of Schlesinger's influential friends intervened and ended the delays. "I could not but reflect, however, on the fate of innocent persons falsely accused who did not have the good luck to have a powerful newspaper publisher as a friend. The incident increased doubts about the entire loyalty program."[cccliii] Those doubts did not prevent Schlesinger from defending it "in an imperfect world of spies and traitors [in which] a Government must be conceded the right of self-protection."

Earlier that year, however,

before his own troubles in this matter, Schlesinger had proposed a solution to the conflict between civil liberty and national security. His article *Not Left, Not Right, But a Vital Center* was published on April 4, 1948, in *The New York Times Book Section*. Schlesinger begins this article with an argument associated with Walter Lippmann and Hannah Arendt, the identity, or similarity, of "totalitarian" regimes, regardless of ideology. According to Ellen Schrecker, they, and "the New York intellectuals developed a new interpretation of Soviet Communism. Again a single word [like "Stalinism"], 'totalitarian,' recapsulates that understanding. It underscored the New York intellectuals' moral revulsion against Moscow by making few distinctions between Stalin's crimes and Hitler's and stressing the similarities rather than the differences between Communism and fascism."[cccliv] As Schlesinger put it: "In certain basic respects - a totalitarian state structure, a single party, a leader, a secret police, a hatred of political, cultural and intellectual freedom - fascism and communism are clearly more like each other than they are like anything in between." He calls forth the term "the non-Communist Left," which for this audience he identifies with European Socialism, claiming that officials in the State Department and others recognize this as "among the strongest bulwarks in Europe against communism."

For Schlesinger, the Left, as it existed in Europe in 1948, consisted of the Communist Party (and its sympathizers) on the one hand, and the Socialist parties, on the other. From this he deduces that "A united Left is an illusion: the question of freedom vs. totalitarianism cannot be compromised . . . the non-Communist Left and the non-Fascist Right share a common faith in free political society - a faith that the differences between them over economic issues can be best worked out by discussion and debate under law . . ." Given the defeat of Fascism in the Second World War, and therefore the existence on the Right of *only* a "non-Fascist Right" (outside of the Iberian Peninsula), it follows that Schlesinger is arguing that he finds little effective difference between the European non-Communist Left and the European Right, between, say, Social and Christian democratic parties, both of which were supported, from time to time, by U.S.

funding, and which some years later would form the habit of Grand Coalitions, as if to make Schlesinger's point. Applying this analysis to American politics, and given the minuscule and shrinking American Communist Party, Schlesinger's political analysis comes down to an American democracy with only one political formation: two ideologically similar political parties, Republican and Democratic, which he calls the "Vital Center," a term that would be popular for a few years in the early 1950s.

The Vital Center: The Politics of Freedom, Schlesinger's once famous book-length exposition of these ideas came out at the beginning of 1949.[ccclv] Despite the congressional election victories of the anti-New-Deal-Republicans (in virtual coalition with the segregationist southern Democrats), Schlesinger wrote in the first pages of this book: "During most of my political consciousness this has been a New Deal country. I expect that it will continue to be a New Deal country."[ccclvi] It was to be a forlorn expectation. However, it was in this vein that he began his argument from a position that was becoming increasingly unseasonable: "I am persuaded that the restoration of business to political power in this country would have the calamitous results that have generally accompanied business control of the government; that this time we might be delivered through the incompetence of the right into the hands of the totalitarians of the left . . ."[ccclvii] Presumably anticipating another Depression brought on by what he believed to be the incompetence of businessmen in government, Schlesinger anticipated that another Red (or at least Pink) Decade would follow. The reason that "business" is incompetent in government, according to Schlesinger, is that businessmen are not just interested in making money, they are only interested in making money for themselves. "The capitalists have not been, in the political sense, an effective governing class. They have constituted typically a plutocracy," which Schlesinger defines in opposition to his clerisy: "A plutocracy is a possessing class founded, not on the complex values of status which arise in a stable and interdependent society, but on the naked accumulation of money . . . The plutocracy thinks in terms of class and not of nation, in terms of private profit and not of social obligation, in terms of business dealings and not of war, in terms of security and not of honor."[ccclviii] He declares that "The fight on the part of the 'humble members of society' against business domination has been the consistent motive of American liberalism."[ccclix] (Perhaps he meant "on behalf of" rather than "on the part of" the humble (sic) members of society.) Thus in opposition to the plutocracy, "American liberalism" thinks in terms of nation, not class, social obligation, not private profit, war, not business dealings, honor, not security. Such was the self-image of this son of the Cambridge, Massachusetts, professorial inheritors of the Puritan ascendency.

In sum, Schlesinger's objection to business (read, Republican Party) control of the country was that it was not fit to form a party of government and would fall to a Communist putsch during the anticipated post-World War II depression. However, there was hope: "In America when the chips were down the businessmen have always been bailed out by the radical democracy, often under aristocratic leadership."[ccclx] Schlesinger was thinking back to FDR, but, as it happened, anticipating his hero-worship of John Kennedy. Schlesinger believed that the Roosevelt Administration had demonstrated that state power could be used, contra Marx, to alleviate the evils of capitalism. "As a passive instrument of capitalistic power, the state in Marx's judgment was incapable of acting independently of the business community.

> But history in this case . . . betrayed Marx . . . through using the state power, the other classes have been able to promote the systemic redistribution of wealth . . . Through using state power, the other classes are even

now within measurable distance of the means of avoiding economic crises.[ccclxi]

Such was Schlesinger's view of the state of the country in 1949.

Having begun a line of argument by declaring the unsuitability of the business community, the plutocracy, to govern and declaring his belief in and commitment to a continuing New Deal, Schlesinger then produced the apparent *non sequitur* of an alliance between the plutocracy and of those he refers to as liberals. Because "liberals have values in common with most members of the business community—in particular a belief in free society—which they do not have in common with the totalitarians,"[ccclxii] therefore an alliance between the business plutocracy and liberals will defeat the threatening power of the then perhaps 10,000 members of the Communist Party of the United States. With the example of the Labour Government close at hand, Schlesinger was optimistic: "Britain has already submitted itself to social democracy; the United States will very likely advance in that direction through a series of New Deals . . ."[ccclxiii] However, there were to be no more programs in the United States like those of the New Deal until the Lyndon Johnson administration. It is unimportant that this historian, like others, was not a prophet, but it is important that Schlesinger used his inaccurate prophecies to justify his analysis of the political situation in 1949.

Schlesinger, in the course of a long diatribe against fellow-traveling Progressives, moved from his initial condemnation of contemporary businessmen to a defense of "the robber barons," Rockefeller and Carnegie, by comparing the benefits of their activities, industrial and philanthropic, with the horrors of Stalinist industrialization.[ccclxiv] He makes the contrast more vivid as he does not mention either the slaughter of the Carnegie Steel Company Homestead Strike, or the Rockefeller Ludlow Massacre, the working conditions in the Pennsylvania steel mills or those in the Colorado mines. Following his doctrine of equivalence between Left and Right, Fascism and Communism, Schlesinger claims that "Conservatism in its crisis of despair turns to fascism; so progressivism in its crisis of despair turns to Communism."[ccclxv] The key word here is "despair." In a move collapsing the

Aristotelian hierarchies of human action later explicated by Hannah Arendt (the political, the social and the intimate), Schlesinger diagnoses adherence to "totalitarian" parties of the Left and Right as having psychological origins: "Most men prefer to flee choice, to flee anxiety, to flee freedom," claimed Schlesinger, invoking Sartre, Kierkegaard and Fromm, despite the fact that at least the first two of these emphasize the necessity of choice.[ccclxvi] ("Anxiety" was not a frequently used term in American English before 1940, after which its use rose steadily to a plateau circa 1960. There was not a similar pattern in the rate with which the term appeared in British English.)

Schlesinger then goes further, attributing the very existence of "the totalitarian state," that is, for him the political commonality of Nazi Germany and the Stalinist Soviet Union, to these psychological causes, rather than to, say, historical conditions and the actions of political parties and their leaders: "The totalitarian state, which has risen in specific response to this fear of freedom, is an invention of the twentieth century. It differs essentially from old-style dictatorship, which may be bloody and tyrannical but yet leaves intact most of the structure of society. Totalitarianism, on the contrary, pulverizes the social structure, grinding all independent groups and diverse loyalties into a single amorphous mass."[ccclxvii] This nightmare description of the consequences of "fear of freedom" is highly problematic. Nazi Germany, if anything, multiplied social and governmental structures, while leaving the capitalist economy of the country largely intact, in some ways strengthened. But Schlesinger's real focus was not the vanished Nazi state, but the then-existing, Stalinist, Soviet Union, which he describes in the tendentious terms of the day. "Lenin's terror, being attached to objective conditions, like a still-existing capitalism, had some limits. But Stalin's terror, operating after the liquidation of capitalism, is directed at thoughts . . . it is consequently unlimited in its application."[ccclxviii]

The key Western Cold War term, "totalitarianism," used to assert the equivalency of Nazi Germany and Soviet Communism, first appears in English language publications circa 1935.[35] The frequency

---

[35] Lippmann's *The Good Society,* which first employed the term, appeared in 1936.

of appearance of "totalitarianism" in American publications rose to a 1944/45 peak and declined only slightly thereafter.

It was clarified in December, 1951, when "twelve Congressmen, including McCarran and Walter, wrote to [Attorney General] McGrath protesting that the term 'totalitarian' used in the [McCarran] act was not meant to apply to former Nazis and Fascists . . . In 1953 it was finally established in the courts that the Nazi and Fascist parties did not fall within the act's definition of 'totalitarian' parties."ccclxix

Schlesinger, continuing his psychological framing of political life, also invokes homosexuality in his discussion of totalitarianism and its charms: "totalitarianism . . . perverts politics into something secret, sweaty and furtive like nothing so much, in the phrase of one wise observer of modern Russia [Isaiah Berlin?], as homosexuality in a boys' school: many practicing it, but all those caught to be caned by the headmaster."ccclxx Totalitarianism, that is, Stalinism, is similar to homosexuality. Or is it visa versa? *The Vital Center* is unclear on this point. As a matter of fact, the simile is also unclear. Who is the headmaster? How can totalitarianism be practiced in secret? The story seems to be deployed only to associate Soviet Russia with the pariah group of homosexuals.ccclxxi (With "homosexuality," as with "totalitarianism," trends in British and American usage differ. The American frequency rises through the 1940s, peaking during the witch-hunt years of 1951 to 1956, then declining to the 1950 level. The frequency of the use of homosexuality, the word [not necessarily the practice], in British English shows a simple upward slope from

1945 onward.)

Closely following Erich Fromm's argument in *Escape from Freedom,* Schlesinger claims that many ex-Communists, "once they make the break, have become so dependent emotionally on discipline that, like Louis Budenz and Elizabeth Bentley, they rush to another form of discipline in the Roman Catholic Church, moving from one bastion to another in their frenzied flight from doubt."[ccclxxii] In regard to Budenz, the ex-Communist who was one of the key figures of the persecution of the leaders of the Communist Party of the United States of America, then of rank and file members of the Party, and finally of those whose actions, words and indeed thoughts "followed the Communist line," Schlesinger wrote: "When the Communists used to insist on all or nothing, it seemed to him insupportable intellectual tyranny; now he remarks with evident pleasure, 'There is no compromise in the Church's stand. Catholic faith and the Catholic view must be accepted whole . . . A Catholic has an obligation to live and act in a special manner . . . We had to be sure that our whims and wishes did not supersede our duties to the Catholic cause."[ccclxxiii] After the publication of his *God and Man at Yale,* William F. Buckley, Jr.'s professors spoke similarly of Buckley's need to submit to the discipline of his Church.

In what amounts to an aside, Schlesinger states his belief that "it is fatal not to maintain an unrelenting attack on all forms of racial discrimination."[ccclxxiv] He allows that "the USSR stands plausibly— and many thousands of individual Communists have stood honestly and courageously—for racial equality. The shocking racial cruelties in the United States or in most areas of western colonialism compare unfavorably with the Soviet nationalities policy . . . and with the long Russian traditions of racial assimilation."[ccclxxv] And elsewhere Schlesinger concedes that "high in CPUSA priorities is the drive to organize the Negroes. As the most appalling social injustice in this country, the Negro problem attracted Party interest from the start . . . in countless small ways across the country Communists performed commendable individual acts against discrimination." Small ways. But he then takes back that compliment: "The top leadership . . . continued to view the race problem mainly as a valuable source of propaganda."[ccclxxvi]   Including,

171

no doubt, the African-American members of the top leadership of the Party. In *The Vital Center* Schlesinger claims that the majority of White Southerners were in favor of equal rights for African-Americans: "where Truman and the neo-Confederate Thurmond were on the same ticket, Truman ran ahead almost two to one. This result suggests that the [White] South on the whole accepts the objectives of the civil rights program as legitimate, even though it may have serious and intelligible reservations about timing and method."[ccclxxvii] This was not true. Thurmond won 80% of the vote in Alabama, 49% (to Truman's 33%) of the vote in Louisiana, 87% of the vote in Mississippi and 72% of the vote in South Carolina. In all of these except Alabama, Truman as well as Thurmond was on the ballot. The White voters in the South did not accept "the objectives of the civil rights program as legitimate," as they were making it, and would continue to make it, perfectly clear.

Early on in *The Vital Center* Schlesinger had declared his faith: "The concept of the free society—a society committed to the protection of the liberties of conscience, expression and political opposition—is the crowning glory of western history."[ccclxxviii] Perhaps influenced by Reinhold Niebuhr's theological teachings, Schlesinger wrote later in the book: "In the years after the Second War Americans began to rediscover the great tradition of liberalism . . . the tradition of a reasonable responsibility about politics and a moderate pessimism about man."[ccclxxix] Optimism about "man," was (is) the hallmark of the Enlightenment, pessimism, the conviction of sinfulness, that of its enemies. Whether he was fully conscious of it or not, this Niebuhrian formulation moved Schlesinger's political philosophy out of the great tradition of Western liberalism, giving its name to something much darker with its roots in Prussian absolutism.

Moving toward his conclusion, anticipating Sidney Hook's argument in *Heresy, Yes; Conspiracy, No,* Schlesinger cites Charles Evans Hughes's comment on the New York Socialist case (contesting the expulsion of five Socialist members from the State Assembly): "guilt is personal and cannot be attributed to the holding of opinion or to mere intent in the absence of overt acts."[ccclxxx] Further, "We must tolerate dangerous opinions, [as] jurists Holmes and Brandeis [said] . . . even when their eventual tendency, should they win out by democratic methods, would be to extinguish freedom. But we must draw the line at opinion which results in the immediate and violent obliteration of the conditions of subsequent free discussion."[ccclxxxi] This implies for Schlesinger that *"Due process of law* and *the clear and present danger* test . . . constitute the framework of freedom secured by our ancestors and ratified by the Supreme Court." However, "We are confronted with the spread of a ruthless *totalitarianism* abroad and with the propagation of opinions at home which may well undermine our own faith and sap our capacity to resist foreign tyranny. A fanatical minority is engaged in a cruel *conspiracy* to end forever the whole conception of a society based on free discussion (emphasis added)."[ccclxxxii] And yet, "There is no 'clear and present danger' resulting from the political agitation of Communism which could not be handled by constitutional methods. And there is a 'clear and present danger' that Anti-Communist feeling will boil over into a vicious and unconstitutional attack on nonconformists in general and thereby endanger the sources of our democratic strength."[ccclxxxiii] As he threads this needle, Schlesinger seemingly weakens the case for loyalty tests, oaths and Anti-Communist investigations.

Schlesinger, moreover, and bravely, scoffs at HUAC-style Anti-Communism: "Does anyone seriously believe that even the Communist Party is absurd enough to contemplate a violent revolution in the United States?"[ccclxxxiv] On the other hand, "The performance of the House Committee on Un-American Activities . . . has shown clearly the dangers to civil freedom of a promiscuous and unprincipled attack on radicalism . . . The impact of these committees and of their amateur imitators can be seen most clearly in the field of education."[ccclxxxv] Consistently with his faith in the great and good, Schlesinger cites Harvard President Conant as a defender of academic freedom, while "Popular ignorance about civil liberties is jeopardizing free discussion for everybody . . . threatening to turn us all into frightened conformists; and conformity can lead only to stagnation."[ccclxxxvi] At this point Schlesinger's argument again becomes very confused. He supports loyalty tests, loyalty boards and termination on suspicion of disloyalty, even in the absence of a clear and present danger, in national security executive agencies, e.g., the Department of State, but not in the Post Office and such.[ccclxxxvii] He opposes the style of HUAC, but supports some of its actions, relying on the Establishment, and such men as Conant, to protect civil liberties. Schlesinger concludes the book by turning to an elitist version of Fromm, dissolving the political in the psychological: "We [sic] must somehow give the lonely masses a sense of individual human function, we must restore community to the industrial order . . . Totalitarianism has scotched the snake of anxiety, but not killed it; and anxiety will be its undoing."[ccclxxxviii] Embracing as appropriate for post-war liberalism what was certainly a Communist, then Nazi, goal, but never that of his ancestral Progressives, Schlesinger asserts that "the reform of institutions can never be a substitute for the reform of man."[ccclxxxix]

The Vital Center, then, is not so much a political manifesto on behalf of the goals of the New Deal as a despairing surrender of the political, a retreat into exactly the atomized individuality of anxiety, its causes and cures. In so far as it does offer a political program, that program is for an alliance of "the non-Communist Left" and the "non-Fascist Right," in other words, in the United States as it actually was at mid-century, an alliance between the Democratic Party, shorn of its progressive and fellow-traveling elements, and the Republican Party.[ccxc] After the election of 1948, the main political parties did effect a *de facto* merger: the Dulles brothers working first for Truman, then for Eisenhower; both parties hoping to secure Eisenhower as their nominee in 1952; the Kennedy family becoming perhaps literally intimate with Joseph McCarthy, Robert working for him, two of Joseph Kennedy's daughters "dating" him. The Republican Party had long been the representative of Wall Street; the Democratic Party had become its mask. As *Animal Farm* concludes in the original version:

> *The creatures outside looked from pig to man,*
> *and from man to pig, and from pig to man again;*
> *but already it was impossible to say which was*
> *which.*[ccxci]

The Vital Center was famous in its time, widely publicized and distributed not only in the

United States by Schlesinger's Americans for Democratic Action, but also internationally by the Central Intelligence Agency and British secret intelligence.[cccxcii] In the years that followed, Schlesinger at first believed that he was participating in a decision by the American establishment to continue on the New Deal path toward the sort of arrangement that had been instituted in the United Kingdom by the Attlee Government: "We all felt that democratic socialism was the most effective bulwark against totalitarianism. This became an undercurrent—or even undercover—theme in American foreign policy during the period."[cccxciii] But he soon enough abandoned his respect for Socialists and others on the non-Communist left, adopting the attitudes and vocabulary of the intolerant Right. On September 2, 1951 he wrote, in regard to a group of those he considered "fellow travelers": "None of these gentlemen is a Communist, but none objects very much to Communism. They are the typhoid Marys of the left, bearing the germs of infection even if not suffering obviously from the disease."[cccxciv] Who were these Typhoid Marys? The artists, musicians, composers, actors, scientists and writers who had attended the Waldorf Conference? The directors and executives of the New Deal agencies? Schlesinger does not stay for an answer.[36]

Schlesinger's deployment of the phrase "typhoid Marys" is but one example of his use of the key terms of Cold War, Anti-Communist language. It aligns with his references to Communism as a religion; to the "infection" of Communism, as if it were a disease rather than a political entity; of the non-Communist "free societies" exemplified in the United States by Jim Crow and abroad by the old European empires; of "totalitarianism" equating Communism and National Socialism and "national security" as a justification for purges of government, education and corporate business.

---

[36] The term "Typhoid Mary" has left no trace in British English between 1940 and 1960. In American English it was present specifically in the witch-hunt years, between 1952 and 1958.

Schlesinger's increasing alignment with the witch-hunters may have coincided with his increasing involvement with the Central Intelligence Agency[37] and its front organizations, such as the Congress for Cultural Freedom (CCF). "He was part of what Stuart Hampshire, Isaiah Berlin and Stephen Spender nicknamed 'the *apparat*, the controlling group' [of the CCF]. (Writing to congratulate Irving Brown after the [June, 1950] Berlin meeting, Schlesinger noted enthusiastically, 'I think we may have an immensely powerful instrument of political and intellectual warfare.')" In addition, "Schlesinger was on the Executive Committee of the CIA's Radio Free Europe from 1950 and 'he became involved in the secret distribution of [Marshall Plan] counterpart funds to European trades unions . . . Schlesinger was one of the handful of non-Agency people who knew from the outset the true origins of the Congress for Cultural Freedom."[cccxcv] In sum, according to Frances Stonor Saunders, he "was a [CIA] source, a consultant (if not a paid one), a friend, a trusted colleague to [CIA officials] Frank Wisner, Allen Dulles and Cord Meyer.

He corresponded with all of them, over more than two decades, on subjects ranging from the American Committee for Cultural Freedom, *Encounter*, and the reception of Pasternak's *Doctor Zhivago*. He was even helping the CIA get coverage for themes it wanted aired, agreeing on one occasion to Cord Meyer's suggestion that he Schlesinger, "suggest to the editor" of an

[37] Meeting with CIA leadership as early as 28 September, 1948, while with ECA. Document Number (FOIA) /ESDN (CREST): CIA-RDP80R01731R002700030031-0

Italian journal "that he run a series of articles on the problem of civil liberties inside the Soviet system as companion pieces to the articles on the status of civil liberties inside the US."[cccxcvi]

Schlesinger's career was part of the tragedy of American liberalism that led from anti-Stalinism in the City College cafeteria to Anti-Communist witch-hunts, from "containment" of the Soviet Union to endless wars from Vietnam to Angola. The vital center was, in the end, an ethical void that was filled not by, repeated New Deals but by neo-conservatives, "plutocrats," and reckless right-wing politicians of whom Richard Nixon was only the most notorious.

Notes

cccxl Review: The Age of Jackson: After Forty Years. Reviewed Work: *The Age of Jackson* by Arthur M. Schlesinger, Jr. Review by: Donald B. Cole. *Reviews in American History* Vol. 14, No. 1 (Mar., 1986), pp. 149-159. Published by: The Johns Hopkins. DOI: 10.2307/2702131. Stable URL: http://www.jstor.org/stable/2702131

cccxli Schlesinger, Arthur M., Jr. A Life in the 20th Century: Innocent Beginnings, 1917-1950. New York: Houghton Mifflin, 2000, pp. 334; 335.

cccxlii To Schlesinger's credit: "I was also disturbed by the alacrity with which Frank Wisner seemed to be preparing for the Third World War. While I was vigorously anti-Stalinist, I thought we should do our best to get along with the Soviet Union if only to make sure that, when the break came, the world would have no doubt which side was to blame . . . I was especially disturbed when I discovered that Wisner, in his anti-Soviet fixation, was beginning to draw on Nazi intelligence operatives and sources. " Schlesinger, Arthur M., Jr. A Life in the 20th Century: Innocent Beginnings, 1917-1950. New York: Houghton Mifflin, 2000, pp. 349-50.

cccxliii Schlesinger, A Life in the 20th Century, p. 324.

cccxliv Schlesinger, A Life in the 20th Century, pp. 376-7.

cccxlv Schlesinger, A Life in the 20th Century, p. 399.

cccxlvi Schlesinger, A Life in the 20th Century, p. 346.

cccxlvii *The New York Times,* January 5, 1947.

cccxlviii Schlesinger, A Life in the 20th Century, p. 433.

cccxlix Durr, Virginia Foster. Outside the Magic Circle. Ed. Hollinger F. Barnard. The Autobiography of Virginia Foster Durr. University of Alabama Press, 1985, p. 218.

cccl Arthur Schlesinger Jr., What is Loyalty? A Difficult Question, *The New York Times*, November 2, 1947.

cccli Caute, David. The Great Fear: The Anti-Communist Purge Under Truman and Eisenhower. New York: Simon and Schuster, 1978, p. 320.

ccclii Caute, pp. 410; 425.

cccliii Schlesinger, A Life in the 20th Century, p. 469.

cccliv Schrecker, Ellen. Many Are the Crimes: McCarthyism in America. Princeton University Press, 1998, p. 81.

ccclv Schlesinger, Arthur M., Jr. The Vital Center: The Politics of Freedom. Second Edition. New Brunswick and London: Transaction Publishers (the Riverside Press, 1949), 1998.

ccclvi Schlesinger, The Vital Center, p. xx.

ccclvii Schlesinger, The Vital Center, p. xxii.

ccclviii Schlesinger, The Vital Center, p. 13.

ccclix Schlesinger, The Vital Center, p. 172.

ccclx Schlesinger, The Vital Center, p. 25.

ccclxi Schlesinger, A Life in the 20th Century, pp. 152-3.

ccclxii Schlesinger, The Vital Center, p. xxii.

ccclxiii Schlesinger, The Vital Center, p. 154.

ccclxiv Schlesinger, The Vital Center, p. 44ff.

ccclxv Schlesinger, The Vital Center, p. 50.

ccclxvi Schlesinger, The Vital Center, p 52. "Especially among moderates and liberals, the notion that Communism was some kind of psychological disorder came to be quite common." Schrecker, Ellen. Many Are the Crimes: McCarthyism in America. Princeton University Press, 1998, p. 145.

ccclxvii Schlesinger, The Vital Center, p. 53.

ccclxviii Schlesinger, The Vital Center, p. 77. Schlesinger, as we have seen, was an apologist for the interrogation of the thoughts of governmental employees, other than himself (but not those of Hollywood script writers).

ccclxix Caute, p. 254.

ccclxx Schlesinger, The Vital Center, p. 151.

ccclxxi But see: Pease, Donald E. Cat on a Hot Tin Roof: Restoring Tennessee Williams's Production of the 1950s Primal Scene. *Boundary 2*, 2015. Volume 42, Number 2: 25-56.

ccclxxii Schlesinger, The Vital Center, p. 106.

ccclxxiii Schlesinger, The Vital Center, p. 106, footnote, citing Louis Budenz, *This is My Story,* New York, 1947, pp. 352, 351.

ccclxxiv Schlesinger, The Vital Center, pp. 190-1.

ccclxxv Schlesinger, The Vital Center, p. 230.

ccclxxvi Schlesinger, The Vital Center, p. 120-1.

ccclxxvii Schlesinger, The Vital Center, p. 190.

ccclxxviii Schlesinger, The Vital Center, p. 8.

ccclxxix Schlesinger, The Vital Center, p. 165.

ccclxxxSchlesinger, The Vital Center, p. 197; 1921 brief to the Assembly from the NYC Bar Association.

ccclxxxi Schlesinger, The Vital Center, p. 199.

ccclxxxii Schlesinger, The Vital Center, p. 201.

ccclxxxiii Schlesinger, The Vital Center, p. 210.

ccclxxxiv Schlesinger, The Vital Center, p. 129. "By 1949 communism was a negligible political and intellectual force in the United States." Schlesinger, A Life in the 20th Century, p. 495.

ccclxxxv Schlesinger, The Vital Center, pp. 204-5.

ccclxxxvi Schlesinger, The Vital Center, pp 208. Conant's record in this regard was hardly exemplary. His biographer found that "His failure of nerve at key moments was very important in the general failure of the American educational establishment" in the fight for academic freedom and against the Anti-Communist hysteria," James G. Hershberg, author of James B. Conant: Harvard to Hiroshima and the Making of the Nuclear Age, quoted in *The Harvard Crimson,* December 14, 1993.

ccclxxxvii Schlesinger, The Vital Center, pp. 214-8ff.

ccclxxxviii Schlesinger, The Vital Center, p. 247.

ccclxxxix Schlesinger, The Vital Center, p. 250.

cccxc "The overwhelming rejection of Henry Wallace in the 1948 campaign and the emergence of Americans for Democratic Action (ADA) marked the beginning of a new political era in which the left was in virtual eclipse and in which the distinction between liberals and conservatives became one of method and technique, not fundamental principle." "American Politics and the origins of 'McCarthyism,'" Griffith, Robert in Griffith, Robert and Athan Teoharis. The Specter: Original Essays on the Cold War and the Origins of McCarthyism. New York: New Viewpoints, 1974, pp. 12-3.

cccxci The Log of Director of Central Intelligence Bedell Smith, notes under 20 November 1951, the Log carried a notation that "Between 28 and 31 October 105,000 copies of 'Animal Farm' were distributed through Austria as an insertion in a CIA-subsidized newspaper. A sellout at the news-stands necessitated an extra run of 15,000 copies." And under 7 December 1951, that "The circulation of a CIA-subsidized Vienna paper, DIE PRESSE, has increased over one-third in a single month . . . This circulation boost is attributable, in part, to the fact that an insert carrying George Orwell's 'Animal Farm' was included with 1 edition of the paper." https://www.cia.gov/library/readingroom/docs/CIA-RDP80R01731R002700090001-7.pdf

cccxcii "Heinemann brought out *The Vital Center* in Great Britain the next year under the title *The Politics of Freedom* [sic], with a generous introduction by Malcolm Muggeridge." Schlesinger, A Life in the 20th Century, p. 518. Muggeridge was notoriously "close to" British secret intelligence agencies.

cccxciii Saunders, p. 63.

cccxciv Navasky, Victor S. Naming Names. New York: Hill and Wang, 2003 (Viking, 1991), p. 54.

cccxcv Saunders, p. 90-1.

cccxcvi Saunders, p. 379.

A Cold War Theologian: Reinhold Niebuhr

The Irony of American History

Reinhold Niebuhr, in some ways a nineteenth-century figure, lived far into the twentieth century, becoming increasingly influential until, at the height of that influence in 1952, he had the first of a series of strokes that led to his slow decline and his eventual death as late as 1971. He was by far the most often mentioned during the Cold War of the three figures considered here and even today the frequency with which his name appears in the Google book collection exceeds those for Arthur Schlesinger, Jr., and Sidney Hook.

The Niebuhr family business was the German Evangelical Church in Missouri and Illinois, in which his father, a German immigrant, was a pastor. The language in the Niebuhr home was German, as was the language of their church's services until the First World War. The German Evangelical Church was the American branch of the Evangelical Church of the Prussian Union, a government-enforced merger of the Lutheran and Reformed churches in Germany. It had a strong Pietistic flavor, emphasizing individual character and "inward" religious devotion. After his father's death, Reinhold Niebuhr succeeded him in his pulpit. Niebuhr's education took place in German language schools until he went to Yale in 1914 to study Divinity. He preached for thirteen years in a church in Detroit, then in 1928 moved to New York, becoming a professor at Union Theological Seminary, where he remained. While his younger brother, Helmut Richard Niebuhr, who was also prominent in the church, eventually becoming a professor at the Yale Divinity School, was a "theologian's theologian," Reinhold Niebuhr was very much a public figure, first as a much-traveled preacher, then as a theologian, and finally as a public intellectual.

Niebuhr's rapidly expanding church in Detroit was in a White, upper middle class neighborhood. There, Niebuhr began what would be a decades-long routine of preaching and lecturing (a distinction, in his case, without a difference), wherever requested to do so, depending on family members and assistants for the day-to-day operations of the church. Niebuhr's move from the isolated German cultural environment of the small town Midwest to Detroit, then the industrialization center of the United States, brought him into direct contact with the conflict between the owners of the factories and the people who worked in them. His first impulse was to conceive of this relationship in moral terms. According to his biographer, Richard Wightman Fox, "The raging battle between capital and labor was caused, he asserted, by human selfishness.

> Granted, capital earned too much and labor too little. But socialism was no better than capitalism since it merely put the selfishness of the "underclass" in place of that of the "upper classes." As long as most people were selfish there could be no solution . . . On both sides love was the answer.[cccxcvii]

This was a position from which he would move radically to the left, then eventually return to a place somewhere in its ethical vicinity. However, in this period, as he became more involved with the life of the city, he became increasingly convinced that it was not a matter of a balance between individual attitudes that was central to the issues of modernization in Detroit; it was the determination of the owners, represented preeminently by Henry Ford, to extract as much wealth as possible from the labor of their employees. This experience eventually brought him to a prominent role in the Socialist Party.

In 1928 Niebuhr accepted a professorship at the Union Theological Seminary in New York. The following year the system that had produced such figures as Ford and his peers collapsed. By 1930 Niebuhr was writing, *a propos* of the work of the young German theologian Dietrich Bonhoeffer: "Any other interpretation of 'ethical' than one which measures an action in terms of consequences and judges actions purely in terms of notions empties the ethical of content and makes it purely formal."[cccxcviii] Becoming ever more radicalized, Niebuhr wrote in *Harper's* in June, 1932, that "it will be practically impossible to secure social change in America without the use of very considerable violence."[cccxcix] In that year's presidential election, he opposed both Hoover and Roosevelt, thinking the latter a shallow politician, and worked instead for his close associate Norman Thomas, the Socialist Party candidate. Over the remainder of the decade of the 1930s Niebuhr himself stood for a variety of local offices on the Socialist ticket. After the 1932 election of Franklin Roosevelt, in *Moral Man and Immoral Society* (December 1932), Niebuhr asserted once more "that the responsible Christian had to accept the use of force—otherwise he would have to withdraw from politics altogether—and that the use of force logically implied the use of violence in certain situation."[cd]

By the following year Niebuhr had gone yet further, calling "himself a 'Marxian' as well as a 'Christian'."[cdi] In December, 1933, J. B. Matthews—that hyperactive joiner of Communist, then Anti-Communist, organizations—was fired as Executive Secretary of the Fellowship of Reconciliation, an organization working for world peace, for advocating violence. Niebuhr, who was chairman of the Executive Council of the Fellowship of Reconciliation, agreeing with Matthews "that the working class might some day have to use violence" resigned from the organization's Executive Council.[cdii] In what was apparently his closest approach to support for the Communist Party, Niebuhr wrote in the winter 1935-6 issue of *Radical Religion* that "Communism may be a corruption of prophetic religion but it is not its antithesis . . . It does not at least identify the principle of evil with a certain race but only with *the bearers of a particular form of social organization.*"[cdiii] He was still opposed to Roosevelt, still a stalwart of the Socialist Party. But, just a year or two later, at the Oxford Conference in June, 1937, Niebuhr returned to his Pietist roots. His "passionate speech centered neither on the world crisis nor on the injustices of bourgeois capitalism. [It] centered on the fact of sin in the individual life."[cdiv] He seemed to have suddenly given up on political action, and Socialism, as having the potential to improve the world. And two years after that, his Gifford Lectures in the late spring of 1939, "made clear . . . that Niebuhr had no [longer any] affection for the radical left."[cdv]

183

Nonetheless, Niebuhr reacted to the Hitler/Stalin Pact as if from a Socialist or Trotskyite position, criticizing Stalin's sacrifice of Communist ideals to national survival.[cdvi] The following year, moving toward the center, he endorsed Roosevelt in the 1940 election, definitely abandoning Socialism, and in 1941 Niebuhr helped found the Union for Democratic Action, a group of New York City leftist interventionists from which members of the Communist Party were banned.[cdvii] Despite this ban, according to Fox, Niebuhr had to defend "the UDA against Congressman Martin Dies's charge that it was Communist inspired. Dies was troubled by the organization's tolerance for former Communists . . . and by its campaign against conservative Congressmen like himself. It was politically advantageous [for Dies] to label the UDA 'red.'"[cdviii] At this point, just as he had made a definite break with his radical past, Niebuhr became the object of attention of the F.B.I.[cdix] But in the wider world, "Niebuhr's popular reputation was taking on a life of its own: the preacher of man's impotence to guide his fate. 'Niebuhrian' was coming to mean 'pessimistic,' even 'resigned.'"[cdx]Niebuhr's Evangelical Church, which had been created by the fiat of the Prussian King, by definition supported the state. Niebuhr, after his Socialist interlude, was returning to his family's evangelical roots. From this moment on, Niebuhr's "pivotal contribution to the intellectual life of the [nineteen] forties was the somber assertion of built-in limits to human existence.

> The "responsible" self struggled for justice but did not expect fulfillment; his commitments were qualified by skepticism about the delusions to which all individuals and groups were prone; human history was not an arena for perfecting communal fellowship. Responsibility connoted for Niebuhr a simultaneous engagement and retrenchment, a giving of commitment and a holding back, a willingness to act but only within the tragic boundaries of human life.[cdxi]

All this was in direct opposition to the Marxism, with its utopian aspirations, that had inspired him since his ministry in Detroit.

With the end of the Second World War Niebuhr became increasingly Anti-Communist and anti-Soviet. An October, 1946, article in *Life*, picked up by

Time and by the right-wing, mass-circulation, *Reader's Digest,* carried the subtitle: "A distinguished theologian declares America must prevent the conquest of Germany and Western Europe by the unscrupulous Soviet tyranny."[cdxii]   According to Frances Stonor Saunders, "Reinhold Niebuhr [had become] . . . a Cold War 'realist' who believed that the establishment of a calculated balance of power was paramount, with foreign policy the exclusive responsibility of an elite authority . . .

> Niebuhr served up liberal [sic] helpings of theology to *Time-Life* readers, winning Sidney Hook's approval for successfully reviving the doctrine of original sin as a political tool, and making '"God an instrument of national policy."[cdxiii]

Hook, a Marxist as well as Pragmatist philosopher, was presumably an atheist. In June, 1947, Niebuhr wrote that "the one right decision we have made . . . is our evident intention to stay in Europe and prevent the Russian power from inundating the European continent."[cdxiv] And just before the 1948 election, he declared that "poor Henry [Wallace] is really a prisoner of the Commies."[cdxv] Niebuhr, like Schlesinger a few years earlier, used the signature Anti-Communist term the Communist Party of the United States to mark his conversion to that camp. Norman Markowitz observed that "Niebuhr, the apostle of sober choices and the consistent enemy of utopianism, emerged as the major thinker of a 'new liberalism' whose main thrust was essentially escapist and conservative.

> Niebuhr's own philosophy, rooted in the "crisis theology" of European Protestant Orthodoxy, was well suited to the dour mood of cold-war liberalism. It stressed both the complexities of life and the persistence of sin—a world where man neither Prometheus nor the Noble Savage and in which evil was a reality.[cdxvi]

The earliest parts of Niebuhr's key text, *The Irony of American History,* were presented as lectures at Westminster College, Fulton, Missouri, in May, 1949, three years after Winston Churchill inaugurated the Cold War with his Iron Curtain speech at the same college. (The college's endowment required a speaker of "international reputation," which is an indication of Niebuhr's standing at the time.) In the book's 1952 "Preface" Niebuhr defines irony as consisting "of apparently fortuitous incongruities in life which are discovered . . . to [be] not merely fortuitous . . .

> If virtue becomes vice through some hidden defect in the virtue; if strength becomes weakness because of the vanity to which strength may prompt the mighty man or nation; if security is transmuted into insecurity because too much reliance is placed upon it; if wisdom becomes folly because it does not know its own limits—in all such cases the situation is ironic.[cdxvii]

In this Niebuhr is once again the preacher of Pietism, that inward-looking faith, warning the citizens of the new superpower of the limits to that power and the limits that each person must be aware of as they make their way through the world. But after this he quickly turned to the political situation of the world crisis of the early 1950s with an application of his concept of irony to "communism." The word "communism" as used by Niebuhr in the following quotation, has two, or perhaps three, referents. It is an ideology, with dreams of justice and virtue; a government practicing tyranny, and once more an ideology (falsely) projecting universal peace. "Insofar as communism tries to cover the ironic contrast between its original dreams of justice and virtue and its present realities by more and more desperate efforts to prove its tyranny to be 'democracy' and its imperialism to be the achievement of universal peace, it has already dissolved irony into pure evil."[cdxviii]

"Evil," for the secular mind of, say, Arthur Schlesinger, Jr., was an ethical category applied to actions: to bad as opposed to neutral or good actions. Hitler, or Stalin, were evil because of actions they performed. If they had not performed actions that those in the secular world can categorize rhetorically as evil, then they would not have been evil men. That is not what Niebuhr meant. As a minister of the Evangelical Church, he was taught, and taught, that for Calvin, "believers are recognized to be the sons of God by bearing his image, so the wicked are properly regarded as the children of Satan, from having degenerated into his image."[cdxix] Evil, for Calvin, was a state of predestined being—evil actions were merely a sign of that state. Similarly, for Luther, "Good works do not make a good man, but a good man does good works; evil works do not make a wicked man, but a wicked man does evil works."[cdxx] Thus, as "communism," by which Niebuhr means the system then in place in the Soviet Union and the areas it controlled, was doing evil things in his judgment, it was by that sign in itself evil, an ally of Satan. One term for this style of thought is reification, making actions into objects.

Therefore, while Niebuhr may begin with a political statement: "We are defending freedom against tyranny and are trying to preserve justice" he immediately collapses this into a theological definition: "trying to preserve justice against a system which has, demonically, distilled injustice and cruelty out of its original promise of a higher justice."[cdxxi] Communism, "a demonic religio-political creed,"[cdxxii] has an ironic existence, in Niebuhr's rhetoric, because it presents itself as an Enlightenment ideology, while it is, in fact, a work of Satan.[38] Therefore, "If only we could fully understand that the evils against which we contend are frequently the fruit of illusions which are similar to our own, we might be better prepared to save a vast uncommitted world, particularly in Asia, which lies between ourselves and communism, from being engulfed by this noxious creed."[cdxxiii] Giving the Devil his due, Niebuhr reminds us that the "communist movement against which the whole world must now stand on guard was intended as a scheme for giving man complete control of his own destiny."[cdxxiv] But, "In any event we have to deal with a vast religious-political movement which generates more extravagant forms of political injustice and cruelty out of the pretensions of innocency [sic] than we have ever known in human history."[cdxxv]

Having defined communism as the religion of Satan and, apparently, the Soviet Union as Satan himself, Niebuhr then moves on to a consideration of the condition of the United States. He notes that "We find it almost as difficult as the communists to believe that

---

[38] The Evangelical preacher Billy Graham also held "that 'Communism is . . . master-minded by Satan . . . I think there is no other explanation for the tremendous gains of Communism in which they seem to outwit us at every turn, unless they have supernatural power and wisdom and intelligence given to them.'"

anyone could think ill of us, since we are as persuaded as they that our society is so essentially virtuous that only malice could prompt criticism of any of our actions."[cdxxvi] Less ironically, as it were, Niebuhr identifies the cause of that virtue: "For it can hardly be denied that the fluidity of our class structure, derived from the opulence of economic opportunities, saved us from the acrimony of the class struggle in Europe, and avoided the class rebellion, which Marx could prompt in Europe but not in America."[cdxxvii] This is in itself rather ironic given Niebuhr's own political beliefs in the 1920s and 1930s, firmly rooted as they were in a class analysis of American society and culminating in advocacy for, or at least toleration of, violence. Perhaps this was why reading the manuscript of *The Irony of American History* Schlesinger, to his credit, "suggested that Niebuhr include the abysmal treatment of the Negro in this country as one of many ironies of American democracy deserving attention."[cdxxviii] Be that as it may, continuing with his praise for the United States, at that point dominant over the Americas, Western Europe, East Asia— everywhere, in fact, out of the reach of the Soviet military, "we do not have a strong lust of power . . . Our lack of the lust of power makes the fulminations of our foes against us singularly inept."[cdxxix] (This practice of stating as irrefutable truths matters that were obviously not the case was shared by the propaganda of both sides in the Cold War.) Richard Wightman Fox concluded that *The Irony of American History* "reduced communism to a demonic religion while allowing democracy its historical diversity." He also noted that "It was a sign of the times [1952] that none of [its] liberal reviewers challenged his blanket denunciation of communism . . ."[cdxxx]

Aside from references to "Commies" Niebuhr used few of the typical verbal signs of Cold War language in *The Irony of American History*, but he did repeatedly turn to the set of religious metaphors frequently used by the Anti-Communists. Niebuhr went further the most in this, identifying the Soviet Union with Satan and Communism as a Satanic force, a corruption of religion. Here, he was in agreement with the Popes of his time, but few others went so far.

The Rosenbergs' atomic espionage trial and their execution appear to have incited Anti-

Communists like Niebuhr to a nearly literal witch-hunter's fanaticism. (Judge Kaufman, sentencing the Rosenberg's, referred to "this diabolical conspiracy to destroy a God-fearing nation."[cdxxxi]) Channeling Salem's Reverend Samuel Parris, Niebuhr wrote that "'Traitors are never ordinary criminals and the Rosenbergs are quite obviously fiercely loyal Communists . . . Stealing atomic secrets is an unprecedented crime.' Europeans like Sartre—'only recently turned fellow traveler'—were deluded in imagining this was another Dreyfus affair. The Rosenbergs ought to be executed."[cdxxxii] Niebuhr, at this time, was teaching and preaching Christian doctrine at Union Theological Seminary.

The frequency of references in American English to "atomic secrets," an obsession of the Anti-Communists, rose and fell with the Cold War.

The *New Leader* published Niebuhr's article entitled "The Evil of the Communist Idea" ten days before the execution of the Rosenbergs.[cdxxxiii] Quite aside from the present view that Ethel Rosenberg was innocent of the charges and that the punishment was so singular in American history as to violate the Constitution's injunction against cruel and unusual punishment, it does seem ironic that a minister and former leader of the Fellowship of Reconciliations should have taken such a bloodthirsty stand. Of course by that time Niebuhr was affiliated with quite a different group of organizations, including the State Department's Policy Planning Staff, that is, the directing group of Cold War covert activities, of which he was the chairman of the Advisory Committee.[cdxxxiv]

The Language of Anti-Communism

In 1956 Niebuhr criticized Picasso's *Guernica*, against theologian Paul Tillich's admiration for the painting, as the production of "a well-known fellow traveler."[cdxxxv] Writing to Schlesinger on May 7, 1957, Niebuhr said "that, when he spoke to Oppenheimer about 'Einstein's childlike naïveté in all political matters,' Oppenheimer 'said very simply, "actually I think that kind of naïveté is a resource for physical scientists. It gives them a very pure vision." I thought that remark was very revealing."[cdxxxvi] Niebuhr apparently meant that Oppenheimer, also, was naïve. Be that as it may in regard to Oppenheimer, in regard to Einstein's political views, a summary of a collection of his writings states: "Einstein [was] not the ineffectual and naïve idealist of popular imagination, but a principled, shrewd pragmatist whose stands on political issues reflected the depth of his humanity."[cdxxxvii] Einstein, like Eleanor Roosevelt, was—nearly—safe from effective personal attack, or its consequences, even by the most unscrupulous of witch-hunters. Therefore his views had to be stigmatized and disregarded. It was common during the Anti-Communist hysteria of the 1950s to call those not swept up in it and too eminent to attack directly "neurotic" or "naïve," rather than engaging them politically. In Einstein's case, as we have seen, references to his unkempt hair were also commonly used *non sequiturs* to discredit his political positions.

Niebuhr suffered a major stroke in 1952 and entered a long decline, punctuated by more strokes and other illnesses, dying in 1971. At his November 1, 1971 memorial service, Arthur M. Schlesinger, Jr. gave an address entitled "Prophet for a Secular Age," in which he said that "Niebuhr's influence . . . was . . . in his capacity to restate historical Christianity in terms that corresponded to our most searching modern themes and anxieties."[cdxxxviii] Or, to put that another way, Niebuhr's role in the Cold War was to deploy the resonance of Pietism, that theology of inwardness, in the service of the worldly ideology of Anti-Communism. The Prussian King, Frederick William III, who had united the Lutheran and Reformed Churches in 1817 into the Evangelical Church of the Prussian Union, would have been pleased.

The Non-Communist Left

The Language of Anti-Communism

Notes

cccxcvii Fox, Richard Wightman. Reinhold Niebuhr: A Biography. New York: Pantheon Books, 1985, p. 23.
cccxcviii Fox, p. 125, citing Niebuhr on Dietrich Bonhoeffer, 1930.
cccxcix Fox, p. 138.
cd Fox, p. 137.
cdi Fox, p. 143.
cdii Fox, p. 155.
cdiii Fox, p. 169.
cdiv Fox, p. 178.
cdv Fox, p. 189.
cdvi Fox, circa pp. 190 ff.
cdvii Fox, p. 197.
cdviii Fox, p. 200.
cdix Fox, pp. 207-8.
cdx Fox, p. 202. 1941
cdxi Fox, p. 216.
cdxii Fox, p. p. 229.
cdxiii Saunders, Frances Stonor. Who Paid the Piper? The CIA and the Cultural Cold War. London: Granta Books, 1999, p 281. Hook and Niebuhr were not alone in associating God with American national security. In 1954 Congress "expanded the Pledge of Allegiance to include the words 'One Nation Under God', a phrase which, according to [then President] Eisenhower, reaffirmed 'the transcendence of religious faith in America's heritage and future; in this way we shall constantly strengthen those spiritual weapons which forever will be our country's most powerful resource in peace and war'" The President had done Hook one better by metaphorically weaponizing religion.
cdxiv Fox, p. 232.
cdxv Fox, p. 236.
cdxvi "A View from the Left: From the Popular Front to Cold War Liberalism," Markowitz, Norman, in Griffith, Robert and Athan Teoharis. The Specter: Original Essays on the Cold War and the Origins of McCarthyism. New York: New Viewpoints, 1974, pp. 109-10.
cdxvii Niebuhr, Reinhold. The Irony Of American History. Chicago and London: The University of Chicago Press, 1952, p. xxiv.
cdxviii Niebuhr, p. xxiv.
cdxix Calvin, John. Institutes of the Christian Religion, 1.14.18, Beveridge translation, http://www.ccel.org/ccel/calvin/institutes.iii.xv.html#iii.xv-

Page_153
cdxx Luther, Martin. Treatise on Christian Liberty, Works of Martin Luther: with Introductions and Notes, Volume 2. Jacobs, Henry Eyster and Spaeth, Adolph. Philadelphia: A. J. Holman Company, 1915. p. 331.
cdxxi Niebuhr, p. 1.
cdxxii Niebuhr, p. 3.
cdxxiii Niebuhr, p. 16.
cdxxiv Niebuhr, p. 65.
cdxxv Niebuhr, p. 22.
cdxxvi Niebuhr, pp. 24-5.
cdxxvii Niebuhr, pp. 29.
cdxxviii Rice, Daniel F. Reinhold Niebuhr and his circle of influence. Cambridge University Press, 2013, p. 119.
cdxxix Niebuhr, p. 38.
cdxxx Fox, p. 247.
cdxxxi Caute, David. The Great Fear: The Anti-Communist Purge Under Truman and Eisenhower. New York: Simon and Schuster, 1978.
cdxxxii Fox, p. 252.
cdxxxiii Fox, p. 255.
cdxxxiv Saunders, p 457, footnote 8
cdxxxv Fox, p. 258.
cdxxxvi Rice, p. 135.
cdxxxvii Publisher's note to Rowe, David E. and Robert Schulmann, Einstein on Politics: His Private Thoughts and Public Stands on Nationalism, Zionism, War, Peace and the Bomb. Princeton: Princeton University Press, 2007.
cdxxxviii Rice, p. 144.

The Language of Anti-Communism

A Cold War Philosopher: Sidney Hook

Heresy, Yes; Conspiracy, No

Give me a hundred million dollars and a thousand dedicated people, and I will guarantee to generate such a wave of democratic unrest among the masses—yes, even among the soldiers—of Stalin's own empire, that all his problems for a long period of time to come will be internal. I can find the people.—Sidney Hook, 1949.

The New York Times Magazine of July 9, 1950, carried an editorial cartoon, showing a man labeled "Communist" looking in a mirror at his image, which was labeled "Treason." The message was clear enough: Communists were by definition traitors. The cartoon accompanied an article by Dr. Sidney Hook, some-time chairman of the Department of Philosophy at New York University, disciple of John Dewey, ex-communist, CIA contact and F.B.I. informant, founder of the American Congress for Cultural Freedom, soon to be a active member of the CIA front, the Congress for Cultural Freedom. Hook represented the extreme left of American Anti-Communism, a group of remnants, in a sense, and sometimes literally, of the Menshevik and Trotskyite branches of Russian revolutionary socialism.

Hook had come to the attention of the CIA predecessor organization, the Office for Policy Coordination (OPC), for his role in disrupting the March, 1949 "Waldorf Conference." OPC then paid for him to attend Anti-Communist conferences in Paris and Berlin. Shortly after his return from the excitement of the Berlin conference, Hook published an article by on July 9, 1950 in *The New York Times Magazine* entitled "Heresy, Yes—But Conspiracy, No."[cdxxxix] He began by stating that what he called a "cold war of ideologies" was

195

then taking place in the context of "the hot war" in Korea just beginning. The domestic issue, for Hook was liberalism, whether, what Hook called the freedom of liberal society, must be compromised in order to prevent "communism," as a concept, not as a political activity, from using that freedom to destroy liberal society. After some discussion concerning what liberalism is not, Hook defined it as the willingness to limit one type of freedom in order to preserve another. He then cited Justice Oliver Wendell Holmes as having defined liberalism as the belief "in the free trade of ideas— that the test of truth is the power of the thought to get itself accepted in the competition of the market," amalgamating in this way the vocabulary of the political with that of the economic, democracy with capitalism.[cdxl] Truth makes itself known, for Hook, perhaps metaphorically, by how well it "sells" in competition with alternatives. It is difficult to think of a precedent for this definition of truth. On the contrary, the question calls to mind truth's classical location in the Bible, John 18:38: "Jesus answered . . . To this end was I born, and for this cause came I into the world, that I should bear witness unto the truth." According to Francis Bacon, "Jesting Pilate then responded 'What is truth?' and would not stay for an answer." Neither the Roman nor his interlocutor would have thought that truth was to be found in the marketplace, like a melon or slave.

Holmes's dictum came in the course of his discussion of the limits of free speech, in which he claims strong First Amendment protection for nearly all speech, unless there is insufficient time for the operations of his postulated free market place of ideas. The phrase "free market place of ideas" itself was practically unknown in American English before Hook's article and after 1960 again gradually falls out of use, as illustrated by this Ngram chart:

It is not clear what either Holmes or Hook meant by the concept. It seems to point to a radical relativism, some kind of vote as determinate of truth, or, perhaps, to take the phrase literally, an auction. But then, we might ask, how are ideas priced? It is most likely that the "free market of ideas" was not intended to mean anything, exactly—as Professor Hook might have expressed it in class, it was the connotation, not the denotation, of the phrase that mattered.

In his *New York Times Magazine* article Hook, seemingly identifying himself as a liberal (rather than a Marxist or radical), wrote that "What the liberal fears is the systematic corruption of the free market of ideas by *activities* which make intelligent choice impossible. In short, what he fears is not heresy but conspiracy" (emphasis added). This is an innovation by Hook (one which influenced Schlesinger). There was no similar constraint in the discussion by Holmes, where the free market in ideas is qualified only by something like the familiar boundary case of a clear and present danger. Where Holmes limits freedom of speech, in the widest sense, only by the time constraints of a definitionally rare emergency, Hook limits it by the presence in the market place of an unwelcome actor, a Catiline glowering at the end of one of the nearby Senate House benches, conspiring to seize the free market of ideas for his own benefit.

Proceeding further in this direction, Hook introduces the distinction, fundamental in his thought, between a heresy and a conspiracy: "A heresy is a set of unpopular ideas or opinions on matters of grave concern to the community . . . a liberal society can impose no official orthodoxies of belief, disagreement with which entails legal sanctions of any kind," including here the theory of communism as a heresy. On the other hand, "A conspiracy . . . is a secret or underground movement which seeks to attain its ends not by normal political or educational process but by playing outside the rules of the game . . . And conspiracies cannot be tolerated."[cdxli] In other words, "conspiracy" is not a common noun for Hook, not a reference to a group taking or planning an action, it is a proper noun, and in the absence of other referents, it is understood as simply an alternative name for the Communist Party of the United States. Oddly, for a person who made his living—and reputation—as a teacher of philosophy, Hook's distinction between heresy and conspiracy is based on a category mistake: one does not make a distinction in this way between individual mental processes and groups. (The usual opposition is between "heresy" and "orthodoxy.") One does not say: "On the one hand there is confusion, on the other, a grove of trees." But such quibbles are beside the point. Hook's "distinction" between heresy and conspiracy is not the beginning, but the end of an argument, an assumption presented as a definition.

Hook counsels care in using the law to oppose the Communist Party in government, labor unions, education and elsewhere. The problems the Communist Party causes cannot "be solved by placing the Communist movement and its entire periphery outside the law by special legislation." Hook does not advise this for Constitutional reasons, but simply as strategic: "by labeling all progressive ideas as communistic ["reactionaries"] help the Communist strategy." Hook also dismisses the loyalty oaths promoted by reactionaries (Communists will take them), and, on the other hand, the broad tolerance promoted by those Hook calls "ritualistic," as opposed to "realistic" liberals.

This brings Hook to his prescription: "realistic" liberalism. In a governmental context, according to Hook's "realistic" liberal position, loyalty to a foreign government disqualifies a citizen from government employment. (Hook apparently does not have in mind the Vatican as a foreign government.) He states that in labor matters, however, unions should not rely on governmental intervention, but "should" (not "may") expel

Communists on their own, not for ideological reasons, but merely as disruptive. In education, teachers and scholars with communist beliefs and those teaching communist theories are to be tolerated, those who are members of the Communist Party are not. (Once again the parallel cases of Catholic or fundamentalist teachers are not raised in the article, but in the book-length version of the argument, Hook interestingly states that "There is no academic freedom in Catholic colleges and were the Catholics to constitute a majority of the population, education would in all likelihood lose its secular character."[cdxlii]) Reaching for the vocabulary of disease, Hook writes that "This is a matter of ethical hygiene, not of politics or of persecution," a matter which he states should be dealt with by "the teachers themselves and not with the state or Regents or even boards of trustees." The term "ethical hygiene," assimilating ideas Hook disapproved of to dirt and germs, is not defined. It was apparently Hook's coinage.

Arthur M. Schlesinger, Jr., took issue with Hook's distinction between those educators with communist ideas and those with Communist Party affiliations, the first to be tolerated, in Hook's opinion, the second to be purged. Schlesinger wrote in the *Saturday Review of Literature* in May 1949, that the right of political opposition is the heart of free society. "Those who wished to curtail free speech must demonstrate that such speech created a clear and present danger.

> That did not mean a clear and present danger of changing the nation's mind by argument . . . It meant something quite specific: a clear and present danger of inciting overt acts in violation of law . . . Did Communist teachers create an emergency that warranted extreme measures to ferret them out and discharge them? I did not think so.[cdxliii]

Hook writes the discourse of the philosophy lecture hall with all the appearance of logic and reasonableness. However, a close reading of the article "Heresy, Yes—But Conspiracy, No." shows that in attempting a certain academic level of generality—referring to "a foreign government" rather than to the Soviet Union—the argument reveals a specific intent: banning members of the Communist Party from public life not on the basis of their actions, but simply because of their associations and beliefs.

The American Committee for Cultural Freedom was created in January, 1951, with Sidney Hook as its first chairman. The director of the CIA's cultural operations, Tom Braden, later said that "The American Committee for Cultural Freedom was just a [CIA] front in order to create the impression of some American participation in the European operation,"[cdxliv] that is, the Congress for Cultural Freedom. Reinforcing this relationship, sometime around then, Hook, according to intelligence official Lawrence de Neufville,[cdxlv] became a "contract consultant" for the CIA.[cdxlvi] (Hook, who seems to have been rather busy along these lines, was also an F.B.I. informant.[cdxlvii]) The rather small number of members of the American Committee for Cultural Freedom immediately fell into the sort of conflicts typical of political organizations in New York City at that time. On the one side were the hardliners—Lionel and Diana Trilling, James Burnham, Clement Greenberg, "the Upper West Side kibbutz." On the other side, "[r]epresenting the moderate element of the American Committee were Arthur Schlesinger, the Cold War theologian Reinhold Niebuhr [and Socialist Party leader] Norman Thomas . . .

> Swinging between the two factions were Irving Kristol . . . and Sidney Hook. Hook, in particular, had an interest in maintaining peace between the two groups: he was at this time promoting the Committee's interests with CIA director Walter Bedell Smith . . . For Hook, the American Committee was a bazooka in America's political arsenal, and he worked with his customary zeal to consolidate its position.[cdxlviii]

When the group later attempted to reach an agreed position on the activities of Senator McCarthy it again divided. Some—James T. Farrell, Dwight Macdonald and Mary McCarthy—wishing to take a strong stand against "the witch-hunt," while others—Sidney Hook, Daniel Bell, Clement Greenberg, and William Phillips—refusing to condemn the Senator and his allies. Mary McCarthy analyzed the situation in a letter to Hannah Arendt: "The Committee, acknowledging that there is really no Communist menace here, is principally interested in raising funds to fight Communism in Western Europe, or, rather, to fight neutralism, which is taking first place as a Menace." However, the American Committee—for such as the members of the "Upper West Side kibbutz"—was not *merely* a CIA front. According to Mary McCarthy "there was a feeling that . . . if Hook and Co. relaxed their efforts for a moment, Stalinism would reassert itself in [US] government and education . . .

> They live in terror of a revival of the situation that prevailed in the Thirties, when the fellow-travelers were powerful in teaching, publishing, the theatre, etc., when Stalinism was the gravy-train and these people were off it and became the object of social slights, small economic deprivations, gossip and backbiting . . . In their dreams, this period is always recurring; it is "realer" than today. Hence they scarcely notice the deteriorating actuality and minimize Senator McCarthy as not relevant.[cdxlix]

It was perhaps this context that made Sidney Hook sometimes as much a driver of CIA policy as its instrument.

"Stalinism," interestingly, increased in frequency in publications in American English from 1946 to 1960, in spite of Stalin's death at the mid-point of that period. It was apparently thought most useful as an ideological term retrospectively.

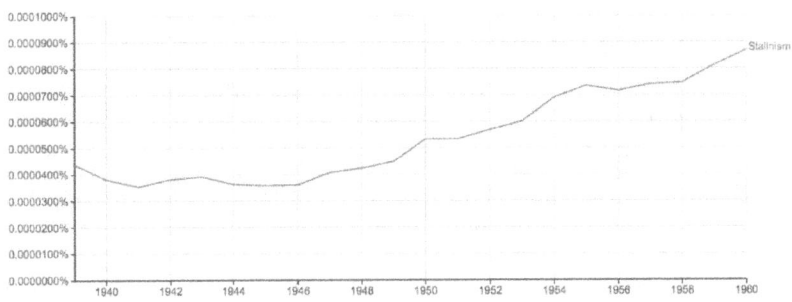

On March 29, 1952, the American Committee held a public debate, again at the Waldorf Astoria Hotel, entitled "In Defense of Free Culture." The group yet again split, with some, such as Mary McCarthy and Dwight Macdonald speaking against Senator McCarthy and "the witch-hunt" and others, led by veteran leftist Max Eastman, denying that there *was* a witch-hunt and defending

McCarthy. On April 4 Arthur Schlesinger, Jr., wrote to Frank Wisner at the CIA, describing the controversy. Wisner, in turn, wrote an internal Agency memorandum, recommending the suppression of the debate within the American Committee as inopportune, and, *inter alia,* noting that the American Committee had been "inspired if not put together by this Agency for the purpose of providing cover and backstopping for the European Effort."[cdl] In the eyes of the CIA, then, members of the American Committee, including Hook, were its agents of influence within the United States, despite the fact that it was, and is, illegal for the CIA to operate within the United States.

In 1953 Hook published a book under nearly the same title as his *New York Times Magazine* article. The book, *Heresy, Yes; Conspiracy, No,* was dedicated to "Norman Thomas, American Heretic and Democrat." Norman Thomas, much celebrated in the early- and mid-twentieth-century as the American face of democratic socialism, was a perennial candidate for President on the Socialist ticket, one of the founders of the Americans for Democratic Action, and on a first name basis with CIA Director Allen Dulles and, like Schlesinger, with other diners at the table of Joseph Alsop.[cdli]

In the "Introduction" to the book, Hook divides the groups he thought to be endangering the United States into "cultural vigilantes" and "ritualistic liberals," the former full of hatred for anyone not sharing every detail of their Anti-Communist and anti-progressive views, the latter overly concerned, in Hooks' opinion, with the state of political freedom as it was besieged by the cultural vigilantes. The epigraph to the book proper is a quietist statement from Hook's mentor, John Dewey, defining freedom not as action but as "freedom of mind." We begin, then, in a Platonic world, far from the Aristotelian—or Marxist—world of action, in the *vita contemplativa*—the refuge of philosophers in times of tyranny, who seek to understand the world—rather than the *vita activa,* highlighted by Hannah Arendt's analysis of the Western political tradition, of those seeking to change it.[cdlii] In the Platonist world of Dewey and Hook, liberalism and its enemies contend on the plane of ideas and "any action which restricts the freedom of ideas to develop or circulate is illiberal."[cdliii] Among those ideas that must be allowed freedom "to develop or circulate" are those that are heretical. "A heresy is a set of unpopular ideas or opinions on matters of grave concern to the community."[cdliv] Heretical—or any other—ideas can develop in the realm of thought, but to circulate they must be expressed in speech or in writing, in lecture halls or magazines. Hook, who chaired a university department of philosophy, who published in *The New York Times Magazine,* who attended conferences in New York and Paris in close association with government secret intelligence agencies, presented himself in this book as a heretic, whose ideas must be protected in a liberal society, which demonstrated its liberalism by, among other things, protecting the ideas of Professor Sidney Hook.

On the other hand, on the mundane level, Hook extended the argument from his earlier article, by explaining that "A conspiracy . . . is a secret or underground movement which seeks to attain its ends . . . by playing outside the rules of the game . . . In general, whoever subverts the rules of a democratic organization and seeks to win by chicanery what cannot be fairly won in the process of free discussion is a conspirator."[cdlv] This would, on the face of it, include as conspiracies, for example, lobbying, influence peddling, the trading of my vote on your motion for yours on mine. However, the legal definition of conspiracy is: "An agreement between two or more people to commit an illegal act, along with an intent to achieve the agreement's goal. Most U.S. jurisdictions also require an overt act toward furthering the agreement."[cdlvi] But that is not what Hook means. He is defining "conspiracy" not as an agreement to commit an illegal act, still less as the illegal act itself, but, again, simply as synonymous with the Communist Party, which he takes to be invariant across time and space: "The Communist *movement . . .* is something quite different from a mere heresy, for wherever it exists it operates along the lines laid down by Lenin as guides to Communists of all countries . . ."[cdlvii] Hook refers to the "Communist movement," but it is quite clear that he is referring to the Communist Party itself. This use of "conspiracy" as a synonym for the Communist Party was common to Hook, Senator McCarthy and such minor characters as Roy Cohn and Richard Arens, the lawyers for the investigatory committees of Congress, as well as the Catholic Church. Hook believed, with the

Popes, and without the need for additional proof, that Communists are conspirators by definition. It is not that Communists may here or there conspire with this or that illegal object; it is that they are everywhere and always conspirators. Hook is therefore opposed to those who object that conspiracy is an action, not a state of being: Those "ritualistic liberals [who] would wait until the sabotage has been carried out before proceeding against Communists." He objects to this view in part as giving aid and comfort to "reactionaries," "who now tend to regard the ritualistic liberals as the dupes or accomplices of the Communists," which in turn confirms "the illusions of the ritualistic liberals that there really is no problem of Communist conspiracy,"[cdlviii] that the charge is simply a stick with which to beat them.[39]

Hook then turns to some of the implications of his reasoning. If it is futile to outlaw the Communist Party, as, according to Hook, it would just change its name and would in any case simply become more insidious, the possible harm done by the Communist Party can be addressed on the level of individual Communists, beginning with government employees: "Because we cannot say '*with exactness*' who is likely to commit acts of espionage and sabotage in all cases, it does not follow that we cannot say with great probability who is likely to commit acts of such a character in some cases." Hook again reaches for the disease metaphor: "Not everybody exposed to a deadly plague will come down with it or transmit it but there is a sufficient likelihood to justify isolating him.

> There are some people, it is true, who come down with the plague who have never been suspected of being exposed to it. Were anyone to argue that therefore we should not isolate those who unquestionably have been exposed to it, he would convict himself of absurdity . . .

The disease and plague metaphors for communism, virtually unknown in British English, rose and fell in frequency in American English with the American Anti-Communist witch-hunt.

---

[39] By the time of the publication of *Heresy Yes; Conspiracy No* the leaders of the Communist Party of the United States (as well as the Hollywood Ten) had been jailed and the Party itself driven underground.

Hook also uses the arson metaphor for Communism: "To punish acts of disloyalty *after they have been committed,* instead of trying to prevent disloyalty, among those who have clearly expressed their intent by membership in the Communist Party, is like saying that instead of trying to prevent a man with the *intent* of committing arson from carrying out his plans, we wait until he has burned the house down and then punish him."[cdlix] As a matter of fact, to take Hook literally, that is exactly what the law of arson requires: "The necessary elements needed to prove arson are: evidence of a burning; and a criminal act which causes the fire."[cdlx] Arson, like most crimes, is a matter of an activity. Intention, without an overt act, is not a crime. And, of course, there is Hook's assumption that simply to join the Communist Party was to show disloyalty, as in the trick-mirror cartoon described above.

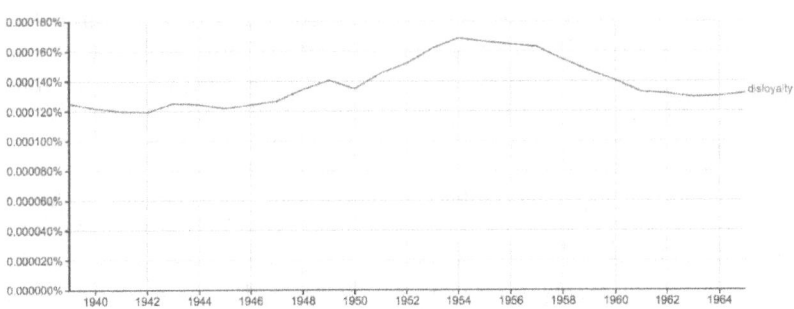

Hook's argument, then, is that members of the Communist Party should be isolated (what that means is not clear) as they have been in the company of those who can be assumed to intend to commit espionage and that disloyalty (undefined) should be punished as a crime as an intention, even in the absence of an overt act. In other words, Hook seems to be saying that it is a crime to be in the company of people who can be assumed to intend to commit a crime. This is not reasoning that would have passed muster in a Philosophy 101 class at Hook's university. But Hook surely knew that he was dealing not in philosophy or logic but in rhetoric, the art of persuasion, in this case using hyperbole and the association fallacy in order to drive home his point that the government should not have to, should not, as a matter of fact, ever, employ members of the Communist Party or even those who may be influenced by communist ideas: "The criteria for establishing 'unreliability' [in government employment] must obviously be less stringent than those which lead us to deprive an individual of his life or freedom."[cdlxi] Suspicion would suffice.

Professor Hook, naturally enough, was particularly concerned with Communists in schools and colleges. He constructs an ideal-type of the Communist teacher in the United States as identical to that thought by him to then exist in the USSR. "It is not his beliefs . . . which disqualify the Communist party teacher, but

> his declaration of intention, as evidenced by official statements, to practice educational fraud . . . to indoctrinate for the Communist Party in classrooms, enroll students in Communist Youth organizations, rewrite textbooks from the Communist point of view, build cells on campuses, capture departments, and inculcate the Communist Party line that in case of war students should turn their arms against their own government.[cdlxii]

The phrase "educational fraud" is another Hookian rhetorical device, implying that Communists cannot, or will not, actually educate their students, but wish only to indoctrinate them. Hook argues that for teachers "membership in the Communist Party is comparable to the action of a physician who has banded himself together with others for the express violation of his Hippocratic oath."[cdlxiii] As to this and the rest of Hook's list of the sins that *must* be committed by an American Communist teacher, none of these in fact were found to have occurred in the twenty years or more of investigations of schools and colleges beginning with those of the New York State Rapp-Coudert Committee in the 1930s, except that of forming "cells" on campuses. According to Stephen Whitfield: "Communists were supposed to be under orders to indoctrinate in the classroom, which is why philosopher Sidney Hook in particular insisted that they show cause why they should *not* be fired. Not a single case of such indoctrination came to light."[cdlxiv] In other words, while teachers in the Soviet Union may have acted in the fashion described by Hook, this was not the practice of Communist teachers in the United States. Nevertheless, Whitefield found that in New York "well over a hundred faculty members were dismissed for political reasons."[cdlxv]

The term "Indoctrination" occurred with increasing frequency in American English in the Cold War years, then with less, as the Anti-Communist fervor lessened.

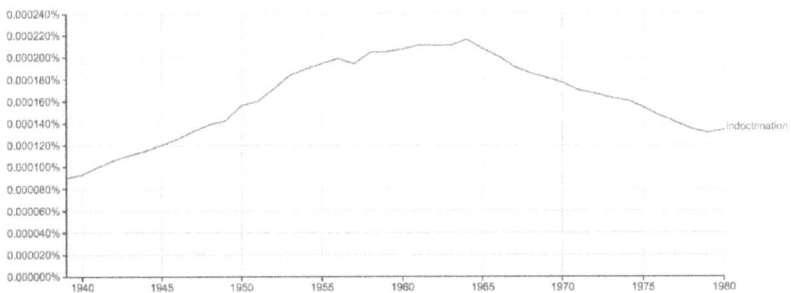

This is even clearer for the phrase "Communist indoctrination":

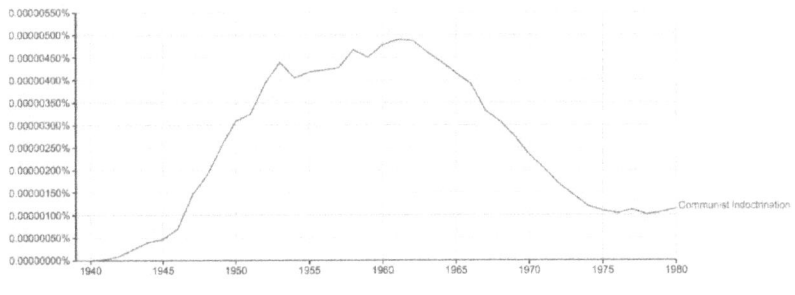

In his dissent in the 1952 Supreme Court case of *Adler v. Board of Education of the City of New York,* Justice Douglas (with Justice Black concurring), set out the argument against Hook's position: "The present law [the "Feinberg" law] proceeds on a principle repugnant to our society—guilt by association.

> A teacher is disqualified because of her membership in an organization found to be "subversive." The finding as to the "subversive" character of the organization is made in a proceeding to which the teacher is not a party and in which it is not clear that she may even be heard. To be sure, she may have a hearing when charges of disloyalty are leveled against her. But, in that hearing, the finding as to the "subversive" character of the organization apparently may not be reopened in order to allow her to show the truth of the matter. The irrebuttable charge that the organization is "subversive" therefore hangs as an ominous cloud over her own hearing. The mere fact of membership in the organization raises a *prima facie* case of her own guilt. She may, it is said, show her innocence. But innocence in this case turns on knowledge, and when the witch hunt is on, one who must rely on ignorance leans on a feeble reed.

The term "guilt by association" came into use circa 1947 with the Attorney General's list and Truman's loyalty boards. Attorney General Tom Clark warned that "It is entirely possible that many persons belonging to such organizations may be loyal to the United States. Guilt by association has never been one of the principles of our American jurisprudence. We must be satisfied that reasonable grounds exist for concluding that an individual is disloyal."[cdlxvi] The term "guilt by association" was used with increasing frequency during the witch-hunt period, rising and falling with the rhythm of Smith Act prosecutions and governmental hearings:

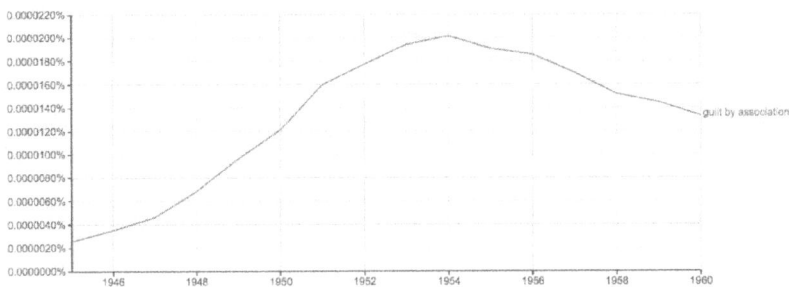

Both "witch-hunt" and "guilt by association" were anti-Anti-Communist terms. No member of HUAC would have referred to its hearings as a witch-hunt. Hook criticized the use of "guilt by association" to criticize anti-Anti-Communists,[cdlxvii] taking strong exception to Justice Douglas's dissent in the Adler case: "At the time Justice Douglas wrote his dissent, virtual war between one section of the Communist International and the United States as part of the U.N. was raging in Korea . . .

> To deny under these circumstances that an organization of some tens of thousands of conspirators [sic], with a reliable periphery of some hundreds of thousands, constitutes a clear and present danger to the security of the nation is to manifest a stubborn will to believe that Providence or luck will protect those who are too blind to protect themselves.[cdlxviii]

Following his usual practice of doubling a term in common use to produce another, similar term, more suitable for his purpose, Hook distinguished between "moral guilt" and "criminal guilt." Thus membership in the Communist Party carries with it "moral guilt," but not necessarily "criminal guilt."[cdlxix]

It is unclear exactly what Hook meant by "moral guilt." In common parlance it would point to a religious judgment or a secular emotion of "feeling guilty," which can arise from anything from forgetting to take out the recycling on a Thursday to an undetected murder, but which is, in any case, subjective. Some people will feel guilty about some action (or nothing at all) while others will not feel guilty about, say, the profitable use of the bankruptcy laws. Perhaps closer to Hook's intention is a judgment made by one person or group of another, outside a legal context. Many people believed that then Secretary of the Treasury Paulson was morally guilty of the 2007 financial crisis because of his actions in the Lehman Brothers bankruptcy, but those judgments had no legal standing. Although "criminal guilt," that is, legal guilt, is a matter for the courts and their judgment, moral guilt is not. A thief can be punished for the fact of the crime, but there is no juridical punishment for the violation of morality that it involves. "Moral guilt," is, nonetheless, in Hook's view, grounds for government action. This is significant, not only for Hook's reasoning, but for that of the entire Anti-Communist movement. Actions, facts, their detection and punishment, were insufficient for their purpose. The Anti-Communists of the period sought to identify and purge those who in their view were morally guilty: members of the Communist Party, fellow travelers, "extreme" liberals, former officials of the New Deal, civil rights attorneys. They did this by collapsing Hook's distinction, by treating moral guilt as legal, criminal, guilt.[40]

In *Heresy, Yes; Conspiracy, No* Hook wishes to argue for the classical civil liberties for everyone except Communists, a classification he usually is willing to restrict to actual members of the Communist Party, except in matters involving governmental employment and teaching, where he extents the boundary to include those ("some hundreds of thousands") influenced by the Party. This involves him in some quandaries having to do with disregarding the legal distinction between intentions and actions. He would remove Communist Party members and those close to them from government and teaching because of their assumed intentions, the former for intending espionage, the latter for intending indoctrination, while he would not have artists, writers and private individuals harassed for their beliefs or assumed intentions in the absence of overt acts.[cdlxx] It is difficult to understand how prosecution for assumed intentions can be squared with the Constitution, and, if so, why elementary school teaching, for example, might be a proscribed profession for Communists and their sympathizers, but screen writing or the

---

[40] This may have been influenced by contemporary discussions of the moral guilt of Germans for the crimes of the Nazi regime.

creation of public art, would not be similarly proscribed.

This is where Hook, unusually, comes down on the side of those he refers to as the "ritualistic" liberals. In the arts (including movies), for example, "Standards of professional conduct should be drawn up by professional associations, and violations punished on professional, not political grounds."[cdlxxi] But Hook has particular logical difficulties with the teaching professions. On the one hand, he argues that Communist teachers should be purged as they are committed to replicating the Soviet system in, say, Brooklyn.[41] Hook calls them "enemies of freedom." And he says that academic fellow travelers play the role of ideological "typhus [sic] Marys," once more deploying the (slightly misstated) disease metaphor.[cdlxxii] On the other hand, "Those who come knocking at the school door with ultimatistic demands or taboos concerning what teachers *should* teach and *how* they must teach, and with ready-made formulas about the meaning of democracy and its alternatives, must be asked to show their professional qualifications as educators before they are taken seriously."[cdlxxiii] As a disciple of John Dewey, Hook was particularly sensitive about criticism of progressive education. "There seems some reason to believe that those who attack progressive education, under the protective coloration of patriotism, are not opposed to indoctrination. What some of the critics really desire is indoctrination for the economic *status quo* and a low tax rate."[cdlxxiv] Hook was a fervent Anti-Communist, but not a fervent adherent of "free enterprise," noting, with Schlesinger, that "neither free enterprise, the New Deal nor any other economic system is part of the American Constitution."[cdlxxv] (Almost unknown before the Second World War, the frequency of the use of the Cold War branding term "free enterprise" for capitalism peaked in 1947 in both American and British English, but was much higher in the former. This chart shows the frequency of use of the term in all English

---

[41] Hook cites Dr. Bella Dodd, who "testified that at one time a thousand members of the New York City teaching staff were members of the Communist Party—most of them in the high schools and colleges." Hook, Sidney. Heresy, Yes, Conspiracy, No., p. 209, citing New York Times, September 9, 1952.

The Language of Anti-Communism

language publications from 1930 to 1960.)

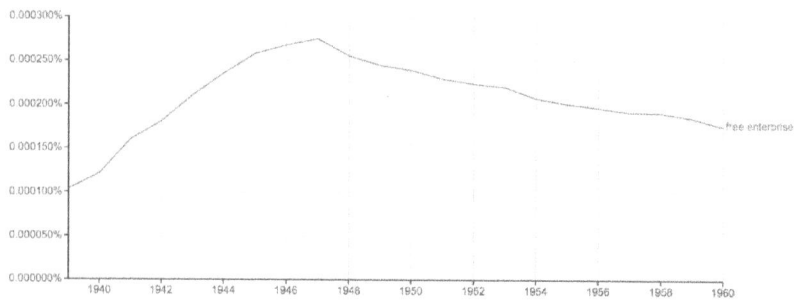

Hook also distinguished his brand of non-Communist left Anti-Communism from the synthetic ideology of "Americanism" promoted by the American Legion, the Knights of Columbus and allied groups: "loyalty to America and to democracy does not mean loyalty to American*ism*" [cdlxxvi] He referred to these who think otherwise as "cultural vigilantes": "Almost every day some incident reveals the growing pattern of cultural vigilantism which invokes the slogans of Americanism while betraying its best traditions. If it remains unchecked, it is not hard to predict the outcome—the rule of the loud shouters, the intimidation and silencing of the thoughtful."[cdlxxvii] Hook does not wish to be associated with "the loud shouters," especially those in Congress: "It is not the [Senator] McCarthys and McCarrans and their allies who can lead the struggle for a free culture against its enemies. For they have a distrust of freedom of thought and therefore of thought itself."[cdlxxviii]

And yet, even as the witch-hunts reached their peak, Hook denied the existence of repression in cultural and educational matters in the United States except for isolated incidents. He was especially disturbed by statements of equivalence, or near equivalence, of the lack of civil liberties in the US and USSR.[cdlxxix] There can be no equivalence, for Hook, because of the unique menace of Communism (again with the disease metaphor): "If communism, as I believe, is the greatest menace to human freedom in the world today, I believe it can be shown in the same way we show that certain growths are cancerous and not benign."[cdlxxx]

212

Ellen Schrecker notes the prevalence of the disease terms at the time: "Disease metaphors were common. Communism was like a plague, the Attorney General noted in 1950; each party member 'carries in himself the germ of death for our society.' For the Minnesota liberal Hubert Humphrey, the CP was 'a political cancer in our society.' For Adlai Stevenson . . . it was worse 'than cancer, tuberculosis, and heart disease combined.'"[cdlxxxi]

Hook believes, then, that his efforts are part of "the war for cultural freedom,"[cdlxxxii] using the CIA-branded term. Which brings him to a defense of the "Smith Act," the Alien Registration Act of 1940, that made it a crime to advocate the overthrow of the United States government. The heart, as it were, of the Smith Act criminalized anyone who: "with *intent* to cause the overthrow or destruction of any such government,

> prints, publishes, edits, issues, circulates, sells, distributes, or publicly displays any written or printed matter advocating, advising, or teaching the duty, necessity, desirability, or propriety of overthrowing or destroying any government in the United States by force or violence, or attempts to do so; or... organizes or helps or attempts to organize any society, group, or assembly of persons who teach, advocate, or encourage the overthrow or destruction of any such government by force or violence; or becomes or is a member of, or affiliates with, any such society, group, or assembly of persons, knowing the purposes thereof. (Emphasis added.)

At first actions under the Smith Act were even-handedly aimed at the

Communist head of the West Coast Longshore and Warehouse Union, Harry Bridges; members of the (Trotskyite) Socialist Workers Party; fascists and Nazi sympathizers, but by the end of the 1940s, the Act was primarily an instrument for the suppression of the Communist Party of the United States, beginning with the trial of the party's leaders, *Dennis v. United States* in 1949.

In *Heresy, Yes; Conspiracy, No,* Hook commented that "The Smith Act is imperfectly phrased. Were it to be interpreted literally it could easily lend itself to abuse," which was, as it turned out, something of an understatement. Hook argued that the "main, if not avowed purposes of the Act—[was] to prevent the organization of the Communist conspiracy from growing to a point where it could become dangerous [and] to make known to the people of the United States the nature of the Communist movement . . ."[cdlxxxiii] The Act, according to Hook, was best seen and used as an educational, not punitive, measure. On the other hand, Hook believed that in regard to the Smith Act, "there is a legal warrant to accept as evidence of conspiracy to do something unlawful, speech, writing and organizational activity"[cdlxxxiv] and the defendants "in the case of Dennis *et al.* . . . are an integral part of a highly organized international conspiracy."[cdlxxxv] A conspiracy so sinister that it justifies the invocation of the Smith Act, which as it "has now been interpreted by the courts . . . applies only to cases in which 'clear and present' danger exists that an attempt at revolutionary overthrow will be made."[cdlxxxvi] There was, as a matter of fact, no evidence at all that the SWP or the CPUSA were planning a "revolutionary overthrow" of the American government.

Sidney Hook was a senior public intellectual during the Cold War years. Like others discussed here, he had a background in political activity on behalf of socialism and as such was a fervent Anti-Communist. Hook's use of the phrase "typhus [meaning "typhoid"] Marys" paralleled Schlesinger's use of that key term of Cold War language. Hook seemed to be particularly fond of such disease metaphors, referring to the need for "ethical hygiene" in response to the "plague" of Communism and the latter as a "cancerous growth." His central idea about Communism, per se, as well as its exemplification in the

Communist Party of the United States (and the COMINTERN) was that it was a "conspiracy" against "the free market of ideas," just as for the popes Communism was a conspiracy against religion. The deployment of this vocabulary was at once intended to be rhetorically effective and a sign to other Anti-Communists that in spite of his Marxism, Hook was one of them. For the public, the readers, say, of *The New York Times,* he spoke and wrote with the prestige of his academic appointment in the philosophy department of New York University. However, for the cognoscenti, there was another Sidney Hook, the contract consultant of the Central Intelligence Agency. He helped the Agency apply the lessons of Willi Münzenberg's Communist Front organizations of the 1930s to create front organizations, publications, conferences and reputations as weapons in the ideological Cold War. The language of Hook the philosopher and public intellectual, replete with metaphors of disease and assertions of conspiracy, revealed Hook's other role to those who could interpret it, that of a propagandist and organizer for Frank Wisner's "Might Wurlitzer," a promoter of that Central Intelligence Agency project, the Non-Communist Left.

Notes

[cdxxxix] Victor Navasky emphasizes the importance of this article: "Underlying all was the doctrine of conspiracy, whose most articulate proponent was the ex-Marxist philosopher Sidney Hook. His 1950 essay 'Heresy, Yes—But Conspiracy, No' was expanded into a book that became the bible for liberals unwilling to fight for the rights of Communists. Hook's argument: Communists were not heretics whose unpopular ideas deserved First Amendment protection, but conspirators who were out to subvert not merely the government but also the very exchange of ideas the First Amendment was designed to protect. Our moral obligation 'is the toleration of dissent, no matter how heretical, not the toleration of conspiracy, no matter what its disguise.' . . . the distinction between the Stalinist espionage apparatus and the legal activities of the Party was eliminated." Navasky, Victor S. Naming Names. New York: Hill and Wang, 2003 (Viking, 1991), p. 43.

[cdxl] However, Holmes says nothing about liberalism in his dissent in the *Abrams* case in which the concept appears. Abrams v. United States, 250 U.S. 616, 630(1919)(Holmes, J., dissenting).

[cdxli] Hook, Sidney. Heresy, Yes—But Conspiracy, No. July 9, 1950, New York Times Magazine. p. 264.

[cdxlii] Hook, Sidney. Heresy, Yes, Conspiracy, No. New York: John Day Company, 1953, p. 220. But Catholic educators in non-catholic settings are not under Church discipline.

[cdxliii] Schlesinger, Arthur M., Jr. A Life in the 20th Century: Innocent Beginnings, 1917-1950. New York: Houghton Mifflin, 2000, pp. 491-2.

[cdxliv] Saunders, Frances Stonor. Who Paid the Piper? The CIA and the Cultural Cold War. London: Granta Books, 1999, p. 203.

[cdxlv] Saunders, p. 157. According to his obituary in the Hartford Courant, July 14, 1998: "Lawrence E. de Neufville had served as a foreign correspondent, a news-magazine editor, a special-forces operative for the World War II office of Strategic Services and as liaison for the Central Intelligence Agency with the U.S. High Commissioner in Germany, and at the European political headquarters of the Marshall Plan in Paris."

[cdxlvi] The CIA files show correspondence between Hook and General Walter B. Smith, Director of the Central Intelligence Agency, in September, 1951. www.cia.gov/library/readingroom/search/site/%22Sidney%20Hook%22

[cdxlvii] "Most of the living authors banned under State Department directives were also the subjects of voluminous . . . files at J. Edgar Hoover's F.B.I.. The activities and movements of Robert Sherwood, Archibald MacLeish,

Malcolm Cowley (in whose file Sidney Hook was named as the F.B.I.'s informant) . . . were monitored." Saunders, p. 194.

cdxlviii Saunders, pp. 158-9.

cdxlix Mary McCarthy to Hannah Arendt, 14 March 1952, in Brightman, Carol (ed.) Between Friends: The Correspondence of Hannah Arendt and Mary McCarthy 1949-1975. San Diego: Harcourt Brace & Company, 1995, p. 5.

cdl "Memorandum of April 7, 1952, From Wisner in Warner, Michael (ed.) The CIA Under Harry Truman. CIA History Staff; Center for the Study of Intelligence, 1994, p. 455

cdli "Norman Thomas, the foremost socialist libertarian in America." Hook, Sidney. Heresy, Yes, Conspiracy, No. New York: John Day Company, 1953, p. 217.
See, inter alia, Dulles to Thomas, 18 October 1960:
https://www.cia.gov/library/readingroom/docs/CIA-RDP80B01676R003700080010-5.pdf

cdlii See, Arendt, Hannah. The Human Condition, 1958.

cdliii Hook, Heresy, Yes, Conspiracy, No. p. 20, citing Holmes.

cdliv Hook, Heresy, Yes, Conspiracy, No., p. 21.

cdlv Hook, Heresy, Yes, Conspiracy, No., p. 22.

cdlvi See *Whitfield v. United States*, 453 U.S. 209 (2005). The illegal act is the conspiracy's "target offense." Legal Information Institute, Cornell Law School.

cdlvii Hook, Heresy, Yes, Conspiracy, No., p. 22.

cdlviii Hook, Heresy, Yes, Conspiracy, No., p. 27.

cdlix Hook, Heresy, Yes, Conspiracy, No., pp. 77-8.

cdlx 18 USCS § 3559

cdlxi Hook, Heresy, Yes, Conspiracy, No., p. 33.

cdlxii Hook, Heresy, Yes, Conspiracy, No., pp. 34-5.

cdlxiii Hook, Heresy, Yes, Conspiracy, No., p. 180

cdlxiv Whitfield, Stephen J. The Culture of the Cold War. Baltimore and London: The Johns Hopkins Press (2nd Edition), 1991, 1996, p. 24.

cdlxv Whitfield, p. 24.

cdlxvi Attorney General Tom Clark to Seth W. Richardson, chairman, Loyalty Review Board, Civil Service Commission, 24 November 1947.

cdlxvii Hook, Heresy, Yes, Conspiracy, No., pp. 84ff.

cdlxviii Hook, Heresy, Yes, Conspiracy, No., p. 112.

cdlxix Hook, Heresy, Yes, Conspiracy, No., p. 88.

cdlxx Hook, Heresy, Yes, Conspiracy, No., p. 72.

[cdlxxi] Hook, Heresy, Yes, Conspiracy, No., p. 45.

[cdlxxii] Hook, Heresy, Yes, Conspiracy, No., p. 242

[cdlxxiii] Hook, Heresy, Yes, Conspiracy, No., p. 128.

[cdlxxiv] Hook, Heresy, Yes, Conspiracy, No., p. 40.

[cdlxxv] Hook, Heresy, Yes, Conspiracy, No., p. 42.

[cdlxxvi] Hook, Heresy, Yes, Conspiracy, No., p. 132.

[cdlxxvii] Hook, Heresy, Yes, Conspiracy, No., p. 47.

[cdlxxviii] Hook, Heresy, Yes, Conspiracy, No., p. 260.

[cdlxxix] Hook, Heresy, Yes, Conspiracy, No., pp. 58ff.

[cdlxxx] Hook, Heresy, Yes, Conspiracy, No., p. 127.

[cdlxxxi] Schrecker, Ellen. Many Are the Crimes: McCarthyism in America. Princeton University Press, 1998, p. 144.

[cdlxxxii] Hook, Heresy, Yes, Conspiracy, No., p. 81.

[cdlxxxiii] Hook, Heresy, Yes, Conspiracy, No., p. 116.

[cdlxxxiv] Hook, Heresy, Yes, Conspiracy, No., p. 99.

[cdlxxxv] Hook, Heresy, Yes, Conspiracy, No., p. 103.

[cdlxxxvi] Hook, Heresy, Yes, Conspiracy, No., p. 104.

A Cold War Cultural Journal: *Encounter*

"I've always had a theory . . . that part of the literary war of the mid 40's, '50's and '60's . . . was somewhat weighted and influenced by . . . a world network of magazines subsidized by the CIA and edited by them to their own interest promoting somewhat liberal but conservative non-revolutionary, non-psychologically visionary, anti-Whitmanic, pro-conservative <u>Eliotic</u> manners . . . I wrote to Spender saying, 'Is or is not *Encounter* magazine funded by the CIA?' And Spender wrote back saying, 'No'. And then it turns out it was.—*Allen Ginsberg*[cdlxxxvii]

The members of Attlee's Labour Government, which unexpectedly came to power in 1945, spanned the ideological spectrum from the Foreign Secretary, Ernest Bevin, who, over his long and dominant career in the trades union movement had acquired Anti-Communist views as strong as those of any Tory, to Stafford Cripps, who had from time to time in the 1930s been expelled from the Labour Party for favoring a coalition between it and the Communist Party of Great Britain. In foreign policy matters, Bevin was an Imperialist, seeking to maintain or even expand the Empire, which reached its largest extent early in his term as Foreign Secretary, while Attlee wished to dismantle it as soon as possible. Bevin was in favor of close ties with the United States, while Attlee and Cripps at first wished to maintain the wartime Anglo-Soviet alliance. Most of the senior Labour Party ministers came into office believing that the Socialist program that they were instituting at home might be leveraged to give Britain a position at the head of a grouping of social democratic states. But the disastrously sudden termination of Lend-Lease by President Truman, with an unexpected demand for repayment, the badly negotiated "British loan" from the United States, eliminating the Sterling Zone and Imperial Preference, followed by the realization of the enormous debt to newly independent India, made it clear that there was no choice beside a dependent relationship with the United States in an anti-Soviet alliance. Instead of leading an international Socialist movement, the nearly bankrupted Attlee Government had to accept social democracy in one country and a client relationship with an increasingly aggressive United States.

The military tasks involved with creating a unified "free world" to confront the post-war Soviet Union were fairly straightforward. American military bases could be strung around the borders of the Soviet Union; British possessions could be utilized as bases, "listening posts," places from which secret operations could be launched. But in the immediate post-war period, the Soviet threat, as seen from Washington, was political, not military, and the linchpin of the struggle was France. On February 19, 1947, the American Ambassador in France wrote to the U.S. Secretary of State: "The long hand of the Kremlin is increasingly exercising power, or at least influence, in all European countries, largely through its principal lever, the French Communist Party and its fortress the CGT.[42]

> All these organizations [such as the World Federation of Trade Unions, Women's International Democratic Federation and the World Youth Federation] function primarily as public pressure machines designed to promote Soviet aims and ambitions, while attacking the "imperialism" of the Anglo-Saxon "capitalist" powers . . . If the Communists [win the next election], Soviet penetration of Western Europe, Africa, the Mediterranean and Middle East would be greatly facilitated, and our position in our zone of occupation of Germany rendered precarious, if not untenable . . . It would appear vital to our security to do everything we can to prevent France from falling under Communist domination.[cdlxxxviii]

CIA money could be used by such as the international American Federation of Labor organizer (and C.I.A. funding conduit[43]) Irving

---

[42] *Confédération générale du travail*, the then-Communist dominated French trade union federation.

Brown to create non-Communist labor unions and political parties in France and elsewhere, but what could be done about French culture, still hegemonic among the ruins of Europe, and increasingly hostile to the United States? "'Who was the real antagonist?' [Carol Brightman] asks . . . What they were really obsessed with was Sartre and de Beauvoir. *That* was "the other side"'."[cdlxxxix] Frances Stonor Saunders thought that "Sartre was the enemy not just because of his position[s] on Communism, but because he preached a doctrine (or anti-doctrine) of individualism which rubbed against the federalist 'family of man' society which America . . . was promoting."[cdxc] It was more complicated than that. Sartre and de Beauvoir were among the dominant intellectuals of the mid-twentieth century and they were neither American nor very impressed by the United States. The sophisticated men who were among the first generation of CIA officers—Cord Meyer, Tom Braden, James Angleton—had a unified theory of Anti-Communism. They realized the important role that cultural figures had in Europe, that it was insufficient to simply make sure that the French or Italian Communist parties did not win elections, insufficient to present the United States as the promised future of refrigerators and elaborate plumbing.

The CIA's answer was to summon into existence through a system of front organizations, publications, conferences, publishing houses and the like, an Anti-Communist culture of favored artists, composers, philosophers, novelists, dramatists and poets: the Abstract Expressionists matched against Picasso and Matisse;[44] Stravinsky matched against Shostakovich; Raymond Aron promoted as superior to Sartre, and so forth. The primary instrument for this was a CIA front, the Congress for Cultural Freedom (CFF), based in

---

[43] A note in Director of Central Intelligence Walter Bedell Smith's log states that Irving "Brown, European representative of the AofL, is the cut-out through which CIA advances funds for the support of various Western European labor unions." CIA Freedom of Information Act Electronic Reading Room, /specialCollection/DCI/Smith\ FOIA/1951-July to September/1951-09-01.pdf

[44] When, arguably, the greatest painter then in the United States was Max Beckmann.

enemy territory—Paris. The Congress for Cultural Freedom's "mission was to nudge the intelligentsia of western Europe away from its lingering fascination with Marxism and Communism towards a view more accommodating of 'the American way'."[cdxci] At the core of CCF operations were a series of grand conferences and a network of magazines. The French magazine was *Preuves,* edited by François Bondy. According to his obituary in *The Times,* "For nearly 20 years François Bondy edited the prestigious literary journal *Epreuves* [sic], one of the decisive weapons of the west in the cultural cold war with the communist East."

> He took the chair there in 1951, at the height of the Cold War. At stake in Europe at that moment was the allegiance of the influential French intelligentsia, which was felt to be wavering dangerously. The loyalty, especially of Jean-Paul Sartre, whose influence was worth many a battalion, was in serious doubt.

The British CCF magazine was *Encounter,* originally co-edited by Irving Kristol and Stephen Spender, the first paid from CIA funds, the second from British (Foreign Office, International Research Department) funds.

From the CIA's point of view, while *Preuves* dealt with Sartre and his battalions, the purpose of *Encounter* was to weaken the influence of British leftist intellectuals and politicians without appearing to be an instrument of American (and right-wing British) policy. One might say that the place of *Encounter* in mid-twentieth century British literary circles was analogous to that of the burlesque star Gypsy Rose Lee in similar groups in New York. Intellectuals were comfortable in the company of both and the way in which they were each financed was carefully ignored. Just as everyone knew that Ms. Lee made her living by removing her clothes in public—an activity traditionally understood as close to prostitution—so everyone who wanted to know knew that *Encounter* was funded by the gentlemen of the Central Intelligence Agency and their British associates—a dependency understood as that of a screen for the activities of the second oldest profession. Just as Ms. Lee was admired for her wide reading and other cultural interests, so many of

The Language of Anti-Communism

Encounter's readers said that they looked to it for its cultural articles and, like readers of *Playboy,* to vary the comparison, claimed to ignore the photographs, just skipping over, in this case, the more obviously propagandistic pieces. But the point of interest of Ms. Lee was that she was a stripper, as the raison d'être of *Encounter* was its role as a propaganda vehicle for the CIA's Cold War in Europe. Ms. Lee and *Encounter* were also similar in that the intellectual credentials of each were exaggerated. Gypsy Rose Lee was very intelligent *for a stripper. Encounter* was a very good magazine *for a propaganda organ.* With *Encounter* (but not with Ms. Lee), there was a "blowback" effect: propaganda intended for Europe filtering back into the United States, nourishing the intellectual bona fides of the CIA's Non-Communist Left, "promoting somewhat liberal but conservative non-revolutionary, non-psychologically visionary, anti-Whitmanic, pro-conservative <u>Eliotic</u> manners" in literature and literary studies.

Some of the famous Anti-Communist literary works of the immediate postwar period were commissioned, encouraged or distributed by British and American governmental agencies. A section of the British Foreign Office, the Information Research Department (IRD) distributed 50,000 copies of *Darkness at Noon* in 1948.[cdxcii] *"The God that Failed,"* to name another, "was as much a product of intelligence as it was a work of the intelligentsia . . . [It] was distributed by US government agencies all over Europe . . . The Information Research Department also pushed the book."[cdxciii] CIA also helped fund the New York-based left-wing magazines *The New Leader* and the *Partisan Review* in the early 1950s. These were Anti-Communist magazines run by ex-Communists.[cdxciv] "The purpose of supporting leftist groups was not to destroy or even dominate, but rather to maintain a discreet proximity to and monitor the thinking of such groups; to provide them with a mouthpiece so they could blow off steam; and, *in extremis,* to exercise a final veto on their publicity and possibly their actions, if they ever got too 'radical'."[cdxcv]

During World War II officials of the nascent American secret intelligence service had sat at the feet of the veterans of the various British services, especially those in MI-6 specializing in foreign intelligence operations, counterintelligence and propaganda. The last of these, in the immediate postwar period, was the responsibility of the British Foreign Office's Information Research Department, which had its origins in Second World War political warfare efforts involving both "White" (more or less truthful) and "Black" (not truthful) propaganda. After the war, the latter was then promoted for use against the Soviet Union by Christopher Mayhew, a Foreign Office official "close to [Prime Minister] Attlee, sharing his Haileybury [public school] background and love of cricket."[cdxcvi] Mayhew believed that "one of the tasks of the IRD was to persuade its American counterparts that, when it came to propaganda, it was a bad idea to be too aggressive. An IRD 'draft brief' of 1953 defines the British position. 'We regard the Stalinist communists alone as the enemy, and all other shades of political opinion and peoples, other than fascism or Nazism, as potential allies.

In policy therefore our aim is to drive a wedge between communist parties and those most likely to support them, i.e. leftwing socialists, pacifists and certain intellectuals in Europe, and nationalists in Asia, the Middle East and Africa. We make no emotional appeals to those already converted, and we regard propaganda issued by right-wing elements as dangerous to us and helpful to the enemy.[cdxcvii]

According to Richard Aldrich, "The importance of IRD is difficult to overestimate. Before 1950, when defence programmes were being cut and the secret services were pleased to hold their programmes steady, it was expanding rapidly. By the early 1950s, IRD, working closely with SIS [the Secret Intelligence Service, MI-6] constituted the largest department of the Foreign Office."[cdxcviii] Frances Stonor Saunders adds that the purpose of the Information Research Department "'was to produce and distribute and circulate unattributable propaganda . . .' Working on the trickle-down theory, IRD compiled 'factual' reports on all manner of subjects for distribution among members of the British intelligentsia, who were then expected to recycle these facts in their own work." In addition to this effort at disguise, the IRD "was not allowed to 'attack or appear to be attacking any member of the Commonwealth or the United States.'"[cdxcix] Matthew Spender found that "In the 1950s IRD worked closely with . . . the International Organisations Department of the CIA against remarkable range of targets . . .

> IRD in particular undertook some extraordinary interventions on the British domestic scene in areas such as student affairs and trade union politics, and the CIA eventually followed suit.[d]

Among those interventions, it is said, were some on behalf of the Gaitskell (right-wing) branch of the Labour Party against the Bevan (left-wing) faction. "Both Irving Kristol and Mel Lasky [editors of *Encounter*] later boasted that they'd helped to push the British Labour Party towards the centre . . . *Encounter* was the perfect magazine for Tony Crosland's [pro-Gaitskell] articles."[di] Lasky, according to Hugh Wilford, was a "witting" CIA agent.[dii]

Some people think it important to differentiate between secret intelligence services and other governmental organizations, between spies, agents, sources and the like and diplomats, civil servants, the great and the good with clean hands. This is not always useful. The Raj itself was famously a secret agency state (cf. Kipling's Kim), a vast Indian Empire ruled by a ridiculously small number of foreigners by means of elaborate networks of informers, the occasional hanging or massacre, vast filing systems, honors, banquets and elaborate uniforms ("ornamentalisim"). Things were not much different at the center of the British Empire, where small numbers of men,[45] many related, nearly all of whom who had been at school together, served interchangeably in the Foreign and Colonial offices and the various intelligence services, "retiring" into Oxbridge colleges, City boardrooms or journalism.[diii] During the Second World War their young American cousins in O.S.S. (from James Angleton to Arthur Schlesinger, Jr.) came under the spell of all this: the knowing glance, the studied understatement, the bespoke suits, the nursery food served in clubs with officious servants and highly restricted memberships. They were greeted with characteristic condescension by such as Malcolm Muggeridge: "Ah, those first O.S.S. arrivals in London! . . . All too soon they were . . . indistinguishable from seasoned pros who had been in the game for a quarter of a century or more"; Muggeridge playing a complicated

---

[45] And at least one notable woman, Gertrude Bell.

rhetorical game here, condescending to the American intelligence officers as newly corrupted prostitutes compared to whom he and his colleagues were as old whores. Fair enough. Muggeridge was still on the game after the war, lecturing, for example, on communism to intelligence officers at Worcester College, Oxford in the summer of 1948.[div] A few years later he was to provide liaison between CIA and IRD in Congress for Cultural Freedom matters.[dv]

The basic vocabulary for what became the joint Anglo-American Anti-Communist propaganda campaign was laid out in a series of IRD documents beginning with a memorandum from F. R. H. Murray, soon to be Director of the Information Research Department, to Christopher Warner, Undersecretary of State, dated 5 August 1948.[dvi] "Ministers have on several occasions spoken of the desireability of having a glossary of terms or catch-phrases to offset the Communist employment in a pejorative sense of "imperialism", "colonialism", "bourgeoisie", "war-mongering", "dollar diplomacy", "fascist", "right-wing socialist" etc. and their derivatives . . .

> I submit below some proposals, including two new phrases which may perhaps commend themselves. I have assumed as axiomatic that the phrases required must be comprehensible, or at least must convey a strong impression to the meanest intellect [sic]; that they should, if possible, have some quality of alliteration or assonance which is transmissible in a number of languages; and that they should refer to the fundamental themes of our criticism of the Communist regimes.

In addition to suggesting the use of the phrase "Communo-Fascism" and "Communo-fascist imperialism/colonialism" Murray suggested "we make a real effort to brand the U.S.S.R. and satellites as 'police states.'" Warner commented on 7 August: "I wonder if 'Red Fascism' wd. not go better than Communo-Fascism . . . I also think that 'Kremlin' can be effectively used in such contexts as 'Kremlin democracy', 'Kremlin imperialism'." "Police state" was soon in wider circulation in British English:

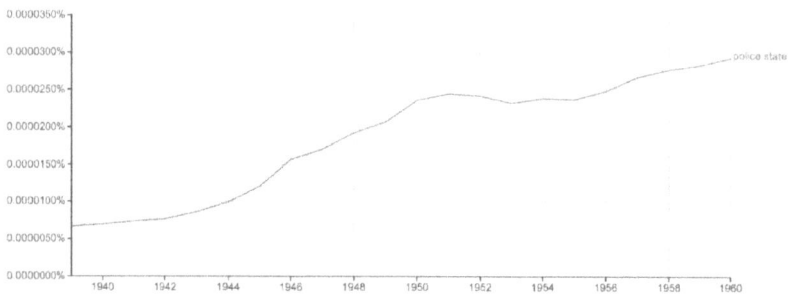

After some months of percolating through the Foreign Office, on 7 April 1949 a formal Confidential "MEMORANDUM ON THE USE OF WORDS IN PUBLICITY ABOUT COMMUNISM" was sent to embassies, major consulates and the BBC. It began with a rationale: "The persistent use of particular words or phrases to convey a meaning is an elementary step in any organized publicity.

In the present battle for world opinion, which has unfortunately been thrust upon us by Soviet policy and propaganda, it is essential that we should have recourse to this technique. It has, of course, long been used by Communist propaganda, in the case of words like "imperialism," "colonialism," "reactionary," "war-mongering," and even the appropriation of the word "democratic," with outstanding and dangerous success.

In order to concentrate and to sharpen our publicity about Communism it is important that a number of words, crystallizing the judgments or information which we wish to convey to world opinion, should be used extensively, and that other descriptions and variation should be avoided as far as possible.

Below is a list of words . . . divided into two main groups: first, words to describe Soviet internal practices, and second, words to describe the impact of the U.S.S.R. on the outside world. It is recommended that these . . . words should be used wherever practicable and politic in public statements, hand-outs, information or news bulletins, conversation and correspondence with appropriate persons . . .

The approved—and disapproved—words and the commentary

attached to them are appended to this chapter.

It is, perhaps, unnecessary to underline the importance for the study of the language of the Cold War that there was an official list of words to be used by the Foreign Office, a linguistic armory, as it were. This was then taken up by the U. S. State Department. During the Tripartite Foreign Ministers Conference in May, 1950, it was agreed that the U.S., U.K. and France would coordinate propaganda efforts "and other phases of our policy toward the Soviet Union and the satellites."[dvii] Specifically, in regard to propaganda: "We must bring our propaganda effort into harmony and, by giving increased and continuing expression to our agreed objectives, bring them home to peoples of Europe and Asia.

> In light of high quality of Russian propaganda US is renewing its efforts in information field and wishes to coordinate its efforts with those of France, UK and other countries. We must not allow Russia to have monopoly of peace theme . . . we must counter powerful Communist peace propaganda theme, which is making dangerous headway even in non-Communist circles, by impressing on our own and friendly peoples that we do not prepare for war in order to wage it and that we increase our defenses for peaceful purposes only.

The foreign ministers were careful to specify the importance of the vocabulary to be used: "'Cold war' is inappropriate term indicating we accept Russian challenge to fight on their chosen ground. Our purpose is not to win cold war but to increase security of our peoples through consolidated total defense."[dviii] And again, in something like a "note to self," Secretary of State Acheson wrote under the heading of *"Propaganda.* Must study information programs in order determine how make more effective and how coordinate."[dix]

On May 20, 1950, while Bevin was meeting with Acheson, Christopher Warner and Ralph Murray were meeting with their U.S. opposite numbers to discuss, among other matters, "arrangements for closer cooperation between our services in promoting common objectives and combating Communist propaganda." The Americans informed their British interlocutors that the U.S. was planning to double its propaganda budget in the first year and nearly double it again in the second year. "Mr. Warner stressed the importance attached by the Foreign Office to the use of local channels for the dissemination of anti-communist propaganda, rather than flooding the market with publicly identified British propaganda." He then "described the methods and techniques of anti-communist propaganda.

> Basic materials are developed by a central research staff in London, and processed for specific areas by a group of writers who work through an agency set up outside of the Foreign Office for this purpose. Trade Union organizations and various groups are used to place articles published under the by-line of well known writers; these articles and additional anti-communist materials are then sent to regional field offices in Singapore and Cairo, or to Information officers in individual countries for adaptation to meet local needs. The materials are never used directly by BIS, but are placed in local journals or made available to local groups. Careful attention is given to the selection of the most effective channels and target groups and themes.[dx]

The Anglo-American working group met again two days later, spending most of their time discussing cooperation in radio transmission matters. However, "Mr. Warner indicated considerable concern over the apparent trend toward neutrality on the Continent, particularly in France.

> He felt that the line taken by *Le Monde* was beginning to have effect and he knew that the French Government was very much concerned with the development of the neutrality philosophy.

Finally, "In working on our positive output, it was agreed that we should exchange ideas on all possible common lines of action and give more attention to developing effective slogans."[dxi]

As with the propaganda efforts in the Second World War, these postwar operations were directed at British audiences as well as those in third countries. The U. S. State Department already had in place a well-funded effort to influence British labor unions and key members of the Labour Party itself. The stigma of obviously U.S. government propaganda was avoided by circulating items from the American labor press. Less subtly, an exchange program funded under the Smith-Mundt Act brought British trades union and political leaders to the United States for meetings with their peers and such as, *inter alia,* secret intelligence executive Allen Dulles.[dxii] The success of the labor publication program, and, no doubt, encouragement from higher levels of the U.S. government, set American representatives in Britain to thinking about other possibilities. "By July 1951, the US [Labor Information Officer] in London, Patrick O'Sheel, had developed three 'special projects.'" One, which had originated with T. R. Fyvel, "a key British representative at the Congress for Cultural Freedom" was for a "magazine [that] should attract contributions from 'leading intellectual and political writers on both sides of the Atlantic.'"[dxiii] This was truly a joint effort, as Fyvel "had spent the war working for Eisenhower's Psychological Warfare Board in Europe."[dxiv]

OPC Project QKOPERA, the Congress for Cultural Freedom, was approved by the Project Review Board of that secret intelligence organization in early 1950.[dxv] In other words, the Congress for Cultural Freedom—world-wide sponsor of deluxe conferences, music festivals, traveling art exhibitions and, not least, publications aimed at the non-Communist Left intelligentsia—was a formal, proprietorial, CIA front. Matthew Spender, in the course of researching the lives of his parents, found that "On 15 June 1959 [Foreign Minister] Selwyn Lloyd signed a Foreign Office circular summarizing the communist front organizations in the West,

> and also their 'free-world counterparts', which, as he points out matter-of-factly', are less familiar' . . . [saying] in effect, that the Russians have their front organizations, and we have ours; and they are evenly balanced. This presupposes a major strategic decision going back many years . . . Paragraph 9 discusses the work of the Congress for Cultural Freedom. It reports without comment: "The organization is largely American-financed."[dxvi]

The Congress for Cultural Freedom was initially quite successful. However, "Two British delegates to the [June 1950] Berlin meeting, [historian] Hugh Trevor-Roper and [philosopher] Freddie Ayer . . . immediately recognized that a semi-secret institution was being created. They wanted to know who would be in charge. The British government did not have the money for that kind of thing. Did this mean it would be an American operation?"[dxvii] Only in part. IRD was working closely with the U.S. Office for Policy Coordination and State Department. The former already had in place its American Congress for Cultural Freedom, run by Sidney Hook, with its in-house OPC informant Arthur Schlesinger, Jr. "The Congress for Cultural Freedom (CCF) itself was also active in Britain from 1950, presumably with the informal approval of Whitehall, since a leading light was Malcolm Muggeridge, who maintained links with his wartime service, SIS.

> Britain was one of the first countries to boast a national committee of the CCF, set up by Stephen Spender in 1951, which eventually became the British Society for Cultural Freedom . . . this took hold the following year under the chairmanship of Muggeridge. The Society itself was eclipsed when the CCF decided to put most of its London effort into Fyvel's suggested magazine, which became *Encounter*. [dxviii]

And, perhaps as Ginsberg surmised, because of Anti-Communism itself, its effect on American culture, there were no American intellectual figures to match those in Paris. The dominant position of the intellectuals of the left in Western Europe had to be overcome in other ways, which was, as we have seen, the mission of the CCF. The idea was to publicize anyone except Communists and the *Les Temps Moderne* group. And the CIA had the cash to do it. "Of the multitude of covert projects financed through [CIA agent Irving] Brown, approximately $200,000 (equivalent to [$1.8 million in 2016]) was earmarked for the basic administrative costs of the Congress for Cultural Freedom in 1951. This paid the salaries of Francois Bondy, Denis de Rougemont, Pierre Bolomey . . . an administrator and several secretaries . . . Michael Goodwin, Secretary of the British Society for Cultural Freedom, had access to a monthly subsidy of £700 [$26,000 in 2016], deposited to his account at Westminster Bank in St James's Park."[dxix] Stephen Spender at that point was chairman of the British Society for Cultural Freedom. Goodwin was a contract employee of IRD.

Matthew Spender found that "The English branch of the CCF . . . the Committee for Cultural Freedom . . . acquired about forty members, most of whom were just names on the stationery.

> Stephen [Spender] knew that both the English CCF and [the predecessor to *Encounter*] *Twentieth Century* were both subsidized by the Paris office, "which, in turn, receives its funds from the American Federation of Labor" . . . [Stephen Spender] qualifies this by adding: "To many people, though, it seems that in fact its money comes from the State Department".[dxx]

Pointing to the American Federation of Labor as the CCF's funding source was a reference to Irving Brown and Jay Lovestone, both some-time CIA agents. The CIA itself was not well known in those days. Seeing the State Department behind the screen of the American Federation of Labor was good enough. One of those who was knowledgeable about the CIA was Diana Trilling, who "deduced that, at least outside the USA, the CCF must be subsidized by the CIA, for the simple reason that the Paris office could afford expensive lunches and the New York office could not . . . [indeed] at this stage it was no secret that the CIA was backing the CCF."[dxxi] Who "knew," and when, is a red herring in these discussions. The CCF was a CIA front. Those who ran it and its publications did what they were—in one way or another—told to do . . . or told not to do.

In early 1951, Frank Wisner met in London with MI-6 and Foreign Office officials to decide on the details of collaboration between the American and British secret intelligence agencies. (He was accompanied by the MI-6 Washington liaison officer, Kim Philby, who in his usual way, gave an amusing account of the visit in his memoir.) It was during these meetings that "the question of a high-level publication *aimed at encouraging a leftist lexicon* free of Kremlin grammar was first aired."[dxxii] (Emphasis added.) A year later Christopher Monty Woodhouse of IRD (and SIS) and Lawrence de Neufville and Michael Josselson of CIA reached an agreement to start what became *Encounter*. As "SIS wished to maintain a financial interest in the project . . . Woodhouse suggested that this contribution be earmarked for the salaries of the British editor and his secretary." (Curiously, it appears that the British editor, Stephen Spender, as well as the American editor, Irving Kristol, were selected by the CIA.[dxxiii]) Early in 1953, Josselson wrote from Paris to Spender who was in the United States "saying the American CCF was planning to found a magazine. Irving Kristol would be one of the editors. . . . Soon, [Spender] wrote to Irving [Kristol]: 'looks as if we are both to be employed by the British Committee.'"dxxiv As a matter of fact, although Spender was paid (through cut-outs) by the IRD, Kristol and his successors were paid through the Congress for Cultural Freedom by the CIA. This joint funding was an aspect of the Anglo-American special relationship. Spender's salary was set at £2,500, where it remained throughout his time with *Encounter*.dxxv The average annual earnings of a British worker in 1953 were 500 pounds, and then 1,400 pounds in 1967. According to the Measuring Worth academic website, 2,500 pounds in 1953 in 2016 dollars would be either $63,000 in purchasing power or $160,000 in relation to the earnings of an average worker. In 1967 (when Spender resigned) it would have been the equivalent of $56,800 in 2016 dollars. Perhaps he did not bargain as inflation eroded the value of his fixed salary. Perhaps IRD thought his work of declining value.

Irving Kristol was a Jewish, working class, married, ex-City College Trotskyite from Brooklyn, thirty-three years old in 1953. He had spent the war years as an infantryman and the immediate post-war years as a writer for, and then managing editor of, *Commentary*, the Anti-Communist magazine of the American Jewish Committee. He had also been the Executive Director of Sidney Hook's American Committee for Cultural Freedom. It was from there he was transferred to London to edit *Encounter*. Kristol was famous, or infamous, in New York for a March 1, 1952 article in *Commentary*, "'Civil Liberties,' 1952—A Study in Confusion: Do We Defend Our Rights by Protecting Communists?" The article's heart is in an early paragraph: "there is one thing that the American people know about Senator McCarthy: he, like them, is unequivocally anti-Communist. About the spokesmen for American liberalism, they feel they know no such thing. And with some justification."46 And in an echo of Schlesinger's *Vital Center:* "the antithesis of "left" and "right" no

---

46 The frequency of the phrase "Anti-Communist" in British English in 1940 was about the same as in American English. By 1956 it was nearly twice as common in American English.

longer suits the political realities . . .

> measured by the ideals of the French or even Russian Revolution, Communism today is as counter-revolutionary as Louis XVI or Kolchak ever was . . . if one wishes to defend the civil liberties of Communists (as the Senator does not), one must do so on the same grounds that one defends the civil liberties of Nazis and fascists—no more, no less.[dxxvi]

The position Kristol wished to defend in this article was a form of intellectual McCarthyism, one step on his journey to his late career as "the godfather of neo-conservatism." The next step was London's Bloomsbury, bowler hats, tightly rolled umbrellas and a secret intelligence agency-funded partnership with Stephen Spender.

Spender, to follow the format just used to describe Kristol, was a 43-year-old, upper middle class, ex-Communist, who had spent the war as a volunteer fire fighter in London. He was married with children, lived in St. John's Wood, a fashionable part of London, and conducted a lifelong series of homosexual affairs, beginning with a seduction (or rape) by W. H. Auden. Spender's literary reputation was at first as a minor member of the Auden school. Later, as co-founder of *Horizon,* he became a central participant in the London world of literary magazines, publishing, clubs and international cultural organizations. In 1949 Spender had contributed to the anti-Communist collection of essays, *The God That Failed,* with Arthur Koestler and Ignazio Silone (who were shortly to be among the founders of the CCF), Louis Fischer, Andre Gide and Richard Wright. He is today, perhaps, better known as a friend and publisher of poets than for his own poetry. He "knew everyone" in London and traveled frequently, as far afield as Japan, but most often to and in the United States. His was a career much like that of the CCF head, the minor composer Nicolas Nabokov, both well-known for being well-known, rather than for their artistic achievements. In spite of their very different class backgrounds, Kristol and Spender seemed to work as well together as any in a forced marriage such as theirs. They had their steadily increasing Anti-Communism in common and, perhaps, a certain sympathy on Spender's part for Kristol's non-observant Judaism. (Spender's wife was Jewish, his mother half-

Jewish.) In any case, both were ambitious and both were well-paid to continue the partnership.

Encounter, that joint operation of American and British secret intelligence, was labeled when it first appeared in October, 1953 as published by "Martin Secker and Warburg, Ltd. For the Congress for Cultural Freedom." The title page, listing Spender and Kristol as editors, detailed personnel of the Congress for Cultural Freedom: Honorary Chairmen—Karl Jaspers, Salvador de Madariaga, Jacques Maritain, Reinhold Niebuhr, Bertrand Russell—one German and one British philosopher; a Spanish historian; one French and one American theologian. Denis de Rougemont, a literary historian was listed as the President of the Executive Committee and Nicolas Nabokov as the Secretary-General of CCF.

The first issue of *Encounter,* Spender, perhaps, calling in favors, included contributions from Virginia Woolf, Christopher Isherwood, Edith Sitwell, Denis de Rougemont, C. Day Lewis and Albert Camus, a most distinguished Anglo-French group (even though Woolf, of course, had been dead for more than a decade). Other writers included the Americans Leslie A. Fiedler, Nathan Glazer and the editor Irving Kristol himself. An article on the Rosenberg case by Fiedler, a some-time Trotskyite, who had published in *The Partisan Review* and was beginning a career in the English department of the University of Montana (later emigrating to that of the University of Buffalo), was unusually vitriolic: "The suffering and death of the Rosenbergs were willed by the makers of Communist opinion and relished by them, as every instance of discrimination against a Negro in America is willed and relished, as further evidence that they are right."[dxxvii] He wrote that the Rosenbergs had been "poisoned by Communism" and went so far as to claim, after criticizing Ethel Rosenberg's prose style, that she and her husband "failed in the end to become martyrs or heroes—or even human beings."[dxxviii] Fiedler's vocabulary and rhetoric seemed to be adapted from that of Stalin's prosecutor, Andrey Vyshinsky. His dehumanizing condemnation of the only people executed for espionage in the United States in modern times appears, in retrospect, particularly exaggerated, as the current view is that Ethel Rosenberg, whether on not the possessor of a prose style sufficient for the English Department of the University of Montana, was innocent, executed in an unsuccessful attempt to force her husband to confess. The statement about discrimination against "Negroes" was willed by the Communist Party is simply astonishing.

In the March, 1954 issue, Fiedler reminded the magazine's readers that "Under the Soviet system of mass culture, you [the European intellectual] would have to choose among conformism, silence, or death!"[dxxix] Fiedler was still writing from Missoula, Montana, where, it might be said, under the system then prevailing in the United States, the choices were limited to conformism or silence, unless your name was Rosenberg, in which case the third alternative applied. In July, 1954, Fiedler devoted an extraordinarily lengthy essay to at once attacking Senator McCarthy and attacking his opponents, criticizing both reactionaries and Communists, the uneducated mob and the "red-tinged" intelligentsia. He mentioned "the Communist Menace," "Communist infiltration" of government and unions and coupled "Communists and fellow-travellers," and "Communists and liberals." (The frequency of the phrase "Communist menace" in Cold War American English was ten times that in British, where it was chiefly deployed in a colonial context.) Google's Ngram shows us that in all English language books published between 1940 and 1960, the phrases "Communist infiltration" and "fellow travelers" rise in frequency with the development of the Cold War, then decline. (The British spelling, "fellow Travellers," when charted alone, does not show this pattern, being virtually flat over the period.)

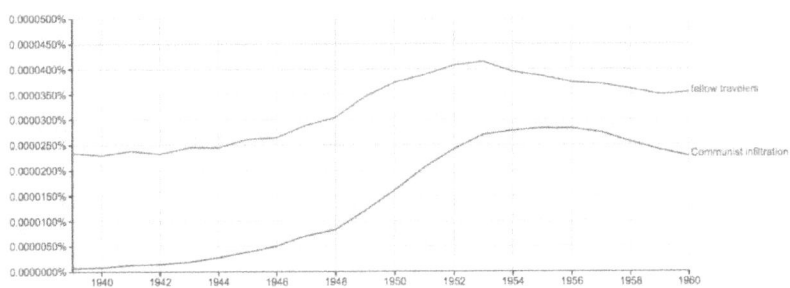

Fiedler's own position in this article was perhaps made deliberately obscure, but his rhetoric appeared to divide the American political scene at the point occupied by then-Vice President Nixon, everyone to his left suspect or foolish, everyone to his right . . . well, there was only one prominent person to Nixon's right: Senator McCarthy.[dxxx]

Spender was concerned that the Fiedler article had revealed the hidden hand of American backers of *Encounter*. "The *Times Literary Supplement* accurately detected an obsession with the evils of communism, which resulted in a sort of 'negative liberalism', while T. S. Eliot dismissed it as American propaganda hidden under a veneer of British culture."[dxxxi] Mary McCarthy, as was her custom, was blunt. Writing to Hannah Arendt: "Have you seen *Encounter*? It is surely the most vapid thing yet, like a college magazine got out by long-dead and putrefying undergraduates."[dxxxii] Given the negative reaction to the first issue, Spender wrote to Josselson that "the kind of reputation we have to try and live down of being a magazine disguising American propaganda under a veneer of British culture . . . any direct Anti-Communist sentiments simply defeat their own ends."[dxxxiii] Of course, *Encounter* was, precisely, "a magazine disguising American propaganda under a veneer of British culture." The contributors to *Encounter* shared a lexicon along the lines of that developed by the IRD. The United States and its allies and their colonies were always referred to as "the free world," in contrast to "the Soviet Regime," "the Communist world," or "totalitarian governments." This branding of the term "free world" was announced by Irving Kristol in an Editorial in the January, 1954: "As against the Communist world, ours is the free world . . ." The frequency of the term "free world" in English language publication rose through the first years of *Encounter*. As we have seen earlier, it had hardly been used in American English before 1948.

238

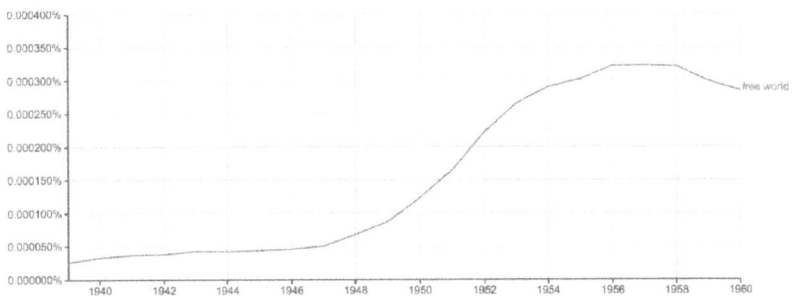

Never to be outdone in matters of invective, Arthur Koestler informed the readers of *Encounter's* second issue that "The totalitarians . . . are the forces of death assailing our civilization,"[dxxxiv] adding the common trope that "Communism . . . has the dynamism of a secular religion." The frequency of references to Communism as a religion rose and fell with the Anti-Communist activities of the IRD, the CIA and magazines like *Encounter*. Koestler was to return to the pages of *Encounter* for the last time in May, 1955, with an article entitled, in the Koestlerian manner, "The Trail of the Dinosaur." Franz Borkenau, the Austrian ex-Communist writer of *The Spanish Cockpit*, with a personal history, views and temperament similar to those of Koestler, predicted in the February, 1954, issue, with that other common trope of Anti-Communism, disease, that "As the Soviet regime continues to decline, it will be less and less able to conceal its festering diseases . . ."[dxxxv]

Spender, in spite of his self-fashioned image as a naïve and non-political poet, wrote in his "Notes from a Diary," in the November, 1955, number: "*Anti-Americanism.* Sometimes based on a simple idealistic wish that America would perform some act quite different from anything else in history . . . this feeling of resentment that America has not accomplished an absolutely disinterested act—an act outside historic materialism and therefore disproving it . . . How could such an act be possible?" Spender's February, 1956, "Notes from a Diary" asserted that "the co-existence which is talked of so glibly today, is in fact an almost unattainable ideal." Spender later referred to "the twisted pattern of Soviet dialectic" in his

239

increasingly Anti-Communist "Notes from a Diary." In a 1958 issue of *Encounter* Spender referred to Pasternak as the last surviving Russian poet. This was rather premature, as a possibly greater poet, Anna Akhmatova was to live until 1966, by which time there was also a new generation of Russian poets, such as Joseph Brodsky. It was, however, consistent with the general CCF line, contrasting the cultural achievements of the West and those of the ancien régime in Russia with the supposed lack of such in Communist societies.

Encounter published few articles by Kristol apart from editorial notes and reviews. One of those reviews, in August, 1956, juxtaposed "Communist totalitarianism," as against "the free world," while in the February, 1957, number he tried his hand at Parisian philosophy: "One suspects that the attitude of so many French intellectuals toward Sade has some connection with their attitude toward Communism. In both cases, they find themselves apologizing for hideous cruelty as being, in some dialectical way, liberating."[dxxxvi] T. R. Fyvel came out from behind the scenes in the April, 1954, *Encounter* to describe the then recently deceased American official, Harry Dexter White alternatively as pro-Communist or a Stalinist agent, engaged in "pro-Soviet activities," presumably during his negotiations at Bretton Woods to found the International Monetary Fund and the World Bank as instruments for American financial hegemony.[dxxxvii] In the October, 1955, issue Fyvel returned to refer to "the endless and scintillating argumentation of M. Sartre in favour of Communism [which] has by now an almost provincial and musty flavour." This is an unusual, perhaps unique, use of the term "provincial" to refer to Parisians.

Fyvel's colleague, Hugh Seton-Watson, informed readers of the April, 1954, issue of *Encounter* that "The Bolsheviks were . . . the first who not only genuinely cast off all moral inhibitions but also had, and used, the opportunity to try out their beliefs on the living flesh of a hundred million men and women,"[dxxxviii] deploying connotations of torture and, perhaps, cannibalism. Seton-Watson, who had worked variously for the Foreign Office, the Special Operations Executive and other British secret intelligence agencies before settling into university life in Oxford and the University of London, was a frequent contributor of fervently Anti-Communist articles to *Encounter.* In July, 1954, for example, maintaining IRD vocabulary discipline, Seton-Watson referred to "Stalinist totalitarianism." The usage of the phrase "totalitarianism," as we have seen, had steeply increased after the Second World War, reaching a plateau in the early-1950s, declining in parallel with the fortunes of *Encounter* in the 1960s.

In July, 1954, also maintaining lexical discipline, Raymond Aron referred to the "Soviet regime," rather than the Soviet government. "Soviet regime," was a particularly American locution, declining in frequency from 1944 to 1960 in British publications, other than *Encounter,* while rising to a 1954 peak in American publications. Aron's article, "Nations and Ideologies," in the January, 1955, issue of *Encounter* deployed a dense IRD-approved vocabulary: "Soviet régime," "Communist infiltration," "conspiracy and infiltration," "espionage and conspiracy," and "pinks." (As a matter perhaps of slight interest, the frequency of the appearance of "Raymond Aron" in English language publications rose steadily during the covert years of *Encounter*, peaking circa 1970, and declining after *Encounter*'s relationship with the CIA became known. The frequency of references to Sartre, whom Aron was intended by CCF to supplant, or rival, reached a plateau in 1965 and stayed at a level more than three times that of references to Aron, thereafter.)

The November, 1954, *Encounter* included an article by Peregrine Worsthorne entitled "America—Conscience or Shield?" Worsthorne, who was, perhaps uniquely, an English aristocrat supportive of Senator McCarthy, referred in this article to "the Communist menace," "the Communist conspiracy," and, notably, to "the Communist God which, on closer examination, turned out to be a devil."[dxxxix] (The use of the term "Communist menace," little known before 1945, reached a high point in 1955 before declining after 1965 along with the frequency of the use of the term "Soviet totalitarianism." The phrase "Communist God," while not infrequent in American usage during this period, was virtually unknown in British publications, its use by him perhaps a sign of Worsthorne's sensitivity to American political orientations and vocabulary.) Anticipating by twenty years Henry Kissinger's question in regard to

241

Chilean democracy, in the January, 1956, *Encounter,* in an essay entitled "Democracy v. Liberty?" Worsthorne asked "Why should the Indo-Chinese people be free to choose tyranny?" a sentiment Irving Kristol may be taken to have referred to the following month as "that spirit of candour and forthrightness, which is the free world's most valuable asset."[dxl]

Three and a half years later, in May, 1958, Worsthorne was quoted as stating that "the cause of the cold war [was] Russian penetration, political and military"[dxli] The frequency of the term "Communist penetration" in American English rose steeply from virtually nothing in 1940 to a peak in the early 1960s, then fell away as dramatically and followed a similar curve in British usage. "Russian penetration" in American usage was on a plateau throughout the Second World War, then rose to a high point in the mid-1950s, by 1980 falling below the 1940 level. On the other hand, British usage of that phrase appears to have been more exclusively connected with the wartime advance of the Red Army and its activities.[47]

In May, 1955, G. F. Hudson of St. Antony's College, Oxford, referred to "Communist dictatorship," the "Sino-Soviet block," "Communist aggression," and the "Western powers" in an article entitled "Divided We Stand." In the number of *Encounter* for November, 1955, Edward Shils declared victory, perhaps prematurely, in a "Letter from Milan: The End of Ideology," that "Communism had lost the battle of ideas with the West," which may be why Christopher Sykes, in a December, 1955, review of "The Whispering Gallery" by John Lehmann, felt confident enough to refer to the "current Marxist nonsense." (Shils had been attending a CCF conference in Milan, much documented in CIA files. Lasky was also there, about whom Mary McCarthy commented in a letter to Hanna Arendt: "Lasky is a strange person, appallingly vulgar but with curious convictions. He hates all of us, I think, and yet he has become in the last months very heatedly anti-Anti-Communist, I

---

[47] The "Freudian" interpretation of the fear of Soviet "penetration" and the various references to "hard" or "soft" political stances hardly requires further elaboration.

suppose it is his practical side, which now looks on the [ex-Communists] Bert Wolfes and Hooks and Sperbers as absurd visionaries."[dxlii])

In the June, 1955, *Encounter*, Sir David Kelly, former British ambassador in the Soviet Union, referred diplomatically to "the Soviet threat," "the Soviet Empire," "the Soviet camp," and "the totalitarians." In the August, 1955, issue, Russian émigré historian Max Beloff's referred to "the threat to freedom . . . from the Soviet world," and "the Communist yoke." This was an adaptation of the terms the "Russian" or "Tartar yoke", which had been more frequently used in the early-twentieth century in anti-Czarist Russian propaganda than Beloff's Anti-Communist version would be in the middle years of the century, when its use in English had already peaked four years earlier.

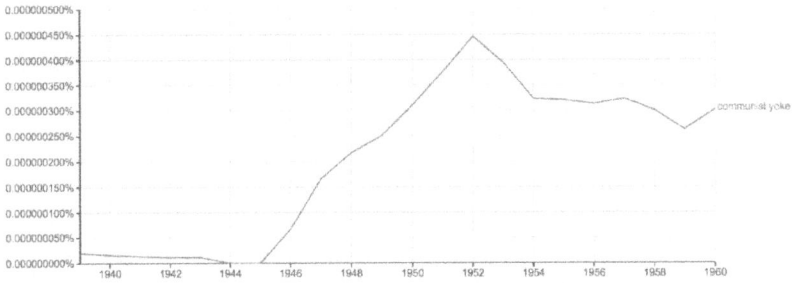

In a common application of the time of a psychiatric expression to politics, in April, 1956, *Encounter* Michael Swan said of Forbes Burnham, who would become president of Guyana: "Burnham was not treated well when he studied law in England and he now has a neurotic hatred of the English."[dxliii] "Neurotic hatred" was, however, otherwise an almost exclusively American term, peaking in frequency in the early Cold War years, and therefore presumably a political as well as psychiatric usage.

The "Thaw" was anticipated by German historian and journalist Richard Lowenthal, who, in the May, 1956, issue of *Encounter,* rather surprisingly wrote that "The recognition that world war is no longer inevitable . . . marks no basic change in policy . . . the Soviet government always strove to avoid involvement in world war." In August, 1956, while Kristol continued to follow IRD's guidance, juxtaposing "Communist totalitarianism," as against "the free world," other articles in the issue were devoted to reports from the Soviet Union, Poland, etc. on the end of Stalinism, the closing of the camps, the opening of intellectual life, etc. In May, 1957, to its—and her—credit, *Encounter* included an anti-Anti-Communist essay by Mary McCarthy, defending Arthur Miller: "to the ordinary newspaper reader, every witness who used the Fifth Amendment was a dyed-in-the-wool member of what was felt to be a Communist conspiracy " while "for Mr. Miller, it was not in reality a question of betraying specific people [to which he objected] . . . but of accepting the *principle* of betrayal as a norm of good citizenship."[dxliv]

Nonetheless, from late 1957, *Encounter* began to run anonymous articles[48] about the Soviet Union, Poland, etc. called "From the Other Shore," which were written with a uniformly unreconstructed Cold War rhetoric and a relentless focus on the virtues of the anti- or non-Communist Polish intelligentsia and literati. Along this line, in the October, 1958, issue of *Encounter,* long after the death of Stalin, Robert Lowenthal in an article on Yugoslavia uses the terms "Stalinist mire," "unrepentant Stalinist," and "Stalinist reaction."[dxlv] And in November, 1958, Stuart Hampshire (whose connections with British secret intelligence dated from the Second World War) in an article called "'Doctor Zhivago: As from a lost culture" referred to the Soviet Union as "a cultural desert." On the other hand, there was another essay in the November issue, this by George Steiner, praising the Marxist (and one-time-Stalinist) literary critic Georg Lukács.

The November 1958 *Encounter* was the last edited by Kristol, who returned to New York to a career in publishing and neo-Conservative politics. The CIA replaced him with its agent Melvin Lasky. Spender continued as the IRD's editor of *Encounter*. The change in political editors was immediately evident, as despite their

[48] Edited by Leopold Labedz, an Anti-Communist Polish writer, resident in England, veteran of the Polish exiled Anders Army.

common New York City Trotskyite, anti-Stalinist background, Lasky appears to have decided on a more subtle tone for *Encounter* than that orchestrated by Kristol. John Kenneth Galbraith, for example, was allowed to report from Poland in the January, 1959, issue: "Geography makes a socialist economic order more or less an imperative.

> Even the least reconciled do not talk of much change here [Poland]. While good relations with the U.S.S.R. are essential, even the most ardent Communists with whom I talked consider themselves Poles first. Certainly the notion that all Communists take their orders willingly and automatically from Moscow . . . can be a prime source of error.[dxlvi]

"From the Other Shore," with its ironic comments and excerpts from Soviet bloc press, etc., was the only feature in this issue maintaining Cold War attitudes. The following month Richard Lowenthal went so far as to declare that "The crisis of 1948-9 marked the end phase of Stalinist post-war expansion in Europe."[dxlvii] Continuing this retreat from Cold War rhetoric, in March, 1959, *Encounter* included a report by Edward Shils, that the Congress for Cultural Freedom Conference at "Rhodes (Greece) was remarkable for many things. Not the least of these was the small place accorded to the dangers of Communism . . ."[dxlviii] And F. R. Allemann noted that "The Soviets may rattle their atom bombs, but they have no intention of risking a real conflict."

By the Spring of 1959, Cold War rhetoric was disappearing from *Encounter* except for "From the Other Shore" and Spender's diaries. In June, "Moscow Notebook," by Andrew Boyd, is a typical example of an *Encounter* travel article of the time. He depicts Moscow as odd, amusing and confusing, but not especially evil. Even in the "From the Other Shore" feature in this issue there is a "Letter from Leipzig," by the Swiss journalist F. R. Allemann, who notes that political conditions in the German Democratic Republic were growing worse, but economic conditions were growing better. By August, 1959, there was a very favorable review of the magazine's former bête noir Simone de Beauvoir's *Memoirs of a Dutiful Daughter* by J. G. Weightman and in October there was a travel essay by Walter Laqueur, who was favorably impressed by Sochi in the Soviet Union. Five years earlier, in the June, 1954, issue, Laqueur, writing under the pen-name Mark Alexander, in an article entitled "New Directions in Soviet Literature?" had referred to "totalitarian regimentation, thought control . . . Stalinist . . . glorified servitude."[dxlix]

While Reinhold Niebuhr appeared only once in the pages of *Encounter*, perhaps for health reasons, Arthur M. Schlesinger, Jr., was a rather frequent contributor and the magazine published twenty of Sidney Hook's contributions. These began with a review of Alger Hiss's *In the Court of Public Opinion* in July, 1957. There were travel stories—India, we are informed by Hook, is exotic—and philosophical interventions. In an essay in August, 1961, Hook engaged with an earlier article by Michael Polanyi, an *Encounter* stalwart, referring to the (there linked) "Monstrous Bolshevik and Nazi Revolutions" and "totalitarianism or nihilism" (seen as identical). Hook's article is a defense of the Enlightenment, and Marx, against Polanyi's *post hoc ergo propter hoc* irrationalism. He similarly defends "revisionist" Marxism against both Western and Soviet vulgarizations of Marx in "Revisionism at Bay," published in September, 1962. His interventions, often philosophical, more usually polemical, continued annually or more frequently until ending with "The Case of Lillian Hellman," in February, 1977.

Schlesinger's first *Encounter* article was a review of his friend Isaiah Berlin's *The Hedgehog and the Fox* in November 1953. After that the magazine published his reviews approximately annually until 1967. In September, 1970, he reviewed a re-issue of his own *The Vital Center*. Recounting the circumstances of the writing of the book, Schlesinger mentions the Marshall Plan and the re-election of President Truman as having at the time given cause for optimism about American liberalism. He also recalled that "I was much influenced by Reinhold Niebuhr, first by [his books] . . . later by close personal association with this wise and noble man in 'Americans for Democratic Action' and elsewhere." Niebuhr had taught him, Schlesinger wrote, that pessimism, rather than optimism about the perfectibility of mankind, was the best stance to take in opposition to the "totalitarianism." He then turned to a discussion of the effects of technology on society, which, in 1970, he takes to be more important than the conflict between capitalism and communism. After this Schlesinger pointed out the differences between communism in 1949 (which he says is better thought of as "Stalinism") and the various national communist governments of 1970. He wrote that, ironically, as it were, "At the same time, nationalism has also terminated the American effort to dominate the non-communist world." After two decades, Schlesinger had changed his mind about "the Communist threat," and the dominance of ideology: "I think it essential to distinguish between rational and obsessive Anti-Communism:

[B]etween Anti-Communism as an element in a larger position, an element addressed to specific situations and graduated in mode and substance according to the character of the threat; and Anti-Communism as a total position, addressed to some great, all-pervading evil and requiring the subordination of every other consideration and value.

And, citing the work of Soviet authors such as Solzhenitsyn and Sakharov, he admits that the extreme view of the omnipotent force of "totalitarianism" had been mistaken.

The preceding pages of this chapter have picked out the Cold War language of *Encounter*, largely passing over in silence the non-political articles, which remain, in many cases, informative and a pleasure to read. *Encounter* was a well-regarded magazine of the mid-twentieth-century with a reputation for excellent, authoritative, literary essays and a right-of-center political stance. It was the Lasky/Spender *Encounter* of 1959 and the years following, as the political Cold War continued, but the cultural Cold War was winding down, that is remembered in this way as a magazine of cultural affairs and general interest, the London counterpart of *The New Yorker*. Did *Encounter* succeed in its dual missions of helping shift the presumably left-wing British intelligentsia to the center and the Labour Party to the right? The CIA and Foreign Office continued to fund it for more than a decade. They must have judged that they were getting what they paid for.

The Language of Anti-Communism

From FO 1110/191

WORDS DESCRIBING SOVIET INTERNAL PRACTICES

KREMLIN

This is thought to be the most useful single word for general audiences in order to fix in people's minds the cruel, backward, tyrannical and centralizing aspects of the Communist movement as it now exists in Russia. It is also applicable to Russia's foreign policy (see below). A further advantage is that it may provide a useful peg for graphic propaganda.

STALINIST
STALINISM

These words also suggest both control from Russia and the perversion of Communism by Stalin; they are more suitable for intellectual audiences.

DICTATOR

This proved very useful against Hitler and is suitable for general audiences.

TOTALITARIAN

The use of this word should perhaps be confined largely to European audiences as it is not widely enough understood for general use.

POLICE STATE

Another useful phrase, which underlines this sometimes over-looked but essential aspect of the system.

BACKWARD
OUT-OF-DATE
THEORY

These words, which have already been launched by Mr. Bevin, can with elaboration be applied to most aspects of Soviet internal policy; they are not only useful for European audiences by rebutting the Communist claim to be progressive, but also have an effective sting.

THE REVOLUTION
BETRAYED

This phrase and concept is particularly useful for European audiences on the fringe of Communism against whom our publicity must be especially directed. It crystallizes the criticism to which the Soviet system must and should be exposed from the extreme Left and the most humanitarian point of view.

THE STRANGLING OF ART AND SCIENCE

This is an issue which we should do our utmost to keep alive and on which fresh material is daily reaching us from Moscow. It is of great importance to convince the "intellectuals" that they would have no freedom of expression under Communism and would be expected to produce only work in tune with the Party line and "popular democratic" idiom.

FORCED LABOUR

This is an issue on which the Russians are particularly vulnerable and have no effective answer. In order to get the idea across to the public it is essential to build up the names of one or two well-known camps until they are as familiar as Dachau or Belsen. **Karaganda,** the remote coal-mining region of Central Asia which is worked almost entirely by forced labour, is considered the most promising name to use in this context. It is, moreover, the name most familiar to the Russian public.

Words which should be avoided

Communist

This word is not considered suitable because of its vague attraction for many waverers. Insistence on it, moreover, is not necessary.

Red

This is liable to cause confusion with Socialist Parties and tends to be used as a term of reactionary abuse.

Tyranny

This word is not as effective as dictatorship.

The Language of Anti-Communism

Slavery   This is a difficult accusation to substantiate,
                        but "the new serfdom" might be useful.

Stalin   The figure of Stalin himself should not be
                        built up on the analogy of Hitler, as great
                        efforts are made by Soviet propaganda to turn
                        him into a popular and friendly figure with the
                        masses. It is, however, important to explode the
                        fallacy that Stalin is a benevolent realist who is
                        prepared to over-rule the rasher and more
                        intransigent decisions of his subordinates and
                        with whom one can talk peace with a
                        reasonable chance of success.

Words to describe the impact of the U.S.S.R. on the outside world

KREMLIN   This is a graphic and sinister term that can
IMPERIALISM   be employed to cover the entire field of
                        Soviet foreign policy.

SATELLITE   This is thought to be the most suitable and
STATES   the most readily understood of various
                        alternatives and should therefore be used
                        exclusively to describe the states of Easter
                        Europe and the Far East under Kremlin
                        control.

PUPPETS   This is another graphic and well-established
                        phrase.

RUSSIAN ASIA   This corresponds to "German Europe,"
                        which was used with success in the war. It is
                        a potentially useful and much-needed phrase
                        to describe the actual parts of Asia under
                        Russian control and will help to get the issue
                        across to other Asiatic countries including the
                        three Asian Dominions.

THE VETO ON   This phrase has already been widely
PEACE   successfully adopted by the Labour Party to

describe Soviet behaviour in the general field of international settlement since 1945 and "veto" has a useful Soviet flavour.

THE BETRAYAL OF PEACE

This and the phrase above outline the essence of developments in foreign policy since 1945 far more clearly than any lengthy analysis.

Words which should be avoided

Soviet Imperialism

This term, which is already in wide use, has less implications than "Kremlin imperialism" and has been given certain favourable overtones by Communist propaganda.

Protectorate
Dependency
Colony

These are technical terms for our own possessions and should therefore not be used to describe areas under Kremlin control.

Expansionism
Aggrandisement

Not as good as "imperialism"

Exploitation

The allegation of "exploitation" of a state or area by the Soviet Union is not quite compatible with Soviet economic policy generally, which tens rather to economic *gleichschaltung,* and this word should not be loosely used.

Note:--It is important not to stress Russian strength; phrases such as "the Soviet fear belt" should be avoided.

Notes

[cdlxxxvii] A class in Ed Sanders's "Investigative Poetics" series, led by Allen Ginsberg. Jack Kerouac School of Disembodied Poetics, published June 9, 1977.
http://ginsbergblog.blogspot.com/2013/11/investigative-poetics-10-conclusion.html

[cdlxxxviii] United States Department of State / Foreign relations of the United States, 1947. The British Commonwealth; Europe (1947), pp. 709-712.

[cdlxxxix] Saunders, p 101.

[cdxc] Saunders, p 121

[cdxci] Saunders, p 1.

[cdxcii] Saunders, p 60.

[cdxciii] Saunders, pp. 65-6.

[cdxciv] Saunders, p. 163.

[cdxcv] Saunders, p. 98.

[cdxcvi] Aldrich, Richard J. The Hidden Hand: Britain, America and Cold War Secret Intelligence. Woodstock and New York: The Overlook Press, 2002, p. 131.

[cdxcvii] Spender, Matthew. A House in St John's Wood: In Search of My Parents. London: William Collins, 2016, P. 142, citing FO 1110/533.

[cdxcviii] Aldrich, p. 131.

[cdxcix] Saunders, p. 59.

[d] Aldrich, p. 443.

[di] Spender, p. 237.

[dii] Wilford, Hugh. The CIA, the British left, and the Cold War: Calling the Tune? London: Frank Cass, 2003, p. 275.

[diii] This happened on the American side as well. ". . . those running the CIA and other covert warfare programmes were also running the foundations . . . In 1954 Nelson Rockefeller, who helped to fund [the MOMA art program] took over from C. D. Jackson as Eisenhower's special adviser on Cold War operations. Meanwhile John McCloy, the American High Commissioner in Germany, and his Publicity Chief, Shepard Stone, moved seamlessly from the Cold War front line to become Directors [sic] of the Ford Foundation."[diii]

[div] Aldrich, p. 149 citing Bright-Holmes, J. (ed.) Like It Was: The diaries of Malcolm Muggeridge.

[dv] Saunders, p 108.

[dvi] The National Archives, FO 1110/191. A similar document had been released in Washington on December 9, 1947, as NSC 4: National Archives

and Records Administration, RG 273, Records of the National Security Council, NSC Minutes, 4th Meeting. Confidential. Copies sent to the President, the Secretaries of State, Defense, the Army, the Navy, and the Air Force, and the Chairman of the National Security Resources Board. See also documents contributed to the Cold War International History Project by A. Ross Johnson, available through digitalarchive.wilsoncenter.org.

[dvii] Foreign Relations of the United States, 1950, Western Europe, Volume III. Paper Prepared in the Department of State WASHINGTON, April 28, 1950. Top Secret U.S. Objectives and Course of Action in the May Meetings. Cfm Files: Lot M–88: Box 149: May FM Meeting A Series https://history.state.gov/historicaldocuments/frus1950v03/ch4subch6https://history.state.gov/histo.ricaldocuments/frus1950v03/d511

[dviii] Foreign Relations Of The United States, 1950, Western Europe, Volume III. https://history.state.gov/historicaldocuments/frus1950v03/d510https://history.state.gov/historicaldocuments/frus1950v03/d512 396.1 LO/5–850: Telegram The Secretary of State to the Acting Secretary of State PARIS, May 8, 1950—10 p. m.

[dix] Foreign Relations of The United States, 1950, Western Europe, Volume III https://history.state.gov/historicaldocuments/frus1950v03/d512https://history.state.gov/historicaldocuments/frus1950v03/d514 396.1 LO/5–950: Telegram The United States Delegation at the Tripartite Foreign Ministers Meeting to the Acting Secretary of State LONDON, May 9, 1950—midnight. According to the "Informal Minutes of Meeting of Director and Consultants Interdepartmental Foreign Information Organization," December 5, 1950, a topic was "the question of terminology in characterizing the Russians in speeches and general propaganda output." https://www.cia.gov/library/readingroom/docs/CIA-RDP80-01065A000500130030-6.pdf

[dx] Foreign Relations of the United States Document 707 https://history.state.gov/historicaldocuments/frus1950v03/d706https://history.state.gov/historicaldocuments/frus1950v03/d708 611.41/5–2250 Notes on the First Meeting Between Messrs. Christopher Warner and Edward Barrett, at London, Saturday May 20, 1950.

[dxi] https://history.state.gov/historicaldocuments/frus1950v03/d708

[dxii] Wilford, pp. 173-4

[dxiii] Aldrich, , pp. 448-9.

[dxiv] Aldrich, p. 449.

[dxv] Saunders, p. 86.

[dxvi] Spender, p. 229 citing FO 1110/1726, FO Circular no. 37.

[dxvii] Spender, pp. 105-6.

[dxviii] Aldrich, p. 450.

[dxix] Saunders, p 106.

[dxx] Spender, p. 108.

[dxxi] Spender, p. 107.

[dxxii] Saunders, p. 167.

[dxxiii] Saunders, p. 169.

[dxxiv] Spender, pp. 127-8.

[dxxv] Saunders, p. 328.

[dxxvi] Kristol, Irving. "'Civil Liberties,' 1952—A Study in Confusion: Do We Defend Our Rights by Protecting Communists?" *Commentary*, March 1, 1952.

[dxxvii] Fiedler, Leslie A. A Postscript to the Rosenberg Case, *Encounter*, October, 1953, Vol.1.No.1, p. 14.

[dxxviii] Fiedler, p. 21.

[dxxix] Fiedler, Leslie A. "The 'Good" American," *Encounter*, March, 1954, p. 53.

[dxxx] Fiedler, Leslie A. *Encounter*, August, 1954, "McCarthy," pp. 10ff.

[dxxxi] Aldrich, p. 450.

[dxxxii] Brightman, Carol. Between Friends. San Diego: Harcourt, 1995. MM to HA, 4/10/53, p. 14.

[dxxxiii] Saunders, p 187.

[dxxxiv] Koestler, Arthur. *Encounter*, November, 1953, "A Guide to Political Neuroses," p. 25

[dxxxv] Borkenau, Franz. "The Secret History of Communism," *Encounter*, February, 1954, p. 76.

[dxxxvi] Kristol, Irving. "The Shadow of the Marquis: Notes on Some Possibly Related Matters," *Encounter*, February 1957, p. 4.

[dxxxvii] Fyvel, T.R. "The Broken Dialogue," *Encounter*, April, 1954, p. 45.

[dxxxviii] Seton-Watson, Hugh. *Encounter*, April, 1954,"Cossacks of Destiny," p. 66.

[dxxxix] Worsthorne, P. G. "America—Conscience or Shield?" *Encounter*, September, 1954, p. 22.

[dxl] Kristol, Irving. "Indian Excitement," *Encounter*, February, 1956, p. 3.

[dxli] "Books: Long Haul to Where?" Donald Tyerman, quoting Does

Democracy Disengage? by Peregrine Worsthorne, *Encounter,* May, 1958, p. 74.

[dxlii] Brightman, MM to HA, 5/29/55, p. 36.

[dxliii] Swan, Michael. "Politics and Pork-knockers. British Guiana," *Encounter,* April, 1956, p. 70.

[dxliv] McCarthy, Mary. "Naming Names: The Arthur Miller Case," *Encounter,* May, 1957, p. 23.

[dxlv] Lowenthal, Robert. "Tito's Gamble," *Encounter,* October, 1958, p. 61

[dxlvi] Galbraith, John Kenneth. "Heresy Revisited," *Encounter,* January, 1959, p. 50.

[dxlvii] Lowenthal, Richard. "The Crossroads: Letter from Berlin," *Encounter,* February, 1959, p. 4.

[dxlviii] Shils, Edward. "Old Societies, New States," *Encounter,* March, 1959, p. 34.

[dxlix] Alexander, Mark. "Counterfeit Freedom," *Encounter,* October, 1953, p. 42.

The Language of the Non-Communist Left

Arthur M. Schlesinger, Jr., Reinhold Niebuhr and Sidney Hook were among the most prominent American public intellectuals of the Cold War period. One was a historian, another a theologian, the third a professional philosopher. All three were ideologists, occupied with creating and promulgating the ideology of the Cold War. *Encounter,* that Anglo-American cultural journal, was similarly during those years a vehicle for the promulgation of Cold War ideology and ideological language along the lines frankly discussed by the Information Research Department of the British Foreign Office and agreed to by the American State Department and the secret intelligence agencies of both countries.

An ideology is a kind of second nature, a lens through which we view the world. More literally, it is a storehouse of words and phrases, ideas and images that form our understanding of the structure and events of the world. Just as the Puritans and Pietists saw in the world God's design and in its events His Will, so those living in a pre-capitalist society divided into classes understood their society as one in which there were real differences in human nature that could be described in class terms, quite aside from such matters as income and wealth. "It's in God's hands," or "Everyone has his place," are ideological statements that are simultaneously descriptions and injunctions. During the Cold War Schlesinger told his readers that American political space had become one-dimensional: there was only "the vital center." Niebuhr preached his pessimistic, ironic, vision of humanity, that the world as it is cannot be otherwise, that the improvement of human conditions was unthinkable. Hook simply ruled the Communist Party and its sympathizers out of American society; those ten thousand Party members, those hundreds of thousands of sympathizers, did not differ for him politically, the Party members were by definition criminals, the sympathizers potential criminals or collaborators. *Encounter* carried out its mission negatively, by not publishing articles critical of American and British foreign policy and society, and positively, by means of a relentless series of articles critical of the foreign policy and society of the Soviet Union, of non-Soviet Communist parties and individuals insufficiently critical of communism.

The Non-Communist Left in Europe, as a set of organizations like the Congress for Cultural Freedom, publications like *Encounter,* certain fashions in art, scholarship and literature, was to a large extent the creation of American and British secret intelligence agencies. Although its goal was to prevent Western Europe from adopting Communist forms of government, the Non-Communist Left refused to consider Communism politically and resorted instead, time after time, to the imagery of disease and religion, and psychology. However, the Western European Communist parties were mass organizations. It made little sense, especially to their members, to think of them as semi-religious cults or analogous to disease. The Cold War Communist parties of France and Italy remained large and influential, politically and culturally, kept out of government only by sheer military and economic pressure, supplemented, as needed, by bribery. *Encounter* best served the British and American intelligence services and their governments as an instrument for influencing the culture, the ideological atmosphere, of their own countries. In Britain this meant putting a thumb on the scales in the contest within the Labour Party between the pro-American Gaitskell and the less tractable Bevan. In the United States it meant bringing the prestige of a segment of the British and European intelligentsia to legitimize Anti-Communism, to delegitimize what remained of the left.

Although arguably successful in Britain, the sophisticated Cold War ideologists of the Non-Communist Left had little enduring influence in the United States. Niebuhr and Hook are barely remembered; Schlesinger chiefly as a courtier in Camelot. At best they may have constructed a comfortable ideological way station for

The Language of Anti-Communism

intellectuals moving from left to right, from the politics of social transformation to the everyday practices involved with "making it," from Socialism to soirees chez Jacqueline.

The Non-Communist Left

Epilogue

The language of American Anti-Communism was similar to and derived from that of the Catholic Church, on the one hand, and from that of Nazi Germany, on the other, with a specific admixture of the vocabulary of Southern racism. For those Anti-Communists who were themselves ex-Communists, there were also the vulgarities they brought with them from Party meetings and publications. We have the "conspiracies" of the encyclicals, the vermin and disease images of Lenin and Ley, Trotsky and Goebbels, the sexual hysteria of the likes of Senator Eastland. Coughlin recycled Nazi publications, but it is not clear that the Nazi vocabulary was consciously deployed by other Anti-Communists. It could be they just produced it on their own, in parallel, as it were. It was in the air, a stench, to use a favorite Anti-Communist term, closely related to anti-Semitism, that clung to the language of American Anti-Communism to the end.

There were two sources of the specifically American language of Anti-Communism. One was anti-intellectualism, typified by the attacks on Einstein and Oppenheimer, the Berkeley physicists and Harvard professors, exemplified in the sneers about "so-called" liberals, "so-called" intellectuals, "eggheads" and the like. The other was the increasingly desperate racism of the defenders of "the Southern way of life," the Eastlands, Rankins and Bilbos, the Daughters of the Confederacy, and the Young Businessmen's clubs, and in the North the members of "Americanism" committees, horrified by interracial dances in Detroit, Black speakers on public platforms, the possibility of a Black man asking a White woman for a date.

The language of Anti-Communism, the language of conspiracy, dehumanization, anti-intellectualism, sneers and bullying, seemed, at the end of the last century, to have faded from the public sphere. So it seemed. But as Victor Klemperer himself found, the corruption of language is not restricted to a single political system or moment. It is there, ready at hand, to express the resentment of those whose lives have been embittered by shattered hopes, to be diverted from the plantation owners to the share-croppers, from the bankers to the intellectuals, from the property developers to any group that can be branded as "other," registered, imprisoned or expelled.

Bibliography

Aldrich, Richard J. The Hidden Hand: Britain, America and Cold War Secret
   Intelligence. Woodstock and New York: The Overlook Press, 2002.
Arendt, Hannah. The Human Condition. Chicago: University of Chicago Press,
   1958.
Barnhisel, Greg, Cold War Modernists: Art, Literature, and American Cultural
   Diplomacy, 1946-1959, New York: Columbia University Press, 2015.
Braden, Anne. House Un-American Activities Committee: Bulwark of
   Segregation. National Committee to Abolish the House Un-American
   Activities Committee; 1St Edition (1963).
   http://www.crmvet.org/info/64_braden_huac-r.pdf
Brightman, Carol (ed.) Between Friends: The Correspondence of Hannah
   Arendt and Mary McCarthy 1949-1975. San Diego: Harcourt Brace &
   Company, 1995.
Brown, Sarah Hart. Standing Against Dragons: Three Southern Lawyers in an
   Era of Fear. Baton Rouge: Louisiana State University Press, 1998.
Caute, David. The Great Fear: The Anti-Communist Purge Under Truman and
   Eisenhower. New York: Simon and Schuster, 1978.
Durr, Virginia Foster. Outside the Magic Circle. Ed. Hollinger F. Barnard. The
   Autobiography of Virginia Foster Durr. University of Alabama Press, 1985.
Feffer, Andrew. "The Rapp-Coudert Investigation, Liberals, and the
   Countersubversive Tradition, 1939-1942".
   https://www.academia.edu/29380443/Feffer_The_Rapp-
   Coudert_Investigation_Liberals_and_the_Countersubversive_Tradition_19
   39-1942.
Finley, Keith M. Delaying the Dream: Southern Senators and the Fight Against
   Civil Rights, 1983-1965. Baton Rouge: Louisiana University Press, 2008.
Fox, Richard Wightman. Reinhold Niebuhr: A Biography. New York: Pantheon
   Books, 1985.
Gilmore, Glenda Elizabeth. Defying Dixie: The Radical Roots of Civil Rights,
   1919-1950. New York: Norton, 2008.
Gleason, Abbott. Totalitarianism: The Inner History of the Cold War. New
   York: Oxford University Press, 1995.
Griffith, Robert and Athan Teoharis. The Specter: Original Essays on the Cold
   War and the Origins of McCarthyism. New York: New Viewpoints, 1974.

Hershberg, James G. James B. Conant: Harvard to Hiroshima and the Making of the Nuclear Age.

Hinds, Lynn Boyd; Windt, Theodore Otto, Jr., The Cold War as Rhetoric: The Beginnings, 1945-1950. New York: Praeger, 1991, pp. 114-5.

Hofstadter, Richard. Anti-Intellectualism in American Life. New York: Vintage Books, 1963.

Hook, Sidney. Heresy, Yes, Conspiracy, No. New York: John Day Company, 1953.

Hook, Sidney. Heresy, Yes—But Conspiracy, No. July 9, 1950, *New York Times Magazine.*

Jenkins, Philip. The Cold War at Home: The Red Scare in Pennsylvania, 1945-1960. Chapel Hill: University of North Carolina Press, 1999.

Ley, Robert. *Pesthauch der Welt* (Dresden: Franz Müller Verlag, 1944) trans. Randall Bytwerk, used by permission.

Luther, Martin. Treatise on Christian Liberty, Works of Martin Luther: with Introductions and Notes, Volume 2. Jacobs, Henry Eyster and Spaeth, Adolph. Philadelphia: A. J. Holman Company, 1915.

Medhurst, Martin J.; Ivie, Robert L.; Wander, Philip; Scott, Robert L. Cold War Rhetoric: Strategy, Metaphor, and Ideology. East Lansing: Michigan State University Press, 1997.

Murrell, Gary. "The Most Dangerous Communist in the United States": A Biography of Herbert Aptheker. Amherst, MA: University of Massachusetts Press, 2015,.

Navasky, Victor S. Naming Names. New York: Hill and Wang, 2003 (Viking, 1991), p. xx.

Niebuhr, Reinhold. The Irony Of American History. Chicago and London: The University of Chicago Press, 1952.

Oshinsky, David M. A Conspiracy So Immense: The World of Joe McCarthy. New York: The Free Press, 1983.

Powers, Richard Gid. Not Without Honor: The History of American Anticommunism. New York: The Free Press, 1995.

Raumer, Frederich von. America and the American People. Trans. William W. Turner. New York: J. & H. G. Langeley, 1846, p. 148.

Rice, Daniel F. Reinhold Niebuhr and his circle of influence. Cambridge University Press, 2013.

Rosswurm, Steve. The F.B.I. and the Catholic Church, 1935-1962. Amherst and Boston: University of Massachusetts Press, 2010.

Rowe, David E. and Robert Schulmann, Einstein on Politics: His Private

The Language of Anti-Communism

Thoughts and Public Stands on Nationalism, Zionism, War, Peace and the Bomb. Princeton: Princeton University Press, 2007.

Sartre, Jean-Paul. Anti-Semite and Jew. New York: Schocken Books, 1995 (1948).

Saunders, Frances Stonor. Who Paid the Piper? The CIA and the Cultural Cold War. London: Granta Books, 1999.

Schlesinger, Arthur M., Jr. A Life in the 20th Century: Innocent Beginnings, 1917-1950. New York: Houghton Mifflin, 2000.

Schlesinger, Arthur M., Jr. The Vital Center: The Politics of Freedom. Second Edition. New Brunswick and London: Transaction Publishers (the Riverside Press, 1949).

Schrecker, Ellen W. No Ivory Tower: McCarthyism and the Universities. New York: Oxford University Press, 1986.

Schrecker, Ellen. Many Are the Crimes: McCarthyism in America. Princeton University Press, 1998.

Spender, Matthew. A House in St John's Wood: In Search of My Parents. London: William Collins, 2016.

Taylor, Clarence. Reds at the Blackboard: Communism, Civil Rights, and the New York City Teachers Union. New York: Columbia University Press, 2011.

Theoharis, Athan. The F.B.I. & American Democracy: A Brief Critical History. Lawrence, Kansas: The University Press of Kansas, 2004, p.33.

Wallerstein, Immanuel. unpublished M.A. essay: "McCarthy and the Conservative," Columbia University, 1954, pp. 46ff.

Warner, Michael (ed.) The CIA Under Harry Truman. CIA History Staff; Center for the Study of Intelligence, 1994.

Warner, Michael. Origins of the Congress for Cultural Freedom, 1949-50. Center for the Study of Intelligence, Central Intelligence Agency, https://www.cia.gov/library/center-for-the-study-of-intelligence/csi-publications/csi-studies/studies/95unclass/Warner.html

Warren, Donald. Radio Priest: Charles Coughlin, The Father of Hate Radio. New York: The Free Press, 1996, p. 30.

Weeks, Stephen B. Department of the Interior. Bureau of Education. Bulletin, 1918, No. 17. History of Public School Education in Arizona. Washington: Government Printing Office, 1918.

Weingarten, Aviva. Jewish Organizations' Response to Communism and Senator McCarthy. London. Vallentine Mitchell, 2008,.

Wheat, George Seay. The Story of the American Legion: The Birth of the Legion. New York and London: G. P. Putnam's Sons, 1919.

Whitfield, Stephen J. The Culture of the Cold War. Baltimore and London: The

Johns Hopkins Press (2nd Edition), 1991, 1996.
Wilford, Hugh. The CIA, the British left, and the Cold War: Calling the Tune? London: Frank Cass, 2003.

The Language of Anti-Communism

Index

A

67, 68, 69, 70, 73, 75, 79, 81, 82,
84, 89, 90, 92, 93, 98, 100, 110,
111, 113, 114, 115, 120, 143,
144, 146, 147, 148, 150, 156,
157, 158, 160, 173, 175, 177,
180, 183, 184, 185, 190, 194,
203, 206, 208, 209, 210, 213,
219, 221, 223, 226, 229, 233,
234, 237, 238, 239, 241, 242,
243, 259
Anti-Defamation League, 71, 76
anti-intellectualism, 79, 259
Anti-Intellectualism in American
    Life, 55, 133, 262
anti-lynching, 78
anti-Semitism, 11, 12, 13, 25, 56, 68,
    69, 70, 76, 93, 259
Arendt, Hannah, 165, 168, 199, 201,
    216, 237, 241, 261
Arens, Richard, 104, 105, 106, 111,
    112, 114, 115, 117, 118, 119,
    202
Arnot, Charles, 86, 87, 131
Aron, Raymond, 240
arson, 204
Asia, 21, 187, 188, 224, 228, 248,
    249
atheistic Communism, 7, 21
Atlanta Journal, 117
Attlee, Clement, 62, 89, 90, 133,
    157, 175, 219, 220, 224
Auden, W. H., 234
Auerbach, Erich, 1
Ayer, A. J., 230

B

Baarslag, Karl, 36, 37, 85
Bacon, Francis, 195
Barnhisel, Greg, 149, 151, 261
Barr, Joel, 94
Beckmann, Max, 221
Belgium, 86
Belknap, Mark R., 15

Bell, Daniel, 199
Bell, Gertrude, 225
Beloff, Max, 242
Bender, George, 110
Bentley, Elizabeth, 77, 171
Berkeley, 79, 80, 129, 259
Berlin, 12, 54, 147, 148, 156, 170,
    194, 230, 245, 254
Berlin, Isaiah, 176
Bernstein, Leonard, 144
Bevan, Aneurin, 156, 159, 225, 256
Bevin, Ernest, 219, 228, 247
Bilbo, Senator Theodore G., 111
Bill of Rights, 161
Bishops' Report, 18
Black, Justice Hugo, 110
bleeding hearts, 95, 103, 117
Blitzstein, Marc, 144
Bloomsbury, 1, 234
Bohm, David J., 79
Bolomey, Pierre, 231
Bolshevism, 11, 13, 33
bondage, 23
Bondy, François, 222
Bonhoeffer, Dietrich, 182, 191
Boorstin, Daniel J., 99
Borden, WIlliam L., 19
Borkenau, Franz, 147, 238, 253
Boyd, Andrew, 54, 55, 244, 262
Braden, Anne, 108, 118
Braden, Carl, 117, 119
Braden, Tom, 199, 221
Bretton Woods, 239
Bridgeport, 71
Brightman, Carol, 216, 221, 253,
    254, 261
British Empire, 87, 225
British loan, 219
British Society for Cultural Freedom,
    231
Brodsky, Joseph, 239
Brooklyn, 68, 210, 233
Browder, Earl, 20, 28, 114

R

racial equality, 64, 66, 108, 171
racist, 11, 50, 69, 81, 117
Rader, Melvin, 163
Radical Religion, 183
Radio Free Europe, 176
Rainey, Joseph, 82
Rankin, John, 11, 70, 71, 73, 74, 75, 76, 77, 78, 93, 109
Rapp-Coudert Committee, 206
Raumer, Friedrich von, 59, 122, 262
Reader's Digest, 184
Red Army, 29, 35, 37, 74, 143, 156, 241
Red Channels, 18, 47, 80
Red China, 107
Red tyranny, 103
Red-fascism, 72
Reds at the Blackboard, 68, 124, 263
Reinhardt, Ad, 144
Republican Party, 69, 78, 83, 84, 124, 167, 174
Reynolds, Walter S., 66, 67
Richberg, Donald R., 83
ritualistic liberals, 201, 203
Rockefeller, John D., 168, 251
Rome, 9, 12, 19
Roosevelt, Archibald B., 103
Roosevelt, Eleanor, 50, 111, 155, 159, 190
Roosevelt, President Franklin Delano, 167
Roosevelt, President Theodore, 33, 155
Root, E. Merrill, 46
Rosenberg, Ethel, 189, 235
Rosenberg, Julius, 79, 94, 188, 253
Rosenberg, Julius and Ethel, 235, 236

Rosswurm, Steve, 18, 28, 31, 32, 262
Rousset, David, 146, 151
Rovere, Richard, 42
Russell, Bertrand, 235
Russia, 11, 12, 14, 17, 21, 23, 35, 41, 121, 148, 170, 228, 239, 247

S

San Francisco, California, 119, 120
Santi Giovanni e Paolo, 19
Sarah Lawrence College, 51
Sarant, Alfred, 94
Sartre, Jean-Paul, 74, 126, 146, 151, 154, 169, 189, 221, 222, 239, 240, 263
Satan, 7, 10, 186, 187, 188
Saturday Review of Literature, 198
Saunders, Frances Stonor, 145, 149, 151, 176, 185, 192, 215, 221, 224, 251, 253, 263
Saunders, Sallie, 64
Scheiner, Leo, 112
Schlesinger, Arthur M., Jr., 3, 148, 149, 150, 154, 155, 156, 157, 158, 159, 160, 161, 162, 163, 164, 165, 166, 167, 168, 169, 170, 171, 172, 173, 174, 175, 176, 177, 178, 179, 180, 181, 185, 186, 188, 190, 196, 198, 199, 200, 201, 210, 213, 215, 225, 231, 234, 245, 246, 255, 256, 263
Schmidt, Emerson P., 72
Schnabel, Artur, 144
Schoenberg, Arnold, 145
Schrecker, Ellen, 31, 64, 84, 108, 129, 130, 137, 165, 178, 179, 212, 217, 263
Scientific and Cultural Conference for World Peace, 144

www.ingramcontent.com/pod-product-compliance
Lightning Source LLC
Chambersburg PA
CBHW072038280526
45788CB00006B/2108